COUNSELS ON THE SPIRITUAL LIFE

Mark the Monk

T0334503

ST VLADIMIR'S SEMINARY PRESS
Popular Patristics Series
Number 37

The Popular Patristics Series published by St Vladimir's Seminary Press provides readable and accurate translations of a wide range of early Christian literature to a wide audience—students of Christian history to lay Christians reading for spiritual benefit. Recognized scholars in their fields provide short but comprehensive and clear introductions to the material. The texts include classics of Christian literature, thematic volumes, collections of homilies, letters on spiritual counsel, and poetical works from a variety of geographical contexts and historical backgrounds. The mission of the series is to mine the riches of the early Church and to make these treasures available to all.

Series Editor
BOGDAN BUCUR

Associate Editor
IGNATIUS GREEN

* * *

Series Editor
1999–2020
JOHN BEHR

Counsels on the Spiritual Life

MARK THE MONK

Volume 1
Translated, with Notes and Introductions, by
TIM VIVIAN

Volume 2
Translated, with Notes and Introductions, by
TIM VIVIAN AND AUGUSTINE CASIDAY

Foreword by the Rt Rev Dr Rowan Williams,
Archbishop of Canterbury

ST VLADIMIR'S SEMINARY PRESS
CRESTWOOD, NEW YORK
2009

Library of Congress Cataloging-in-Publication Data

Mark, the Hermit, d. ca. 430.
   [Selections. English, 2009]
   Counsels on the spiritual life / Mark the Monk ; translated, with notes and introductions, by Tim Vivian.
       p. cm. — (Popular patristics series ; no. 37)
   Vol. 2 translated, with notes and introductions, by Tim Vivian and Augustine Casiday ; foreword by Rt. Rev. Dr. Rowan.
   Includes bibliographical references.
   ISBN 978-0-88141-063-1
   1. Spiritual life—Christianity—Early works to 1800. 2. Theology—Early works to 1800. I. Vivian, Tim. II. Casiday, Augustine. III. Title.

   BR65.M3842E5 2009
   248.409'015—dc22

                                                          2009036694

PRINTED IN THE UNITED STATES OF AMERICA

By the hand of iconographer Joyce Tanner–stpio@sbcglobal.net

Contents

Acknowledgments

We wish to thank Professor Apostolos N. Athanassakis, Fr John Behr, Dr Marcus Plested, and Metropolitan Kallistos (Ware) for advice and suggestions throughout. Any remaining mistakes are our own. We also wish to acknowledge the courteous and prompt assistance of the staff in the Rare Books Room of Palace Green Library, the University of Durham. Finally, we would express gratitude, tinged with regret, to Vladimir Cvetkovic, who provided a copy of the only full-length book on Mark the Monk known to us, which is written in Serbian and which we have not been able to read: *uita breuis, ars longior.*

Foreword

The map of theological and spiritual debate in the late patristic period goes on evolving, and we are all becoming rightly more cautious about some of the textbook categories of yesterday. This excellent translation of Mark's work on both doctrinal and ascetical issues is a helpful reminder that questions about apparently abstruse matters of dogma were regarded in that age as directly relevant to the living of the Christian life. Thus the discussion in chapter two of this collection about what it means to "take responsibility for one another out of love" is inseparably bound in with the subject matter of chapter three, the doctrinal affirmation of Christ's unity. Without the conviction that Christ in his incarnation unites his personal being unreservedly with human nature, we have no real rationale for the unreserved generosity which is the lifeblood of Christ's Body, the Church. It is the divine Word who saves us through the medium of human nature, and we cannot take the discussion to some abstract level where we speculate on what God might do for our salvation while remaining "nakedly" God. As in so many of the debates of the Chalcedonian era, what most matters is the conviction that human nature is—so to speak—saturated by the divine agency in Christ's incarnation and thus decisively changed.

Yet that change is something that, so far from removing our human liberty or dignity, restores our free will to its proper glory. Hence the interest of Mark's discussions of post-baptismal sin, and his rejection of the idea that persisting sin must be the effect of some kind of mechanism, the sin of Adam. It is precisely mechanistic behavior that we are saved from by Baptism; post-baptismal sin is therefore more ours than ever, and so much the more to be combated. Sin takes on a new gravity, because freedom has taken on a new depth and self-awareness. It is not fanciful to see here the roots of a Dostoevskian sense of the frightening character of the freedom Christ offers.

The translators have worked hard to bring to their work a sense of the liveliness and humanity of the debates recorded. The idiom of those debates is not made any the less strange in some respects; we as twenty-first century readers will find things to surprise and occasionally dismay us, and these are not softened. But the reader will also pick up the warmth and even the vulnerability of the speaker, the teacher, portrayed here. These are important texts, not so much as original theoretical exercises (though there are arguments of freshness and interest) but as evidence of the seamless robe of monastic thinking and praying in a formative era for the Christian mind and heart.

†Rowan Cantuar

General Introduction

The brief works here translated are the only known legacy of St Mark the Monk. Mark is known to the modern reader, if he is known at all, as the author of three works found in St Nikodimos the Hagiorite's *Philokalia*: "Letter to the Monk Nicholas," "On the Spiritual Law" and "On Those Who Think They are Justified by Their Works."[1] But Mark is traditionally ascribed a total of eleven writings and it is unfortunately the case that only a relatively small number of scholars are familiar with his corpus as a whole. This situation is regrettable, because Mark's writings are valuable for their spiritual counsels no less than for their theological insight and historical interest. The aim of this translation is therefore to make Mark's complete works accessible in English.

Because Mark is not a well-known Father, we begin by presenting what can be known about him from his writings and from other sources about his life. Since our information about Mark derives chiefly from the works, it will also be necessary to give the works themselves some serious preliminary consideration. In the first place, the best evidence that we have for when Mark lived is derived from estimating when his writings were completed. A preliminary consideration of the works is also relevant because, on the basis of thematic elements in his writings, Mark's modern editor has identified a relatively specific location for where Mark probably lived. (The editor has also argued against attributing to Mark two works that are

[1]Nicodemus the Hagiorite seems to have studied Mark carefully. In addition to including those treatises in the *Philokalia*, his emphasis on Baptism—see, e.g., his *Handbook of Spiritual Counsel* 1 (P. Chamberas, trans., *Nicodemos of the Holy Mountain*, Classics of Western Spirituality [New York: Paulist Press, 1989], 68–69)—continues Mark's emphasis on Baptism.

found in the traditional corpus, and we will need to comment upon that in due course.) Looking at other sources of information about Mark naturally leads us to wonder about who read Mark's works. This question will be treated later in the introduction and will bring the historical component of the introduction to a close.

Following the historical overview, we will look at the character of Mark's teaching. Several important themes emerge from his writings, and it will be helpful to have some idea of how the pieces fit together before moving on to the works themselves. To anticipate, it is at this point that we can appreciate Mark's distinctive contributions to Greek theology through his preoccupation with grace and works. After Mark's life and theology, we will look briefly at some of the reasons he is worth reading today.

Who Was Mark?

The precise identity of Mark the Monk (also known as "the Ascetic" or "the Hermit," although it is generally agreed that in fact "hermit" is a misnomer)[2] has been a vexed question for at least three centuries. Part of the reason for this is the simple fact that the name "Mark" was hardly uncommon during the patristic era. Even if we restrict our attention to monastic figures bearing the name, our situation is not much improved.[3] In fact, the question of Mark's identity has been so divisive that, in an important and influential article on Mark, Jean Gribomont opted to begin by describing the writings and making a

---

[2]Thus, Metropolitan Kallistos (Ware), "Introduction" to C. A. Zirnheld, trans., *Marc Le Moine: Traités spirituels et théologiques*, Spiritualité Orientale 41 (Bégrolles-en-Mauges: Abbaye de Bellefontaine, 1985), ix–li, at ix.; M. Plested, *The Macarian Legacy: The Place of Macarius-Symeon in the Eastern Christian Tradition*, Oxford Theological Monographs (Oxford: Oxford University Press, 2004), ch. 5; G. de Durand, *Marc le Moine: Traités*, Sources chrétiennes 445, 455 (Paris: Cerf, 1999, 2000), 1:29 fn. 1.

[3]For example, Georges de Durand has identified five ascetics named Mark who roughly fit the probable lifespan of our author—and has concluded that our Mark is a different person altogether! See de Durand, *Marc le Moine*, 1:13–15.

somewhat guarded case for the unity of the corpus, which he then took as indirect evidence for a single author.[4] Georges de Durand, who produced the critical edition of Mark's works that is the basis for the present translation, similarly refrained from committing himself to a precise identification.[5] Indeed, in recent times scholars have tended to begin by looking to the collection ascribed to Mark for evidence of his identity, and have typically found that the consistency (both stylistic and theological) across the collection is what one might expect from a single author. So, although we will need in due course to consider what external evidence can tell us about Mark's life, it is wise to begin where the recent experts have begun and look to the collection of Mark's writings for our first clues.

Dating Mark's Works

Internal evidence

Most of the internal evidence for dating Mark's works is, at best, historically imprecise. For instance, at *On Melchizedek* 8, Mark refers to the Council of Nicaea (in AD 325) as an event of the distant past. It is reasonably clear from the language he uses that Mark was familiar with the writings of Evagrius Ponticus (who died c. 399)—to which he is indebted for a great deal of his monastic theory—and with the (pseudo-)Macarian corpus (written c. 370–399). Some scholars have attempted to base arguments about the dating of Mark's works on that evidence, as we shall see. Mark alludes to the Novatians at *On Repentance* 7, but this is not entirely helpful for establishing a date: although Novatus himself was martyred during Valerian's persecutions (c. 257–8), the Novatian communities existed in the East until the seventh century.[6] As it happens, the Novatians are only one of

---

[4]Gribomont, "Marc le Moine," *Dictionnaire de Spiritualité* (Paris, 1932–), 10:279.

[5]De Durand, *Marc le Moine*, 1:13–25.

[6]See M. Walraff, "Socrates Scholasticus on the History of Novatianism," *Studia Patristica* 29 (1997): 170–77.

three groups to which Mark refers in the course of his writings. The other two, Messalian and Melchizedekian Christians, will be discussed in due course.

For purposes of dating the corpus, perhaps the richest vein of material is found in Mark's Christology. In this connection, Alois Grillmeier has argued that *On the Hypostatic Union* (a shortened title for the third treatise of Vol. 2, *On the Incarnation*) is best understood as Mark's attempt to refute Evagrian Christology and that it should be considered part of Theophilus' campaign against the Origenists (c. 399–400).[7] But this argument is unconvincing. Firstly, as Jean Gribomont has noted, the earliest evidence we have for a controversy about Christology associated with Evagrius' teaching took place in the first half of the sixth century;[8] and even then there is no real reason to think that the records of that controversy are historically accurate or adequate.[9] Furthermore, the practice of ascribing to Evagrius himself the doctrines that were eventually condemned in the sixth century has been fundamentally challenged as an error in historical and theological method.[10] What is needed for this purpose—and, in fact, for many others—is an evaluation of Evagrius' Christology that does not depend upon the tendentious claims from the sixth century. Even in the absence of such an account, though, Grillmeier's attempt to date *On the Hypostatic Union* to the "First" Origenist Controversy should be considered unsuccessful. A second, and more fundamental, reason for rejecting Grillmeier's dating has been advanced by Metropolitan Kallistos (Ware).[11]

[7] A. Grillmeier, "Marco Eremita e l'origenismo: Saggio di reinterpretazione di Op. XI," *Cristianesimo nella Storia* 1 (1980): 9–58.

[8] Gribomont, "Marc l'Ermite et la christologie évagrienne," *Cristianesimo nella Storia* 3 (1982): 73–81.

[9] This has been established by Hombergen, *The Second Origenist Controversy: A New Perspective on Cyril of Scythopolis' Monastic Biographies as Historical Sources for Sixth-Century Origenism*, Studia Anselmiana 132 (Rome: Sant' Anselmo, 2001).

[10] See Augustine Casiday, "Gabriel Bunge and the study of Evagrius Ponticus," *St Vladimir's Theological Quarterly* 48.2 (2004): 249–97.

[11] For what follows, see Metropolitan Kallistos (Ware), "Introduction," p. xi.

As Metropolitan Kallistos (Ware) has demonstrated, Mark uses key terms to describe Christ that are common to those used by Cyril of Alexandria (d. 444). Thus, Mark repeatedly uses the expression "hypostatic union."[12] By scholarly consensus, Cyril himself is taken to have coined this phrase, and the earliest established usage of it is found in Cyril's *Second Letter to Nestorius* (430).[13] Mark also uses another Cyrillian phrase to describe the union when he refers to Christ's union "from the womb" (*ek mētras*).[14] And yet we do not find some key phrases in Mark's writings. He never refers to the Virgin as *Theotokos*, nor does he ever explicitly commit himself to the position that after the Incarnation Christ existed "in two natures." In fact, although he does specify that Christ is "from two natures,"[15] and might be thought to imply their distinct existence when he refers to "each nature,"[16] he also sometimes writes as though there were in the Incarnate Lord a simple *physis*.[17] Even so, he does not appeal to the Cyrillian formula, "one incarnate nature of God the Word." Mark's rather fluid language in describing Christ keeps us from being able to situate him with reference to a particular christological milieu,[18] and in any case the use of specific words as evidence for what group an author belonged to is actually not a straightforward matter of ticking off items on a list. Mark may very well have been deferring to the Emperor Zeno's call for silence in matters pertaining to the Council of Chalcedon.[19] We will return to the question of Mark's Christology in the introductory comments to *Melchizedek* and *Hypostatic Union*, but for the moment it is sufficient to say that it

[12]*On Melchizedek* 5; *Incarnation* 13, 17, 21, 26, 31, 34, 42.

[13]Cyril, *ep.* 4.3–4, 6–7 (ACO I.1.i: 26–28).

[14]*On Melchizedek* 4, 5.

[15]*Disputation with an Attorney*, resp. to qu. 7(20): the Incarnate Word "is one and not two (even if he is thought to be united indivisibly from two)"; *On Melchizedek* 5: "Whenever elements are united in a substantive reality, *even if one conceives of them as dual, . . .*"

[16]E.g., *Incarnation* 52.

[17]E.g., *Incarnation* 27.

[18]As noted in conclusion by Metropolitan Kallistos (Ware), "Introduction," p. xi.

[19]Thus, Chadwick, "The Identity and Date of Mark the Monk," *Eastern Churches Review* 4 (1972): 125–30, referring to the *Henotikon* (482).

seems unlikely that Mark coined the technical phrase, "hypostatic union" (as he would have had to do, if he wrote as early as Grillmeier suggested). So we can reasonably suppose that Mark was influenced by Cyril's Christology and therefore wrote after Cyril.

If we turn now to Mark's knowledge of Messalianism and Melchizedekianism, we find that he was certainly preoccupied with their perceived excesses. In fact, he devoted an entire treatise to redressing mistaken belief about Melchizedek and peppered his instruction with affirmations that run counter to Messalian teachings. Indeed, many have followed the insight of Babai the Great (c. 550–628) who, taking Mark's emphasis on Baptism as the source from which every Christian virtue flows as a direct counter to the typical Messalian devaluation of sacraments, claimed that *On Baptism* was an expressly anti-Messalian undertaking.[20]

A word of clarification, however, is in order. In his brilliant study of the Macarian corpus, Marcus Plested has put forward an insightful evaluation of Mark's relationship to the Macarian writings. Plested has shown that Mark's understanding of transgression is deeply consonant with the Macarian teachings.[21] Plested has built upon the claim advanced by Metropolitan Kallistos (Ware) that Mark's teaching, so far from attacking Macarius, actually complements it.[22] One should heed this note of caution and steer clear of confusing the Macarian writings with Messalianism. In any case, it is undeniable that Mark took aim at Messalian teaching—but unfortunately this tells us very little about when Mark wrote, because Messalianism first appeared in Mesopotamia, c. 360, then rapidly spread throughout the Christian East and was a persistent concern in some areas as late as the sixth century.

[20]Babai, *Commentary on Evagrius' Gnostic Chapters* 3.85 (von Frankenberg, ed., *Euagrius Ponticus* [Berlin 1912], 252–53, Syriac text, German translation). For a more recent proponent of this view, see *Liber Graduum* xcv: "Opusculum *De baptismo* placitis Macarii e diametro oppositum est," M. Kmosko, ed., PS 3.1 (Paris, 1926).

[21]Plested, *Macarian Legacy*, ch 5.2.

[22]Metropolitan Kallistos (Ware), "The Sacrament of Baptism and the Ascetic Life in the Teaching of Mark the Monk," *Studia Patristica* 10 (TU 107; 1970): 441–52.

Likewise, we are told by Epiphanius that around the year 375 many in Egypt, fueled by the vague remarks in Scripture (see Gen 14.18–20; Ps 110.4; and Heb 5.10, 7.21) were actively engaged in speculating that Melchizedek was a manifestation of God the Son before the Incarnation.[23] Cyril of Alexandria also wrote against this belief more than a generation later,[24] and a refutation of it appears in the *Sayings of the Desert Fathers*.[25] Mention might also be made of the badly damaged Coptic text, "Melchizedek," which was discovered at Nag Hammadi. According to the analysis by its editor and translator, this document originated from a Christian community, and their beliefs as reconstructed from that text bear a significant resemblance to the beliefs that Epiphanius imputed to the Melchizedekians of Egypt.[26] This might suggest that Mark was writing in Egypt, c. 375–40.

Some have sought to confirm this from a passage in Thomas of Marga's *Book of Governors*, where Theophilus of Alexandria commissions a certain Abba Makarianos to combat an error about Melchizedek which was at that time spreading throughout Scetis, on grounds that, in Syriac, the names "Makarianos" (*MQRYANOS*) and "Markianos" (*MRQYANOS*) could readily be confused; and that, in Greek, the names Markianos and Markos could similarly be confused.[27] (Indeed, as we shall see, it is generally agreed that one of the works traditionally attributed to Mark was in fact written by Markianos of Bethlehem—so confusion of that sort is manifestly possible.) This line of argument is probably the strongest of the three that we have surveyed. Even so, it is not entirely satisfactory.

[23]Epiphanius, *Panarion* 4.9 (Holl and Dummer, eds., *Ancoratus und Panarion* [Leipzig: Hinrichs, 1980], 2:337.21–22).

[24]*Glaphyra in Gen* 2.3–11 (PG 69:84–109).

[25]E.g., Daniel 8, Copres 3 (PG 65:160, 252).

[26]Birger Pearson and Søren Giversen, *Nag Hammadi codices IX and X*, Nag Hammadi Studies 15 (Leiden: Brill, 1981), 38–39.

[27]*Book of Governors* 1.28 (Wallis Budge, *The Book of Governors* [London, 1898], 2:94–95); see O. Hesse, "Markus Eremita und seine Schrift 'De Melchisedech,'" *Oriens Christianus* 51 (1967): 72–77, and Metropolitan Kallistos (Ware), "Introduction," pp. xii–xiii.

In the first place, there is a slight but possibly significant difference between Mark's Melchizedekians and Epiphanius', because Epiphanius states that they are still in the Church, whereas Mark clearly alludes to their excommunication. Furthermore, it is by no means the case that christological speculation about Melchizedek was restricted to Egypt during the fourth and fifth centuries. Timothy of Constantinople, writing c. 600, judges that the Melchizedekians, "now called *Athingani*" (Intangibles), are in need of re-Baptism should they wish to enter the Church.[28] There is also evidence that Syriac Christians were interested in the identity of Melchizedek.

John the Solitary of Apamea (died c. 500) is witness to speculation about Melchizedek's parentage.[29] In fact, it has been suggested that John himself brought Melchizedek into a complicated, heretical cosmology—though some scholars have sharply challenged that suggestion.[30] Be that as it may, André de Halleux has noted that the relevant passage by John is of a piece with such Christian apocrypha as are found in Solomon of Basra's *The Book of the Bee*.[31] In a similar notice in *The Book of the Cave of Treasures*, the compiler is evidently distressed that "the simple folk thought that [Melchizedek] was not a man at all and, in their error, they have said of him that he was God (which God forbid!), since 'there was neither a beginning to

---

[28]*De receptione Haereticorum* (PG 86:34); it is possible that the *Athingani* might not be directly related to the community we are describing—Timothy does not mention doctrinal aberration, merely their adherence to Jewish ritual—but for completeness it seems good to include them.

[29]See John, *Dialogue* 4; R. Lavenant, trans., *Jean d'Apamée: Dialogues et traits*, Sources chrétiennes 311 (Paris: Cerf, 1984), 95–99.

[30]The suggestion hinges on whether one takes Theodore bar Koni to be referring to the same person as the author of the aforementioned dialogue in condemning "John of Apamea in Syria" in his *Liber Scholiorum*. This question has been widely discussed. Irénée Hausherr denied that the names referred to the same person: "Un grande auteur spirituel retrouvé: Jean d'Apamée," *Orientalia Christiana Periodica* 14 (1948): 3–42; Werner Strothmann asserted it: *Johannes von Apamea*, 81–115; and René Lavenant challenged Strothmann's argument: "Le problème de Jean d'Apamée," *Orientalia Christiana Periodica* 46 (1980): 367–90.

[31]A de Halleux, "La christologie de Jean le Solitaire," *Le Muséon* 94 (1981): 5–36 at 18 n 51; Wallis Budge, *The Book of the Bee* (Oxford 1886): 33–36.

his days, nor an end to his life' [Heb 7.3]."[32] In the light of the typological account about Melchizedek in Hebrews, it is reasonable to
suppose that Christians speculating that Melchizedek is God would
have been thinking more precisely that Melchizedek is God *the Son*.
Although we have no conclusive evidence about those people, it is
as feasible to think that the concerns expressed in John's dialogue, in
The Book of the Bee, and in *The Book of the Cave of Treasures* should
be understood as reflecting a common phenomenon; and it is as easy
to suppose that Mark's treatise provides us with further evidence
about the speculation that was taking place along the Greek-Syriac
frontier as it is to suppose that he was writing against Egyptian
Melchizedekians. In fairness, though, it must be acknowledged that
even if this is a plausible line of thinking, it is not conclusive.

   We are therefore not able to restrict Mark's writings to a specific
date on the basis of internal criteria, although it does seem reasonable to suppose that he wrote after Cyril made his contributions to
the Nestorian controversy.

External evidence

One tradition identifies our author as the St Mark who cured the
blindness of a hyena's cub. This legend is attested in the *Synaxarion*
of Constantinople, on March 5;[33] and was incorporated into the
three manuscripts containing Mark's works that begin by offering a
brief life of the author.[34] But the miraculous healing of a blind hyena
cub is ascribed to Macarius of Alexandria, of the fourth century,
by multiple sources and, barring the possibility that many fathers

---

[32]*The Book of the Cave of Treasures* 31.12–13; Su-Min Ri, ed., *La Caverne des Trésors*, CSCO, 486–87, Scrip. Syri, 207–08 (Louvain: Peeters), 1:244 (Syriac text), 2:90
(French translation).

[33]See J. M. Sauget, "Marco, Monaco in Egitto, santo," in *Bibliotheca Sanctorum* 8
(Rome: Pontificia Università Lateranense. Instituto Giovanni XXIII, 1961–69), cols.
708–10.

[34]See de Durand, *Marc le Moine*, 1:13 fn. 1.

of the desert were occupied with the betterment of wild animals, it seems most likely that the legend was simply detached from its original source and attributed erroneously to our author, Mark. Le Nain de Tillemont questioned that attribution nearly three hundred years ago and, so far as we have been able to discover, no one has embraced it since then.[35]

The claim that is most frequently represented, at least in historical terms, relies chiefly on Nicephorus Callistus Xanthopoulos' fourteenth-century *Church History*[36] (which is in turn derived chiefly from the *Chronicon* of George the Sinner, who died before 867).[37] Following information taken from Nicephorus, several historians have claimed that Mark was a disciple of John Chrysostom. This is an appealing move because Nicephorus specifically claims to have seen eight writings by Mark, and that forty of his writings in all were extant. Scholars have gone on to identify him with the Mark whom Palladius and Sozomen mention.[38] This view is found in Nikodimos' *Philokalia*, Gallandius' *Veterum Patrum Bibliotheca*, Fessler's *Institutiones patrologiae*, and somewhat more recently in Argles' entry for the *Dictionary of Christian Biography*.[39] In the early modern period, this view was favored by Protestants such as Vincent Obsopaeus and Matthias Flacius (or one of his circle who retouched the *Magdeburg Centuries*) and opposed by Roman Catholics like Cardinal Bellarmine, on largely ideological grounds that will be mentioned in due course.[40] But this view also attracted scholarly criticism, *sine ira et*

---

[35]Tillemont, *Mémoires pour servir à l'histoire ecclésiastique des six premiers siècles justifiez par les citations des auteurs originaux* (Brussels, 1732), 8:360–61 ("Note 3 on St Macarius of Alexandria").

[36]Nicephorus, *Historia Ecclesiastica* 14.30, 14.54 (PG 146:1157, 1255).

[37]George, *Chronicon* 4.202.16 (PG 110:733).

[38]Palladius, *Historia Lausiaca* 18 (Butler, *The Lausiac History* [Cambridge, 1898–1904], 2:56); Sozomen, *Historia Ecclesiastica* 6.29 (PG 67:1376–77).

[39]Gallandi, *Veterum Patrum Bibliotheca* 8, proleg. 3 (PG 65:893) ; Fessler, *Institutiones patrologiae* 2, 631 (PG 65:897–900) ; and M. F. Argles, "Marcus (14)," in W. Smith and H. Wace, eds., *A Dictionary of Christian Biography* (London, 1882), 3:827.

[40]See G. de Durand, "Études sur Marc le Moine, III: Marc et les controverses occidentales," *Bulletin de Littérature Ecclésiastique* 87 (1986): 163–88.

studio, as is evident in the critical attention of Tillemont.[41] Khalifé has dryly noted that Nicephorus himself never explicitly identified the ascetic Mark as the author of anything at all: it is entirely possible that Nicephorus did not intend for the author whom he mentions to be identified with Chrysostom's disciple.[42] Along similar lines, we might note that de Durand *presumes* that George was referring to our Mark—even though George never attributes any writings whatever to Chrysostom's disciple Mark—before in effect dismissing him as an incompetent historiographer.[43] It is reasonable to suppose that the legendary association of Mark with Chrysostom has prompted readers of George and of Nicephorus to make this connection gratuitously, so it is prudent to refrain from upbraiding them in default of better evidence than has been provided as yet.

In more recent times, however, most scholars have refrained from identifying the Mark mentioned by Nicephorus and George with the Mark mentioned by Palladius and Sozomen. Sauget has noted that if the traditional linking of Mark to Chrysostom is allowed to stand, Mark would have to have flourished (not simply lived, but *flourished*) for well over a century. The motivation to claim that Nicephorus and George on the one hand and Palladius and Sozomen on the other were referring to different people is further driven by internal evidence (particularly the terms used by Mark in describing Christ) which suggests that the texts were written in the mid-fifth century; but we will return to that point in due course.

---

[41]Tillemont, *Mémoires*, 10:350–51 ("Note on Silvanus").

[42]I. A. Khalifé, "Les traductions arabes de Marc l'Ermite," *Mélanges Université St Joseph* 28 (1949–50): 117–224, at 118.

[43]De Durand, *Marc le Moine*, 1:19–20. There is a reference to the treatise *On Melchizedek* by "the divine Mark, Chrysostom's acquaintance" at *Chronicon* 1.12 (PG 110:148–49); but by de Durand's own admission, it is possible that this passage does not go back to George's hand.

A working hypothesis

Despite the rather meager evidence for specifying Mark's location and dates, it is fair to say that at present general consensus seems to favor dating Mark's literary career to the mid-fifth century.[44] This is a reasonable view because, as we have seen, we have evidence that by the sixth century his works were being read and cited by other, more securely datable, authors. Indeed, on the basis of the date assigned to a Syriac manuscript in the British Library which contains Mark's works in translation, we can be confident that he wrote before the year 534, because the translation was copied in that year.[45] Remembering that rapid communication and mass publications are relatively modern, we ought to allow some time for Mark's reputation to gain enough stature to justify a translation—perhaps as much as two generations. This would point approximately to 485 as a likely end point for Mark's literary production. Such an approximation is in keeping with the accepted range of likely dates. But the question of *where* Mark lived as he wrote does not enjoy such a generally agreed answer.

Two locations, as we have seen, are suggested by the tradition. First, there are reasons to suppose that Mark may have lived and written in Egypt. Probably the most salient reason to think this is his treatise against the Melchizedekians. But, as we have seen, christological speculation about Melchizedek was not necessarily restricted to Egypt. Most of the other evidence pointing toward Egypt is frankly circumstantial at best (for example, the suggested emendation to the Syriac that Theophilus commissioned Abba "Markian" to

[44]See J. Kunze, *Markus Eremita, ein neuer Zeuge für das altkirchliche Taufbekenntnis* (Leipzig, 1895).

[45]On Mark in Syriac, see further O. Hesse, "Markus Eremita in der syrischen Literatur," *Deutscher Orientalistentag 1968 in Würzburg*, 2:450–57; W. Voigt, ed., *Zeitschrift der deutschen morgenländischen Gesellschaft*, Supplementa 1 (Wiesbaden: Steiner, 1969). W. Wright dates the translation into Syriac from 534: *Catalogue of Syriac Manuscripts* (London, 1871), 2:633–38. Wright designates the Syriac translation of Mark as Codex 727.2.

write in support of orthodoxy). So while the view is tenable, it is by no means compulsory.

The second possibility suggested by tradition is the linking of Mark to John Chrysostom. Even though it is unlikely that this tradition should be accepted (since it would mean that Mark was extraordinarily long-lived), it has nevertheless inspired in Georges de Durand the rather more plausible idea that Mark may have had connections to Antioch.[46] However plausible that idea might initially seem, though, de Durand has rightly found it wanting: he notes that Mark's scriptural exegesis does not conform to roughly contemporary standards of exegesis as practiced by the masters of Antioch—though he does (somewhat surprisingly) allow that Mark's Christology is solidly "Antiochian."[47] Be that as it may, de Durand is surely right to suggest that the early and apparently strong appeal that Mark's writings had for Syrian Christians (which we will note in some detail below) ought to keep us focused on the Near East as a likely source for Mark's cultural context.

This intuition has been corroborated to a great extent by Marcus Plested's findings that Mark seems to have been a careful and sympathetic reader of the Macarian corpus. Now de Durand has suggested that Mark's exegetical practices, his affinity for Macarian ideas, and the monastic structures that are implied by his writings all correspond neatly to literature originating from Asia Minor.[48] Even though this line of reasoning is in the end no more definitive than the arguments for placing Mark in Egypt, it seems that de Durand's case is provisionally better. We may not be entirely happy with the practice of trying to determine geographical location by correlating ideas or political loyalties, but the least that can be said is that placing Mark in Asia Minor has fewer obvious problems than does placing him in Egypt.

[46]See de Durand, *Marc le Moine*, 1:25–35.
[47]Cf. de Durand, *Marc le Moine*, 1:25–35; for Mark's alleged *antiochénisme*, see p. 33.
[48]De Durand, *Marc le Moine*, 1:27–30.

In the end, then, we are inclined to suppose that Mark probably lived in Asia Minor, and wrote near the end of the fifth century. This supposition is consistent with the available internal and external evidence, and it fits well with the evidence that we have concerning the circulation of Mark's writings.

WHO READ MARK'S WORKS?

It must be said that, having considered what the ancient historians and hagiographers tell us about Mark, the other ancient witnesses who refer to Mark are far more interesting (even if only for indirect evidence).

Dorotheus of Gaza ascribes two passages to "Abba Mark," though they are not perfect in comparison to the modern editions.[49] Abraham of Kaskar, one of the greatest figures in Syrian monasticism, regarded Mark as one of the greatest figures in Christian monasticism (alongside Antony the Great, Arsenius and Isaiah) and incorporated three citations from *Spiritual Law* and *No Justification by Works* into the rule for the monastery that he founded on Mt Izla in 571—and, incidentally, indicates to us that Mark's works were being translated into Syriac at a relatively early date.[50] The works of Mark continued to be influential in the Great Convent, for one of its great abbots, Babai the Great, bishop of Nisibis (c. 569–629), was also familiar with Mark's works.[51] He found in Mark's *On Baptism* a use-

[49]Dorotheus, *Doctrines* 1.10 (cf. *Justification* 197), 8.90 (cf. *Justification* 37); L. Regnault and J. de Préville, eds., *Oeuvres spirituelles*, Sources chrétiennes 92 (Paris: Cerf, 1963), 162, 308. Tillemont (*Mémoires*, 10:351) doubted that the parallels between Dorotheus and Mark prove anything, but Khalifé's estimation is more positive ("Les traductions arabes," 119).

[50]Abraham, *Rule* (A. Vööbus, ed., *Syriac and Arabic Documents Regarding Legislation Relative to Syrian Asceticism* [Stockholm, 1960], 155, 157), quoting *Spiritual Law* 5 and *Justification* 33.

[51]P. Krüger ("Zum theologischen Menschenbild Babais des Großen nach seinem noch unveröffentlichten Kommentar zu den beiden Sermones des Mönches Markus über 'das geistige Gesetz,'" *Oriens Christianus* 44 [1960]: 46–74) thinks that Mark was nothing short of Babai's *maßgeblicher Lehrmeister* (p. 74)—though Krüger had no

ful tool against the "dangerous heresy" of the Messalians.[52] Ebedjesu, in the fourteenth century, tells us that Babai wrote a commentary on Mark's *Spiritual Law*, and that Abraham bar Dasandad (died c. 720) wrote another.[53] Isaac the Syrian, in the seventh century, invoked Mark's authority.[54] Simon of Taibutheh and Dadiso Qatraya were also much impressed by Mark's writings, though in Simon's case at least one of his quotations is not found in Mark's Greek writings.[55] (Dadiso's knowledge seems to have been more precise: he cites Mark some fourteen times in his "On solitude," and nearly twenty times more in his unpublished *Commentary on Isaiah*).[56]

Hesychius of Sinai (7–8th cent.) also seems to have known Mark's works.[57] Theodore the Studite (died 826), offering a list of spiritual teachers, names Mark before Isaiah, Barsanuphius, Dorotheus, and Hesychius.[58] Thomas of Marga quotes Mark's *Spiritual Law*, *No Justification by Works*, and *Repentance* (along with an unidentified pas-

independent knowledge of Mark and supposed that he was a contemporary of Babai's who lived at Matt Izla (p. 47)!

[52]Babai, *Commentary on Evagrius' Gnostic Chapters* 3.85 (Frankenberg, *Euagrius Ponticus*, 252–53 [Syriac text, German translation]).

[53]See J. S. Assemani, *Bibliotheca orientalis* (Rome, 1725), 3.1:96 n. 1, 194. Wright identified one of these commentaries: *Catalogue of Syriac Manuscripts*, 2:482, Cod. 605. Alphonse Mingana considered the attribution of the commentary to Abraham 'very doubtful', though he did not say why (*Early Christian Mystics* [Cambridge, 1934], 185 n. 4).

[54]Cf. PG 65:1113–16 n. 13.

[55]See Hesse, "Markus Eremita," 454–55. The Syriac texts are found in Mingana, *Early Christian Mystics*; see the index nominum, 199.

[56]Hesse, "Markus Eremita," 455, n. 21, 22.

[57]Hesychius, *Cent.* 1.55–60 (PG 93:1497–99 = *Spiritual Law* 117–118), 1.79–81 (PG 93:1504–05 = *Justification* 2, 8). Although this work is ascribed by Migne to Hesychius of Jerusalem (c. 5th c.), this is not possible as the work contains multiple citations from John Climacus and Maximus the Confessor: see Kirchmeyer, "Hésychius le Sinaïte et ses Centuries," in *Le millénaire du Mont Athos, 963–1963: etudes et mélanges* (Chevetogne, 1963), 1:319–29.

[58]*Testamentum* (PG 99:1816); Khalifé ("Les traductions arabes," 117–18) notes that the other names are given in chronological order; and, since Isaiah died around A.D. 488 and Barsanuphius flourished in the first half of the sixth century, he has adduced this as further support for the approximate dating of Mark's works to the mid-fifth century.

sage attributed to Mark) in his *Monastic History* (840).[59] Throughout
this time, Mark's works were quarried for material that was then
included in numerous patristic florilegia and, by the ninth century,
in *Sayings of the Desert Fathers*.[60] According to the colophon of a
manuscript currently at the monastery of Grottaferrata, Nilus of
Rossano copied Mark's *Attorney* in 965.[61] This work was part of the
compilation that Nilus prepared for the edification of a community
of Italo-Greek monks in Calabria living according to the Rule of St
Basil. Significantly, Nilus chose to put Mark's writings at the head of
his collection.[62] As we will have occasion to note, Nilus was not the
only spiritual director who considered Mark's works to be a suitable
foundation for the spiritual life.

Apart from these references to the circulation of specific works,
we have evidence of the works circulating in collections. It would
appear that Mark's works were circulating as a collection by the
seventh century. In a dossier of patristic writings on the incarnation
(*Doctrina patrum de incarnatione Verbi*), we find a list that gives the
lengths of a variety of writings ranging from Scripture to the fathers.
Most of the spiritual writings in the list are also represented in the
Philokalia, but the list of Mark's writings is considerably longer than
what we find in the *Philokalia*.[63] Further evidence for a corpus of
Mark's writings comes from Photios the Great (c. 858), who included
in his *Library* a list of the works of Mark that were available to him:

[59]Thomas of Marga, *Historia Monastica* 4.17 (= *Justification* 157–158; 88–90;
147–148); 5.9 (unidentified), 13 (= *Spiritual Law* 12); 6.1 (= *Repentance*) (Wallis Budge,
Book of Governors, 1:221, 276, 300, 326 [Syriac text], 2:421, 502, 534–35, 570 [English
translation]); see further Hesse, "Markus Eremita," 457 n. 26.

[60]See Gribomont, "Marc le Moine," 279.

[61]See G. de Durand, "Une ancienne stichométrie des œuvres de Marc l'Ascète,"
Revue d'Histoire des Textes 12–13 (1982–83): 371–80, at 371.

[62]Metropolitan Kallistos (Ware), "Introduction," xlvi n. 2.

[63]*Doctrina patrum de incarnatione Verbi* refers to *Spiritual Law*; *No Justification*; *Mind's Advice*; *Repentance*; *Baptism*; *Attorney*; *To Nicholas*; and *Melchizedek* (F.
Diekamp, ed., *Doctrina Patrum* [Münster, 1907], 237–42). By contrast, the *Philokalia*
includes only *Spiritual Law, No Justification,* and *To Nicholas.* Evidence from *Doctrina
Patrum* will be discussed below in connection with de Durand's arguments against
the authenticity of *To Nicholas.*

Spiritual Law, No Justification, Repentance, Baptism, Mind's Advice, Disputation, Fasting, and *To Nicholas.*[64]

At roughly the same time, an anonymous Irish monk undertook to copy *Spiritual Law* and include an interlinear translation into Latin at the abbey of St Gall, c. 850—thus providing us with the oldest surviving text by Mark in the original language.[65] It has been conjectured that Bishop Marcus, his nephew Moengal (or Marcellus), and several other Irishmen may well have brought the Greek text of *Spiritual Law* to Switzerland from Rome, where they had gone on pilgrimage and where they would presumably have been able to acquire a copy from the Greek monks residing there.[66] This possibility is somewhat strengthened by the fact that Moengal taught Greek to Notker Balbulus (thus indirectly contributing to the influence of Greek models on early medieval Latin hymnody), which bolsters the idea that he may have been in contact with Greek monks and could have been interested in bringing Greek material back to St Gall.[67] Around the same time, John Scotus Eriugena seems to have drawn on Mark's *Spiritual Law* as he prepared his *Periphyseon*—but whether he knew the text in Latin or Greek is unknown.[68] Unfortunately, apart from these tantalizingly brief appearances, Mark's works do not appear in Latin until they figure into debates between Catholic and Protestant theologians several centuries later.

But before we turn to references to Mark that occurred in the second millennium, it is worth reiterating an observation made by

[64]Photios, *Bibliotheke*, cod. 200 (R. Henry, ed., *Photios: Bibliothèque* [Paris, 1962] 3:97–99); on the dating for cod. 200, see de Durand, *Marc le Moine*, 1:20.

[65]B. M. Kaczynski, "A ninth-century Latin translation of Mark the Hermit's ΠΕΡΙ ΝΟΜΟΥ ΠΝΕΥΜΑΤΙΚΟΥ," *Byzantinische Zeitschrift* 89 (1996): 379–88. Before Kaczynski's publication, the oldest known copy of Mark in Greek was Lavra *B* 37, completed by the monk Luke on Aug. 8, 970: see de Durand, *Marc le Moine*, 1:46 n. 2.

[66]B. M. Kaczynski, *Greek in the Carolingian Age: The St Gall Manuscripts* (Cambridge, MA: Medieval Academy of America, 1988), 23. The primary source for this information is Ekkehard IV, *Casus S. Galli* 2 (MGH Scriptorum 2:78).

[67]For Moengal's relationship to Notker and Tuotilo, see McCarthy, "Notker Balbulus," in *New Catholic Encyclopedia* (New York: McGraw-Hill, 1967–) 10:525–26.

[68]Cf. the notes to *Periphyseon* 3, lines 111–12, by Jeauneau, CCCM 163:6. We wish to thank Bernice Kaczynski for drawing this reference to our attention.

de Durand. We have mentioned that Babai the Great found Mark especially useful in his struggles against Messalianism, and that Mark's works circulated in Syriac from a relatively early date. Notwithstanding the generally accepted view that spiritual literature circulated across doctrinal boundaries rather freely in the Christian Near East,[69] de Durand has rightly suggested that it is nevertheless difficult to imagine a prominent living author whose works were freely circulating in the rival communities of sixth-century Mesopotamia, without prompting any comment at all regarding his loyalties.[70] This suggestion can be taken as further circumstantial evidence that Mark's career was over long before his works began to circulate in Syriac. Under such circumstances, it would be possible for Mark to be taken as an admirable author by rival communions with no concern that Mark might speak out to clarify matters, or otherwise cause embarrassment by making his loyalties known. More to the point, it would also be possible for Babai to speak highly of Mark and tactfully ignore the anti-Nestorian polemic of Mark's christological treatise all the while.[71]

Even though in surveying the relevant material from the first millennium we have had occasion to note more Syrian than Greek authors, this should not be taken to suggest that Mark was ignored by the Greeks. For example, Nicetas Stethatos (c. 1000–1080) relates that Symeon the New Theologian (c. 949–1022) received a book containing works by "those two marvelous men," Mark and Diadochus, from which Nicetas quotes a passage that corresponds to *Spiritual Law* 69.[72] This was presumably the same incident elsewhere related about the book that was given to Symeon by his spiritual father, Symeon the Pious:

[69]Cf. I. Hausherr, "Dogme et spiritualité orientale," *Revue d'Ascétique et de Mystique* 23 (1947): 3–37.

[70]De Durand, *Marc le Moine*, 1:26.

[71]Cf. Hesse, "Markus Eremita," 457.

[72]Nicetas Stethatos, *Life of St Symeon the New Theologian*; I. Hausherr, ed., *Un grand mystique byzantine: vie de Syméon le Nouveau Théologien (949–1022)*, Orientalia Christiana 12, no. 45 (Rome, 1928), 7.

> The young man also asked of him [*sc.*, his spiritual father] a book containing descriptions of the monks' way of living and their ascetic practices, and the elder gave him the treatise in which Mark the Monk teaches about the spiritual law. The young man received it like a gift from God himself and read the whole thing with diligence and attention, hoping to receive from it as much spiritual fruit as possible.[73]

It is worth noting that Symeon the elder gave Symeon the disciple Mark's book in answer to a request for general guidance. So at the beginning of the eleventh century in Constantinople, no less than in the tenth century in Calabria, Mark's writings were considered the gateway to serious pursuit of the ascetic life.

Anthony Melissa (i.e., "the Bee"), a Byzantine compiler who lived during the eleventh century, quoted Mark's *Spiritual Law, Repentance,* and *Baptism* in his *Spiritual Commonplaces.*[74] Mark's works figure into another eleventh-century Byzantine compilation—Paul Evergetinos' *Synagoge.* Nineteen extracts from *Spiritual Laws, No Justification by Works,* and *Baptism* have been identified in *Synagoge,* book four, alone;[75] for a definitive list, we must await the completion of the Belfast Evergetis project. John IV, patriarch of Antioch, refers to Mark in the twelfth century, and an anonymous Greek poet of perhaps the same period mentions "wise Mark's altogether ascetic works."[76] In the fourteenth century, Gregory of Sinai and the Xanthopouloi brothers cited *Baptism.*[77] The general

[73]Symeon the New Theologian, *Catecheses* 22; B. Krivocheine, ed., *Syméon le Nouveau Théologien: Catecheses,* Sources chrétiennes 104 (Paris: Cerf, 1964), 366.31–38.

[74]*Loci Communes* 1.16 (PG 136:824 = *Spiritual Law* 137), 1.17 (PG 136:832 = *Repentance 7*), 1.39 (PG 136:913 = *Spiritual Law* 163), 2.93 (PG 136:1228 = *Baptism* 5).

[75]See Cunningham, "Creative Selection? Paul of Evergetis's Use of Mark the Monk in the *Synagoge,*" in M. Mullett and A. Kirby, eds., *Work and Worship at the Theotokos Evergetis,* Belfast Byzantine Texts and Translations 6.2 (Belfast, 1997), 134–42.

[76]John of Antioch, *De monasteriis laicis non tradendis* 5 (PG 132:1125); Anon., "Iambs on the Words of the Holy Fathers, or On the Ascetic Saints," line 40 (G. C. Amaduzzi, ed., *Anecdota litteraria ex MSS: Codicibus eruta* [Rome, 1773], 2:28).

[77]Gregory, *De quiete et oratione* 3 (PG 150:1308); the Xanthopouloi brothers, *Methodus et regula* 6 (PG 147:641–44).

level of interest in Mark's works during the first half of the second millennium is eloquently expressed in a slogan that is reported in a fourteenth century manuscript as something that was often repeated by monastics and ascetics: "Sell everything and buy Mark."[78]

Two hundred years later, the circulation of Mark's work in the West becomes relevant. Roughly seven centuries after the Irish monk copied out part of *Spiritual Law* at St Gall, that same treatise was published by Johann Setzer (or Secerius) of Haguenau in 1531.[79] This publication marks the beginning of the sustained Western interest in Mark that has continued up to the translation in hand, and shows signs of increasing sophistication. But it would be a mistake to stress only the scholarly interest in Mark. For even though the positions taken up by Obsopaeus, Flacius and the Centuriators, Schelwig and Oudin on the one hand, and by Bellarmine, Picot, Brasichellanus, Fronton du Duc, and Archbishop Sandoval of Toledo on the other were in the form of historical arguments, they were nevertheless motivated by lively spiritual and theological concerns. These concerns are exemplified by Bellarmine and Schelwig, who respectively represent the Roman Catholic and Protestant sides of the debate. As Bellarmine wrote in response to Protestant arguments that find their culmination in Schelwig, it may be helpful to turn first to Schelwig (even though he wrote a generation after Bellarmine).

Samuel Schelwig (1643–1715) was a leading proponent of Lutheran orthodoxy in the fight against Pietism in Saxony. He was a professor of theology in Danzig and, though he specialized in dogmatics, he appears to have been broadly familiar with Mark's writings. As such, he was part of a line of Protestants who found Mark's emphasis on the utter gratuity of God's grace to be deeply congenial to his own religious outlook. In 1688, Schelwig produced a pamphlet entitled, *Theological theses on justification and good works excerpted from the work "On those who think they are justified by their own works"*

---

[78]MSS Vat. gr. 698f, as cited by Gribomont, DSp 10:279; de Durand (*Marc le Moine*, 1:37 n. 2) notes that the same advice is found in Athens, MSS BN 322 and 547.
[79]The following discussion is based on de Durand, "Controverses occidentales."

of Mark the Hermit, a saint and ancient writer, illustrated with brief notes. Schelwig then argued that Mark's faith was consistent with the Lutheran profession—but also with that of John Chrysostom, Jerome, and Augustine. This looking back to the golden age of the Fathers and finding there *ur-Protestantizmus* (so to speak) is unsurprising. In this, Schelwig was carrying on the legacy of the *Magdeburg Centuries.* The Centuriators followed the traditional dating of Mark, not least because they were motivated to make his teaching as early as possible, and portraying him as the disciple of John Chrysostom was therefore appealing.

Robert Bellarmine (1542–1621) was actively involved in the Counter-Reformation and, along with other Catholic figures, urged that Mark should be read (if at all!) only with extreme caution. Bellarmine's treatment of Mark in *De scriptoribus ecclesiasticis* (1613) was in all likelihood influenced by the exigencies of combating Protestantism. This is perhaps the most charitable explanation for his attempt at identifying Mark with a certain ascetic of the same name mentioned by Zonaras, thus pushing Mark's writings back to 906. Bellarmine has been roundly criticized for this dating. Tillemont found it unsustainable.[80] De Durand has been even more to the point: Bellarmine should have perfectly well known that Photios (c. 815–897) had read Mark's works, since Photios' *Library* had been published in Latin twelve years earlier and Bellarmine's contemporary, the Jesuit missionary Antonio Possevino, had already drawn attention to Photios' notice; in light of this, de Durand dismisses Bellarmine's dating as "a dishonest and ineffective ruse."[81] In de Durand's view, this was a transparent attempt to discredit Mark by making him later than was generally accepted. But it is striking that Bellarmine is representative of the Catholic trend to urge caution in reading Mark, rather than to offer a new reading of Mark. It appears to have been taken for granted by both sides of the debate that Mark was indeed proto-Protestant in his understanding of grace. So it will

[80]Tillemont, *Mémoires*, 10:350–51 ("Note on Silvanus").
[81]De Durand, "Controverses occidentales," 178–79.

be convenient for us to now look at Mark's teaching in context, and assess the merit of that view.

MARK'S TEACHING

It is universally recognized that grace is an extremely important concept for Mark, to such an extent that Mark's position has been compared to Augustine's.[82] Counterpointing his emphasis on grace is Mark's highly developed understanding of sin, which in turn informs his understanding of the salvation that Christ offers. These three themes make up a network that adequately, if not comprehensively, introduces Mark's thinking. So we will take them as a convenient point of entry for describing Mark's theological preoccupations.

The Fall and its consequences

Mark is outspoken in describing the aftermath of the ancestral sin: all humanity is "born under the sin of the transgression" (*Repentance* 10). That phrase, *hypo tēn hamartian*, occurs elsewhere in Mark's writings (*On the Incarnation* 8, page 258) but, as Metropolitan Kallistos (Ware) has noted, it is important to attend carefully to what Mark means by being "under the sin." In the first place, it is clear that the sin in question is not merely hypothetical. For, even if there were no actual sin (i.e., Rom. 3.23 notwithstanding), the sin under which we are born would of itself necessitate repentance: "if not for our *own* sin, then for the sin of the transgression" (see *Repentance* 12). On the other hand, it is equally clear that Mark does not believe that we inherited the actual transgression of Adam. According to Mark, if the transgression itself were transmitted, we would not be blame-worthy for it because transgression (if it is to be culpable) "takes

---

[82]Thus, Metropolitan Kallistos (Ware), "Baptism and the Ascetic Life," 444, 449.

place because of free will and not by necessity" (*Baptism*, resp. to qu. 17). To understand what it is that we have inherited from Adam according to Mark's view, we should begin with what Mark understood Adam himself to have experienced: "an assault that took place according to divine dispensation, a transgression that took place because of Adam's own faithlessness, death in accordance with God's just judgement" (ibid.). As we have already seen, Mark precludes the possibility that we inherited the transgression itself. This leaves the assault, or "suggestion" (*prosbolē*), and death as possibilities. In keeping with the ascetic tradition to which he belongs, Mark understands suggestion to be blameless—suggestion is merely a device used by demons, and as such it reflects badly on them, but not on those who are exposed to it (see *Baptism*, resp. to qu. 5). This leaves death, glossed by Mark as evidence for "the just judgement of God," as a possibility. And in fact it is precisely death, which is "alienation from God" according to Mark, that Adam experienced and that we have as our inheritance from Adam (*Baptism*, resp. to qu. 12).

So Mark teaches that we inherit from Adam the state of being alienated from God, which is, first and foremost, *spiritual* death, but which also necessarily entails physical degradation and eventually biological death. And yet, for Mark, this is not the neutral process that we think of as being inextricably bound up with growth and change. To the contrary, it is sinful and—unexpected though it may be to find such a teaching from the pen of an Eastern spiritual father—guilt attaches to it.[83] Mark characteristically uses the word *enklēma* to describe the human condition (see *Inc* 31.18).[84] Now *enklēma* and related words all refer to an accusation that is made in a case of litigation. So, when Mark says that "No one was exempted from the accusation," he means that we are all liable for the alienation from God that is a blameworthy part of the human condition. Here, then, is Mark's description of what Adam experienced and then passed on to his descendants:

[83]Cf. Metropolitan Kallistos (Ware), "Introduction," pp. xvi–xxi.
[84]See Plested, *Macarian Legacy*, ch. 5.

The first human, after enjoying the aforementioned bounties through created things, was tricked by the Devil's sophistries and disobeyed God. Because of this disobedience, he fell under sin and, because of sin, was handed over to death [Rom 4.25, 5.12]. Because of him, we all have fallen from eternal life, whether sinners or righteous. No human being has escaped accusation because the root of our nature, I mean the first human being, is mortgaged to him. Afterwards, danger was unavoidable; death, likewise, became inescapable (*Inc* 31).

Mark elsewhere reiterates this view. As he explains, we have become "prisoners" who are "being lorded over by the Enemy"; our "harsh captivity" means that we are "ruled by invisible and bitter death" (*To Nicholas* 8.6–9.1). Mark affirms that sin is an "inextricable bond" (*alytos desmos*: see *Inc* 32), and that after the ancestral sin we live in a state of "forced servitude" (*Baptism*, resp. to qu. 5). According to Mark, all the evils that followed Adam's initial transgression are part of "a just sentence" (*Inc* 32). It is clear, then, that Mark, in propounding his view of what was entailed by Adam's sin, did not limit himself to metaphors of impaired growth or of diminished health. To the contrary, he availed himself of the language of accusation, just judgement, and captivity. In other words, Mark uses a rich variety of legal terminology to describe the condition of fallen humanity. (It should also be noted that Mark has recourse to other evaluative language when describing the empirical reality of fallenness, as, for instance, when he observes that "error became more characteristic of [man] than truth" [*Inc* 31].) Even though psychological concepts like "guilt" do not figure into Mark's analysis of the results of the Fall, it is clear that he has a profound awareness of the consequences of sin that can be meaningfully compared to Augustine's—and, as we shall see, to Gregory of Nyssa's and Diadochus of Photike's. It is also clear that Mark holds no hope whatsoever that humans can free themselves from their broken condition:

If the commandment was prescribed, then the condemnation for transgressing it was determined, the judge infallible, his verdict trustworthy, his law truthful, his justice unvarying, repentance impossible because it does not have an undefiled priest. Everyone is liable to condemnation (*Inc* 31).

As Mark relentlessly and tirelessly asserts, this is not a situation from which anyone can extricate himself.

Grace and how it abounds

Freedom from the "inextricable bond" of sin comes through Baptism, according to Mark, for it is through Baptism that Christians mystically receive grace and are thus liberated for the performance of spiritual work. Mark's teaching about the efficacy of Baptism is robust. Jesus Christ, he teaches, "cleanses and renews us through Baptism; he places us in the paradise of the Church; he allows us to eat from every tree in paradise [Gen 2.9]—that is, to love everyone baptized in the Church . . ." (*Baptism*, resp. to qu. 17). It is not for nothing that Mark describes the community that comes into being through Baptism as paradise. Mark has an extremely high estimation of the power of Baptism to restore Christians to the state enjoyed by Adam before the Fall:

Neither God nor Satan forces the will to do his bidding after Baptism (*Baptism*, resp. to qu. 2).

Whatever things Holy Scripture says to us concerning purification, it exhorts us as free persons not to hold onto such defilements but to love liberty, since we have the power to incline whichever way we want, whether towards good or towards evil (*Baptism*, resp. to qu. 3).

And Mark explicitly equates the renewed state of Christians to Adam's state:

> If we and Adam share a single nature, it necessarily follows that his nature accords with ours, and ours with his. [. . .] he was not forced to transgress the commandment because of his nature, but rather wanted to do so of his own free will. Thus just as Adam was susceptible to Satan's assault and had the power to obey or not to obey, so too do we (*Baptism*, resp. to qu. 11).

> By divine dispensation we have an "initial thought," just as Adam did—and we can will to disobey it or not disobey it, just as Adam could (*Baptism*, resp. to qu. 17).

Mark's strong affirmation of the integrity conferred by Baptism is probably part of his polemic against the Messalian idea that Baptism deals with sin only in a superficial way. At this point in Mark's analysis, the parallel with Augustine's teaching breaks down: though they both use similar concepts to evaluate the extent of the damage wrought by Adam's transgression, it is clear that Augustine would not agree with Mark's belief that Christians are restored to an Edenic state of freedom. Late in his life, Augustine maintained that "the guilt [*reatus*] of desire is absolved by Baptism, but the infirmity remains."[85] But it would be misleading to suggest that the difference between the two views is narrowly cultural or otherwise reflects some mysterious difference between Greek and Latin mentalities. In point of fact, Mark's affirmation is extreme even by comparison with other Greek authors. The comparison with Gregory of Nyssa and Diadochus of Photike is instructive. Diadochus agreed that Baptism cleanses us from "the smudge that comes from sin," but thought that even Baptism "does not transform the duality of

[85]Augustine, *Retractationes* 1.14.3; ed. P. Knöll, *Opera* I.ii, CSEL 36 (Vienna, 1902), 73.

our will yet," and so perseverance in a lifetime of ascetic effort is required.[86]

On a similar note, Gregory taught that Baptism brought about "not a total effacement, but a break in the continuity of evil"; he even boldly stipulated that, in cases where the rite is not followed by a Spirit-filled life, "the water is just water, because in what has happened the gift of the Holy Spirit is manifested nowhere."[87] Mark's evaluation of that scenario is importantly different. He writes, "Even if it is not on account of *our* sin but rather the sin of the transgression, we are cleansed when we are baptized and, once we are cleansed, we receive commandments. The person who does not do the latter has profaned the former and 'is forgetful of the cleansing of his past sins' [2 Pet 1.9]" (*Repentance* 12). His view, then, is that we tarnish the perfection of Baptism, or, as he puts it elsewhere, "If we do not keep the commandments, the grace given to us is not revealed" (*Baptism*, resp. to qu. 5). In Mark's mind, there is no possibility of a defective Baptism into the Church,[88] though he knows perfectly well that there are circumstances in which people do not enact the gift of grace that they received at Baptism. This is precisely why Mark insists on the need to "reveal" the grace that is imparted at Baptism— which requires undertaking some ascetic practices, but perhaps even more importantly a willingness to forgive one's neighbors (cf. *Mind's Advice* 4). If we fail to act upon baptismal grace, and neglect the commandments or (worse still) act evilly, then we must not be surprised to find evil at work within us. This awareness adds a note of urgency to Mark's teaching about the perfection of Baptism:

[86]Diadochus of Photike, *Century* 78; J. Rutherford, ed., *One Hundred Practical Texts of Perception and Spiritual Discernment from Diadochus of Photike*, Belfast Byzantine Texts and Translations 8 (Belfast, 2000), 107.

[87]Gregory of Nyssa, *Catechetical Orations* 35, 40 (PG 45:89, 101).

[88]This is not to say that Mark cannot imagine a defective Baptism. The fact that he speaks of "Baptism into the Catholic Church," together with his awareness of communities (such as the Novatianists and Melchizedekians) who are outside the Catholic Church, opens up the possibility that Mark could conceive of an imperfect baptism—which would be one that had occurred outside the Catholic Church. But Mark does not specifically address this possibility.

If sin is destroyed by Baptism, someone will say, why does it continue to work in the heart? We have stated the cause many times: it is not because sin has been left to do its work after Baptism, but because sin is cherished by us because we have neglected the commandments. Holy Baptism provides the perfect release; to bind oneself again because of one's evil inclinations or to be freed from them because one keeps the commandments is a matter of choice and free will (*Baptism*, resp. to qu. 4).

Baptism restores us to a right relationship with God by delivering us from the death we have inherited from Adam, and thus enables us to live in a godly way. It also creates a community in which the conditions for implementing this gift are favorable—that is, the paradise of the Church. But, with his characteristic emphasis on the awesome freedom that abides in Christians, Mark insists that such a life must be deliberately embraced, and sometimes at great cost. This is what it means to put into practice the spiritual law.

Christ's law of liberty

The spiritual laws that must be enacted, like the very grace that enables us to put them into effect, come from Christ himself. Thus, Mark asks,

Have these people not heard that the commandments of Christ, given after Baptism, are a law of liberty [Jas 2.12]? As Scripture says: "Act and speak as those who are to be judged by the law of liberty" [Jas 2.12] (*Baptism*, resp. to qu. 2).

The laws, then, are given by Christ along with the grace without which we cannot practice them—for "grace has been mystically bestowed on those who have been baptized in Christ and becomes active in them to the extent that they keep the commandments. Grace never ceases to secretly help us but it is up to us, as far as it lies within our own power, to do good or not do good" (*No Justification by Works* 56). This image of baptismal grace secretly at work within the Christian is as close as Mark comes to agreeing with the other Fathers whose views on Baptism and sin we have just surveyed. He comes closer to their view, perhaps, in teaching that this grace does not overflow into good deeds (so to speak) automatically. According to Mark, it is imperative that Christians should enact the grace implanted by Baptism, and do so precisely by putting "the commandments" into practice. Mark devotes a considerable number of his pages to these commandments—the "spiritual law"—and it is not necessary to rehearse here what Mark himself has stated with a luminous clarity that a brief summary cannot adequately represent. A better use for these pages would be to present some account of why, according to Mark, Christ is uniquely suited to the task of liberating those who are enslaved to sin.

In a lengthy passage found in *On the Incarnation*, Mark describes Satan's ongoing scheme for implicating humans in his crimes. Mark goes so far as to attribute the following line of reasoning to Satan: "Just as they have become my partners in evil, so too shall they be my companions in punishment. God is just and truthful and does not weaken his own law: just as he cast human beings out of paradise because of their one transgression and handed them over to death, so too shall he condemn them to be punished eternally with me for the additional evils they do" (*Inc* 32). But Mark observes that Satan's keen grasp of God's righteousness is not matched by an understanding of God's power. What Mark demonstrably does *not* have in mind by "God's power," however, is an overwhelming display of divine might. Rather, in keeping with the perennial Christian paradox, Mark claims that God's "strength is perfected in weakness" (2 Cor 12.9). In a return to his use of legal language which we have already noted, Mark takes care to explain how Christ set free those who were captive to sin in such a way as to maintain an emphasis on the justice of Christ's actions. Mark stipulates that, "taking flesh, the Power of God redeemed human beings, not by arrogating power to himself, lest he abrogate justice, but by exchanging himself for us and acting with justice." The continuation of that passage is worth considering in its entirety:

> He was begotten in human fashion,[89] taking upon himself perfect humanity—or, rather, through this unique human being he took upon himself all human beings. He also suffered for us in order to release us from judgement, establish justice, bring to completion what he had promised, and free human beings from death. To do so, he himself died for all and nullified the power of the Devil, without giving him the opportunity to arrogate power to himself and do what he wanted, just as he rescued us without arrogating power to himself but by acting lawfully and using his almighty power (*Inc* 33).

Christ's suffering, according to Mark, nullified the Devil's power in keeping with the law and justice. As he memorably puts it, the law's "perfection is hidden in the cross of Christ" (*Spiritual Law* 29). Although Mark suggests that God, in his omnipotence, could have "arrogated power to himself" and simply overturned his own judgement concerning fallen humanity, he teaches that God's power is expressed in the outpouring of love that is evident in Christ's willingness to suffer on behalf of humanity.

But we should draw back a bit and note at once that, according to Mark, Christ's suffering involved more than his death and the events that led up to it. Mark is also aware of the suffering implicit in the human condition, and he insists that Christ had a share in that suffering, too. Christ, according to Mark, humbled himself and took on

---

[89]Mark uses the same verb to describe divine generation and human birth.

human nature [2 Cor 11.7; Phil 2.8], which had been condemned to dishonorable passions and was subject to divine
judgement. All the punishments imposed upon humankind
by divine decree for the sin of transgression—death, toil,
hunger, thirst, and the like—he took upon himself, becoming what we are so that we might become what he is (*To
Nicholas* 9.1).[90]

Mark's talk of condemnation, subjection, judgement, and punishment for transgression is in keeping with his use of juridical terminology to describe salvation, while the last clause recalls Athanasius'
famous dictum: "He was made human that we might be made divine"
(*Inc* 54.3). Mark therefore sees Christ's Incarnation (no less than his
crucifixion) as an event that transformed the human race: "From the
time that Christ came to dwell with us, the new humanity, made 'in
the image and likeness' [Gen 1.26], is truly made new through the
grace and power of the Spirit, reaching the full measure of perfect
love which casts out fear [1 Jn 4.18] and is no longer able to fall, 'for
love never falls' [1 Cor 13.8]" (*To Nicholas* 9.3). While it is true, then,
that Mark emphasizes the consequences of Christ's death, his words
to Nicholas make it quite clear that Christ's life is no less significant
for the redemption of humankind. But Mark sees Christ's life as being
so deeply significant precisely because of his understanding of who
Christ is. Turning to this topic may help us better understand why the
life and death of Christ in particular has universal ramifications.

To understand Mark's position on Christ's life and death, it is
necessary for us to understand his position on Christ's life. On this
point, he is outspoken: Christ is God the Word become man, "he
is one and not two (even if he is thought to be united indivisibly
from two)" (*Disputation* 7 [20]). Thus, the Incarnation is for Mark a
matter of the hypostatic union of the Word with human flesh.[91] (It

---

[90]The attribution to Mark of *To Nicholas* has been subject to controversy; see
below.

[91]See, e.g., *Melchizedek* 5; *Incarnation* 13, 17, 21, 26, 30, 34, 42.

is quite apparent, however, that Mark intends *flesh* in the sense of complete humanity: he stipulates that the Logos took a human soul in becoming flesh.)[92] The term *hypostasis* has technical significance in Greek, but no obvious meaning in English, so it is perhaps worthwhile to consider how Mark uses it.

As one might expect, his use is clearest in the treatise *On the Incarnation* and from that treatise it emerges that such a union indicates first and foremost the singularity of Christ as a personal subject. Thus, Mark employs the negative language of the Council of Chalcedon—"indivisibly" (*Inc.* 7), "inseparably" (cf. ibid. 17, 52), and "without confusion" (ibid. 51)—so that "'Jesus Christ' defines the indivisible conjoining of divinity and humanity" (ibid. 21). Christ thus issues "from both" natures,[93] and it is owing to this conjunction that Jesus Christ can act as the mediator between God and humanity. The fact that Mark prefers to speak of Christ existing *from* both natures—rather than *in* both natures—gives some support to the claim that Mark's Christology has Antiochian overtones; but it is difficult to accept the assertion that Mark's Christology links him to Antioch on the basis of that similarity alone, particularly since Mark uses numerous terms taken from Cyril, without further comment,[94] and may well have been avoiding the flashpoint of other terms (*e.g.*, *Theotokos, physis*) out of deference to the *Henotikon*, Zeno's imperial prohibition against discussing such problems.[95] So inasmuch as Mark was committed to proclaiming that Christ's personal existence was fully divine and human at once and without compromise, he could readily affirm that the union of human and divine natures in Christ—not to mention Christ's sacrificial death—would have universal implications.

---

[92]*Incarnation* 16: "God the Word took flesh and became human with a soul."
[93]E.g., *Incarnation* 52.
[94]See footnotes 12–14, above.
[95]See Chadwick, "Identity and Date of Mark"; more recently, this theme has been taken up and advanced by Plested, *Macarian Legacy*.

WHY DOES MARK MATTER?

As this survey has shown, some aspects of Mark's thought have an immediate contemporary application—such as his focus on Baptism as the font of Christian life—while others are perhaps somewhat opaque—such as his strident emphasis on the kind of unity evident in Christ. But Mark's works are also interesting in that, as we have seen, they circulated during the Reformation and were closely (if not contextually) read by Lutheran divines and Roman theologians. Apart from the obvious historical interest of Mark's being discussed in the early modern era, these debates are important for our purposes because they call attention to the fact that a number of central themes in Mark's writings resonate with deep concerns for Western Christians, such as the consequences of the Fall and the necessity of grace for good works. As we have suggested, Mark's teaching is unusual for a Greek Father in that he speaks out so clearly on these points. And though it is far from obvious that his teaching can be slotted straightforwardly into the Protestant-Catholic dichotomy, it is nevertheless the case that the historical interest which his writings have had for Westerners may provide a useful point of departure for ecumenical dialogue.

On a related note, there is a great enthusiasm for the writings of monastic spiritual masters these days. Whether it be the *Sayings of the Desert Fathers*, the *Conferences* and *Institutes* of John Cassian, the *Letters* of Barsanuphius and John, the *Lives* of Sts Antony, Mary of Egypt, or Onouphrios, the *Philokalia* or the *History of the Monks of Egypt*—these testaments to the wisdom distilled from a lifetime spent in search of God are appreciated today by an unexpectedly broad readership. But Mark, whose works were deeply valued (as we noted) by Byzantine ascetics, has not been properly introduced to this audience. This is a pity, as his teaching has much of immediate value for modern Christians living in the world, not least of which are his salutary words on love for one's neighbors and his practical— and theologically informed—advice on the need for repentance. In a limited way, this volume of translation aims to set that unfortunate situation aright.

In preparing this translation, we have attempted to be consistent in using English words (or, in some cases, phrases) to render Mark's Greek. Although his Greek is sometimes obscure, he typically uses straightforward grammar, and most of the terms he favors are conventional fare for a Greek ascetic teacher. Mark has a predilection for lengthy sentences, however, and instead of offering a tangle of subordinate clauses and the like, we have opted to translate them as several brief sentences. Similarly, we have reformatted the text into paragraphs at appropriate junctures and added subtitles and internal references to facilitate reading the works. In doing so, we have consulted the French translations by de Durand and Zirnheld. Our aim throughout has been to provide a reliable guide to Mark's work in English, in the hopes that this might promote further study. As for procedure, Dr Vivian prepared the initial translations of Mark's works, which Dr Casiday then revised; Dr Casiday prepared the initial translations of the two brief works not by Mark that have been included and wrote the introductory material, which Dr Vivian then revised. The footnotes emerged from our discussions of the material.

Postscript: Disputed Questions

Three works attributed to Mark in various manuscripts have been subject to scholarly debate for some time: *Fasting, Neptic Chapters,* and *To Nicholas*. For the present volume, the translators have included *Fasting* and *To Nicholas* but have excluded *Neptic Chapters*. Another work, entitled *On Baptism* and ascribed by its editor to the otherwise unknown Jerome the Greek, has also been translated in an appendix to this volume. In the interests of clarity, it seems best to explain the decisions taken by the editors of this collection in regard to these four works.

Our decision to exclude *Neptic Chapters* follows what is, to the best of our knowledge, unanimous scholarly consensus. This consensus is based on the finding that the content of *Neptic Chapters* is derived substantially from Maximus the Confessor (c. 580–662) and from the Macarian Homilies.[96] Even though Mark's relationship to the Macarian Homilies is a complicated matter and it would not be utterly impossible for him to have quoted from those sermons for his own works, it is more reasonable to suppose that *Neptic Chapters* was composed by a later figure who made extracts from the Macarian Homilies and from Maximus than to push back our dating of Mark to enable him to have personally compiled the extracts from Maximos. It seems most likely that the work entered into Mark's corpus at a late stage.

We have opted to include *Fasting* despite a mounting case for attributing it to Marcian of Jerusalem.[97] Marcian is even less well known than Mark. This is probably attributable to Marcian's opposition to the Council of Chalcedon, in consequence of which most of his writings were preserved pseudonymously, in Greek and in Syriac. The editor of Marcian's works has observed that excerpts from *Fasting* 4 appear in the systematic collection of the *Apophthegmata,* and the whole appears in a sixth-century Syriac manuscript, attributed in both cases to Marcian.[98] Without wishing to argue against his conclusions, we have preferred to include *Fasting* in keeping with tradition and in the interest of fullness. From the days of Photios at least, the text was read as a work of Mark's. So even though it seems increasingly likely that the text was not written by Mark, it nevertheless seems good to provide it in English for those

---

[96]This finding is ascribed to Khalifé ("Les traductions arabes"), but we have not been able to consult the relevant article; his findings seem to have been summarized in the index to Maximos and the Homilies given at CPG 6096 (3:186).

[97]See Kirchmeyer, "Le moine Marcien (de Bethléem?)," *Studia Patristica* 5 (TU 80; 1962): 341–59; and Kohlbacher, "Unpublizierte Fragmente des Markianos von Bethlehem (nunc CPG 3898a–d)," in M. Kohlbacher and M. Lesinski, eds., *Horizonte der Christenheit* (FS Friedrich Heyer), Oikonomia 34 (Erlangen, 1994), 137–66.

[98]Kohlbacher, "Unpublished Greek Fragments of Markianos of Bethlehem (†492)," *Studia Patristica* 29 (1997): 495–500, at 499.

whose interest is in the collection rather than the author. We would also note that, because little emphasis has been placed on *Fasting* (both in the tradition and in the present work), our decision does not jeopardize the usefulness of this collection for those whose interest is in the author rather than the collection. Furthermore, it might be hoped that making *Concerning Fasting* available in English will prompt more discussion of its authorship.

As regards *To Nicholas*, we have decided to include it despite two articles by Mark's modern editor, de Durand, that argued against its authenticity. The first publication argued against the attribution on the basis of perceived differences between *To Nicholas* and the several undisputed works by Mark; the second, on the basis of manuscript evidence. We are not persuaded by the editor's arguments on either count. In fact, we have concluded that his arguments are conceptually flawed. Since we have taken *To Nicholas* as a valid source for information about Mark's life, it is appropriate for us to explain here, if briefly, why we have not deferred to the editor. To that end, we will summarize de Durand's articles and respond to them.

In his first evaluation of *To Nicholas*, de Durand argued that the characteristic teaching on spirituality and anthropology found in that writing is different from the teaching that emerges from Mark's undisputed works.[99] De Durand's comments on the psychological foundations of *To Nicholas* are profound and helpful, and it would be churlish to dismiss his scholarly evaluation as merely subjective opinion. To the contrary, his observations about the use of Evagrian ideas in *To Nicholas* are incisive and learned; they provide an excellent point of departure for a thorough evaluation of how much Evagrian influence can be found in Mark's undisputed works.[100]

All the same, we would want to sound three notes of caution. We can accept with gratitude de Durand's insights into *To Nicholas*, but nevertheless wish to dissent from his attempt at contrasting the

[99]De Durand, "Études sur Marc le Moine: I, l'Épître à Nicolas," *Bulletin de Littérature Ecclésiastique* 84 (1984): 259–78.
[100]Cf. de Durand, "L'Épître," 274–76.

advice offered specifically to Nicholas with the principles of spiritual life set down to a general audience in the undisputed works.[101] We can also refrain from concluding that Mark did not write *To Nicholas* even when faced with explicit divergences on the grounds that Mark was as entitled to change his mind or develop his thoughts as anyone is.[102] (It is worth pointing out in connection with that observation that we do not have an established chronology for the writing of Mark's works, which could be helpful in the matter at hand.) Finally, it is entirely reasonable to believe that different literary genres naturally result in different registers of speech, types of argumentation, and even points of emphasis. Since we have no other letters ascribed to Mark with which to compare *To Nicholas*, we could therefore be justifiably reluctant to make the comparisons that de Durand makes without commenting on differences in genre. (These last two points can be taken further by combining them and asking whether there is good reason to suppose that there is a rigid underlying system to Mark's writings that can be extrapolated from his works and stated synthetically. But this is not the place to pursue that question further.)

In another essay, de Durand evaluated the evidence for Mark's corpus that comes from five ancient stichometries (i.e., ancient lists of the length of Mark's writings, given in *stichoi*, or groups of syllables).[103] The manuscript that gives the most complete listing of Mark's works, *Vatopedinus* 507, dates to the twelfth century but, as de Durand concludes, the list itself is in fact much earlier: de Durand shows that Photios' list of Mark's works (dated to 858) depends upon this list, so it must be at least three hundred years older than the

---

[101] E.g., de Durand, "L'Épître," 267–68.

[102] Cf. his comparison of the "three giants" in *To Nicholas* with the looser configuration of temptations in the undisputed works: "L'Épître," 270–71.

[103] De Durand, "Une ancienne stichométrie." The best general introduction to stichometries (not least because of the numerous practical examples that it provides) is still J.R. Harris, "Stichometry," *American Journal of Philology* 4 (1883): 133–57, 309–31. As regards the matter at hand, it is worth just noting that Harris is much less sanguine about the prospects of using stichometric data than de Durand is; and, on a related note, he is much more forthright about how imprecise stichometries are.

manuscript in which it is preserved.[104] The date of the list can be pushed back even further than de Durand allows, however. Unlike the other stichometries surveyed by de Durand, *Vatopedinus* 507 does not contain Mark's works; instead, it contains *Doctrina partum de incarnatione Verbi*, a sixth- or seventh-century compilation of christological texts. We can therefore make a presumptive case on the basis of the evidence in *Doctrina patrum* that the list of Mark's writings goes back to the sixth–seventh century.

While it is true that this section of *Doctrina patrum* is found only in *Vatopedinus* 507, it is equally true that no one apart from de Durand—including the modern editor of the compilation—has given any reason for supposing that this section is a late interpolation into the text. All of the other information found in the relevant passage of *Doctrina patrum* is uncontroversial. In default of good reasons to suppose that the stichometry was inserted into the textual transmission at a later date, it seems arbitrary (not to say question-begging) for de Durand to assert that it goes back only to the ninth century.

Now, given de Durand's interest in isolating *To Nicholas* from the corpus of Mark's works, it is not surprising that he would not be interested in pushing the date for the stichometry back that far: if he were to agree with such an early dating, his argument about *To Nicholas* entering the collection only during Photios' time would fall to the ground. But it is striking that de Durand does not comment on the context in which *Vatopedinus* 507 reports the length of Mark's works. As we have noted, the contents of that manuscript are otherwise datable to the sixth or seventh century. Without firm reasons for supposing that the stichometric reference to Mark is a later interpolation into the material (and none are provided by de Durand), we are at liberty to take it as an authentic witness to Mark's letter at a relatively early date. In fact, questioning the entire passage for the sake of isolating the witness to Mark's works is a dramatic thing to do, like driving in a thumbtack with a sledgehammer.

[104]De Durand, "Une ancienne stichométrie," 376–77.

Furthermore, in the same article, de Durand presents in tabular form an analysis of the *stichoi*. He argues that this analysis shows that *To Nicholas* is unlike the other works by Mark. The *stichoi* for the rest of the works correlate closely to the number of characters in those works as computed by de Durand; but the number of characters in *To Nicholas* is greater than one would expect from the *stichoi*. This finding leads him to take the stichometries as providing further evidence against the authenticity of *To Nicholas*.[105] But de Durand's argument is not as compelling as it seems.

Even though de Durand reports the difference as though it were statistically significant, he does not in fact provide a statistical analysis of the data. The numbers he provides do not actually establish a meaningful pattern, because the sample set that de Durand uses is too small for straightforward manipulations of the kind he has offered to produce conclusive results. In other words, the significance of the numbers that he adduces is impressionistic rather than statistical. And in any case de Durand's table does not reliably report the difference between the stichometries and *To Nicholas*: His figure for the total number of characters in *To Nicholas* (28,217) includes Nicholas' response to Mark, and he offers no figure for *To Nicholas* by itself. This lapse is not necessarily inconsequential for the matter at hand. De Durand specifically notes that many of the manuscripts—at least one of which he included in the table—do not contain Nicholas' *Reply*.[106] If one brackets the *Reply* but otherwise follows de Durand's method for computing artificial values for *To Nicholas* to be compared with the stichometries, then the divergence is less than de Durand has reported and consequently even his impressionistic argument is less striking than it may have otherwise seemed. So de Durand's failure to distinguish the numbers for *To Nicholas* as such from the numbers for Nicholas' *Reply* does not inspire confidence.

[105]De Durand, "Une ancienne stichométrie," 377 (the table) and 378 esp. n. 1.

[106]De Durand, "Une ancienne stichométrie," 378: "Les chiffres fournis par l'ordinateur incluent la *Réponse* de ce même Nicolas, absente pourtant de beaucoup de manuscripts (notamment l'*Atheniensis* 549); compete seule, la *Lettre* ne serait plus longue que de 637 lignes de la *Patrologie*, au lieu de 722."

It is also worth noting that, in the conclusion of a chapter in which he decisively shows that Mark was a careful student of the Macarian literature, Plested has shown that the teaching found in *To Nicholas* is consistent with what he has demonstrated can be found in Mark's other writings.[107] He has queried the decision by de Durand to base his argument against the authenticity of *To Nicholas* on the absence from it of characteristic themes such as Baptism. As Plested rightly notes, *To Nicholas* is the only personal letter attributed to Mark—written, as it seems, to an acquaintance. So there is little reason to join de Durand in thinking that it ought to conform to the patterns that emerge from Mark's other writings, particularly since Plested has adduced a number of recurrent themes that are common to Mark's corpus as a whole and *To Nicholas* specifically. It might also be noted that, if our earlier claim about the relatively early date for the stichometry of Mark's works that appears in *Doctrina patrum* is accepted, then we have good reason for thinking that *To Nicholas* was part of the collection of Mark's writings from a very early stage indeed. This, of course, runs counter to de Durand's claim that the letter entered the collection only around the time of Photios.

In sum, although de Durand has raised a number of interesting points for consideration, it is our view that his case for separating *To Nicholas* from the undisputed works is not compelling. It is commendable for a textual critic to be skeptical when faced with a potentially evolving corpus of ancient writings such as Mark's. After all, no one disputes that at least one treatise that appears in the corpus ought not to be ascribed to him, so it was good for de Durand to ask whether any of the other treatises might have similarly been wrongly incorporated into the collection. But since de Durand's case against the authenticity of *To Nicholas* is inconclusive, it was also good for him to edit *To Nicholas* and to publish it even while expressing his reservations.

---

[107]Plested, *Macarian Legacy*, ch. 5.8.

VOLUME ONE

CHAPTER ONE

A Letter to Nicholas

Introduction

As we have noted in the general introduction, spiritual fathers like Symeon the Pious and Nilus of Rossano recommended that their spiritual children read Mark starting with *On the Spiritual Law*. But we have opted to begin with *To Nicholas* for three reasons: (a) it contains valuable information about Mark's life; (b) in it, Mark offers fundamental principles about the spiritual life; and (c) those principles are stated in a way that is applicable to Christian life in the world no less than to Christian life in a monastery. Let us look at each of those reasons in turn.

First, *To Nicholas* includes the few precious autobiographical details that we have from Mark. Mark mentions having "come to the desert in order to live with the true workers and athletes of Christ, so that we too in some small way may perhaps spiritually contend and compete alongside the brothers who contend against hostile influences and courageously resist the passions" (*To Nicholas* 1.5). He also speaks about an elder who was involved in Nicholas' life and does so in a roundabout way that may suggest he is talking about himself: "Remember how God providentially provided for you to come to Ancyra, and how you were hospitably welcomed with fatherly compassion by a certain freedman, and by divine dispensation became close friends with his very devout son, Epiphanius, in order that *both of you might be guided by a holy man onto the path of salvation and be received by the holy servants of God as true sons*" (6.3). If Mark is obliquely referring to himself in this passage, then it means that he lived in a monastic community in the vicinity of Ancyra before departing for some time to the desert (during which time he wrote *To Nicholas*).

Second, Mark wrote to Nicholas as to a beginner in the spiritual life. By contrast, *On the Spiritual Law* presupposes enough spiritual experience that the reader will be competent to make use of advice given in a somewhat challenging literary form, the "chapters" or *kephalaia*. In *To Nicholas*, Mark is explicit about the foundations of the spiritual life. He exhorts Nicholas to meditate on all God's blessings and always remember them (*To Nicholas* 2.1, 3; 6.1–4). Mark especially recommends meditating on Christ's humility (8.5–10.4), which is a powerful remedy for pride and anger (8.1–4). Meditating in this way will encourage Nicholas to behave piously and gratefully (2.2; 7.1–7)—and to hope that his upright behavior will be rewarded with further blessings (2.5)! But Mark knows very well that devotion and piety are not sustainable, and in fact can be extremely dangerous, when they are hypocritical (4.1–6; 11.1–2). He therefore warns Nicholas to examine his thoughts and to seek guidance from a discerning elder (5.2; 11.3–4). Thus, he will be able to recognize the wiles of the "Three Giants" of Ignorance, Forgetfulness, and Laziness (12.1–3), and ultimately he will be able to defeat them (13.1–3).

Third, despite the fact that some of the manuscripts describe Nicholas as "one living the monastic life" (*monazonta*), the *Letter* itself does not specify that Nicholas was living as a monk. It is possible that Nicholas was a devout Christian in the world who was striving to live spiritually through ascetic practices and who had therefore asked for guidance from Mark, a distinguished elder in a nearby monastery. It is true that Mark says,

> In the end, God guided [the soul] by a clear sign onto the way of salvation, and implanted in the heart a love for the ascetic life, and empowered it with joy to renounce the world and all its deceitful fleshly pleasures, and adorned it with the angelic habit of the monastic order, and provided for it to be readily

received by holy fathers into the organized community of a brotherhood (2.3).

But that does not mean that Nicholas himself had already reached such a stage. In fact, it appears that Mark lived near Nicholas and had previously been available to him for consultation and guidance. But if Nicholas were already living with Mark in a monastery, it is not at all clear why Mark would need to be "physically separated from you 'for a short time, in person, not in heart,' because we have come to the desert in order to live with the true workers and athletes of Christ so that we too in some small way may perhaps spiritually contend and compete alongside the brothers" (5). That being so, the letter can be read profitably by people today who want to lead a spiritual life but who live "in the world" rather than in a monastery.

The recent editor of Mark's works, George de Durand, argued strongly against the authenticity of *To Nicholas*. We, however, have offered arguments of our own in support of the traditional claim that Mark wrote *To Nicholas*. The reader can find a detailed discussion of de Durand's arguments, along with our defense of the traditional claim, in the postscript to the general introduction to this volume.

A Letter to Nicholas[1]

To my much-loved son Nicholas

1 *The purpose of Mark's letter*

(1) Since you have recently become very concerned about your salvation and have been very anxious to live in accordance with God, you have communicated with us and told us about yourself, describing what sort of efforts you have made and with what fervent spirit you have been intending to devote yourself to the Lord through a strict way of life and self-control and great mortification, striving both by keeping long vigils and through intense prayer. (2) You told us about both the pitched battles and the swarms of carnal passions that become aroused because of our physical nature and are stirred up against the soul on account of the law of sin that fights against the law of the mind [Rom 7.23]. You bewailed the fact that you are especially bothered by the passions of anger and lust, and you asked about some kind of method I might recommend and for words of encouragement about what sort of efforts and spiritual struggles you could make use of in order to position yourself above the aforementioned destructive passions.

(3) At that time we advised you, to the best of our ability, in person and with love, offering suggestions and ideas that would benefit your soul, and demonstrating what sort of ascetic efforts and exertions you should make with understanding and enlightened knowledge as your soul wages spiritual battle in accordance with gospel precepts; through faith, aided by grace, it can overcome the interior evils that fill the heart to bursting, especially the aforementioned passions. (4) The soul ought to take up the struggle more vigorously and

[1]Source: de Durand, *Marc le Moine*, 1:106–66.

without ceasing against those passions to which it is especially accustomed through predisposition and habit and by which it is harried and dragged down even more suddenly, until it subdues the fleshly and non-spiritual operations[2] of evil. The soul itself was previously subjected to these and was being dragged down by them and carried off as a prisoner by the continuous remembrance of thoughts and the evil habits brought about by its assent to interior imaginings.

(5) Since we are now physically separated from you "for a short time, in person, not in heart" [1 Thess 2.17], because we have come to the desert in order to live with the true workers and athletes of Christ so that we too in some small way may perhaps spiritually contend and compete alongside the brothers who contend against hostile influences[3] and courageously resist the passions, let us renounce sloth, let us shake off indolence, let us cast away from ourselves indifference, and diligently make every effort as we press on towards our goal of being pleasing to God. (6) Because of this I have been eager to scratch out in letters a little encouragement and advice to Your Sincerity for the benefit of your soul, that it may bear helpful spiritual fruit concerning those things that I talked about with you in person. I appeal to you to consider carefully, as though we ourselves were present, the small words of advice and encouragement that come with our humble letter.

2   *The foundation: Constantly recollecting God's love and benefits*

(1) My son, in order to begin living a life that benefits from being lived in accordance with God, you ought to begin here: You should, with indelible memory, and ever mindful of giving it your unceasing attention, recollect for yourself all the things that God, in his love for humankind, has done for you, and all the special dispensations and benefits he is giving you now for the salvation of your soul. Because

[2]*Energēmata*; see *Concerning Baptism*, notes 10 and 15.
[3]*Energeias*; see the previous note.

of indolence and apathy, the mind is veiled and forgets the evil that one has done; nevertheless, do not be unmindful of the many great benefits that God has given you, and as a result live the rest of your life uselessly and ungratefully.[4] (2) Such unceasing recollections as I have suggested, which like a sting prick[5] the heart, are always prompting it to confession, to humility, to thanksgiving with a contrite heart, to every kind of good effort, and to repaying God with one's godly virtues and practices, with one's heart always meditating with a good conscience on the prophetic saying, "What shall I repay the Lord for all the things he has given me?" [Ps 116.12].

(3) When the soul recalls the benefits it has received from birth from God because of his love for humankind—either how it has often been rescued from so many dangers or how, despite falling into so many evil ways and often willingly slipping into sin, it was not rightfully handed over to deceiving spirits for destruction and death, but instead the long-suffering and benevolent Master, overlooking its sins, protected it, awaiting its conversion—it recalls that, when it willingly enslaved itself to its enemies and to evil spirits on account of the passions, God continually supported it, watching over the soul and providing for it in every way. In the end, God guided it by a clear sign onto the way of salvation, and implanted in the heart a love for the ascetic life, and empowered it with joy to renounce the world and all its deceitful fleshly pleasures, and adorned[6] it with the angelic habit of the monastic order, and provided for it to be readily received by holy fathers into the organized community of a brotherhood.

(4) Who, having a good conscience, and keeping these things in mind, will not at all times persevere with a contrite heart, since he has so many pledges from the benefits he has received in the past,

---

[4]*Acharistôs*, "ungratefully," literally means "without grace" (*charis*).

[5]*Nuttousai*, which is related etymologically to *katanussein*, "spur on, goad," and *katanuxis*, "compunction," an important monastic virtue and practice.

[6]In Greek "adorned" (*katakosmēse*) and "world" (*kosmos*) are etymologically related. Mark is saying that when a person renounces the world, God rewards him by adorning him with the monastic habit; thus the monastic habit and life replace the world.

although he himself has earlier done nothing good? Once he has deliberated on the following, does he not at all times assume a firm faith? "Although I have done nothing good, but have instead committed numerous sins before God, caught in the grip of impurity of flesh and many other evils, 'he has not dealt with me according to my sins, nor has he repaid me according to my iniquities' [Ps 103.10]; instead, he has dispensed all these gifts and graces for my salvation! (5) If, then, I give myself over to serving him completely from now on by living a completely pure way of life and by practicing the virtues, how many good and spiritual gifts will he bestow, guiding me and empowering me for every good work?" Thus the person who preserves[7] such a thought as this at all times, and does not forget the many great benefits that God has given him, importunes himself and directs and urges himself on to every good ascetic practice of virtue and to every work of righteousness, always eager, always ready, to do the will of God.

3   *The chief obstacles to be overcome*

(1) Therefore, my beloved son, since, by the grace of God, you have natural intelligence, preserve within you at all times the following good reflections and meditations:

Do not let your mind be obscured by destructive forgetfulness.

Do not be hindered by laziness that frustrates the mind and turns it away from life.

Do not allow your thinking to be darkened by ignorance, the source of all evils.

Do not be enticed by negligence, which is completely evil.

Do not be dragged down by the pleasures of the flesh.

Do not be worsted by gluttony.

Do not be weighed down by sleep.

---

[7] *Sōzōn*, which also means "saves."

Do not let your mind be taken prisoner by lust, and do not defile yourself inwardly by giving your assent to sexually impure thoughts.

(2) Do not be defeated by anger that causes you to hate your brother. Anger, on account of some pathetic and wretched pretext, causes you both to inflict and to suffer pain, and has you storing up reminders of wicked thoughts about your neighbor, shutting you off from pure prayer directed to God. (3) Reducing the mind to utter slavery, anger has you suspiciously eyeing your brother and soulmate with savage thoughts. It fetters the conscience with irrational impulses controlled by carnal imaginings. It also hands you over for a while to evil spirits to whom you submit yourself for punishment, until the mind, completely at a loss and overwhelmed by sorrow and apathy and, because of the previously mentioned causes, having lost the spiritual progress gained by living in accordance with God, begins again and sets out once more, with great humility taking the first steps on the road to salvation.

(4) Toiling greatly in prayer and with all-night vigils, the mind, by means of humility and confession made to God, frees itself of the causes that have hindered it. Thus it begins once again to come to its senses. Illumined with divine grace through the illumination of gospel knowledge, the mind knows that the person cannot become a true Christian who does not give himself up completely to the cross in a spirit of humility and self-denial, who does not throw himself beneath everyone to be trampled on and despised, wronged and ridiculed and mocked. Nor can that person become a true Christian who does not patiently endure all these things with joy for the Lord, not making any claims on merely human attainments, either glory or honor or praise or the pleasures of food or drink or clothing.

4   *The absurdity of pretended piety*

(1) With such contests and prizes and crowns awaiting us, how long are we going to make a mockery of ourselves by pretending to be pious, serving the Lord as imposters, being seen one way by people but shown to be something else to him who knows in secret [Mt 6.6, 18]? We are thought to be holy by many, while in reality we are nothing but savages in character,[8] having the outward form of godliness while possessing none of its power before God [2 Tim 3.5]. We are thought by many to be virgins and celibates, but to him who contemplates what is hidden [Mt 6.6, 18], we are inwardly defiled by the impurities caused by our assent to lewd thoughts and smeared with the filth caused by the workings of the passions.

Because our ascetic discipline is for show only, we are still bowled over by people's praises and, thus blinded, lose all common sense. How long, then, will we go on with such foolishness, failing to make the spirit of the gospel our own? How long will we fail to know what it means to live according to our conscience and thus fail to eagerly pursue a way of life where we would find confidence because of our good conscience? How long will we still draw strength from the apparent righteousness that we show on the outside and, on account of our lack of true knowledge, deceive ourselves, relying solely on outward appearances, wanting to please people, chasing after the glory and honor and praise they have to offer?

(3) The one who "reveals the things now hidden in darkness and discloses the deliberations of the heart" [1 Cor 4.5] will surely come, the Judge who cannot be deceived. He neither defers to the wealthy nor pities the poor; he strips away a person's outer appearance and reveals the truth hidden within. In the presence of the angels and before his own Father, he crowns those who have lived their lives according to conscience as true athletes and champions. And in the presence of the Church in heaven composed of the saints and of all

---

[8]Mark's contrast involves a play on words: we are thought to be holy (*hagioi*), when in fact we are savages (*agrioi*).

the heavenly forces, like a triumphant general he leads as captives those of counterfeit faith who clothed themselves with the outward form of godliness and the mere appearance of a godly way of life, which they displayed to people, vainly propping themselves up with it, thereby deceiving themselves.

(4) Such persons as these are fearfully dishonored and condemned to the outer darkness [Mt 22.13], like the foolish virgins [Mt 25.1–12] who preserved their outer, bodily, virginity but, in spite of this, were not invited to the wedding feast. No, they also had lamps partially filled with oil—that is, they had a share in certain virtues and external accomplishments and certain spiritual gifts. Thus their lamps were also lit for a while, but because of negligence and ignorance and laziness they did not practice foresight and were not fully aware of the swarm of passions hidden within, operated[9] by evil spirits. (5) No, their thoughts were violated by the hostile powers[10] as they defiled themselves by assenting to such thoughts. They were secretly enticed and defeated by malicious envy, by jealousy that hates everything good, by strife, hatred, quarrelling, anger, bitterness, resentment, hypocrisy, wrath, pride, self-centeredness, flattery, self-satisfaction, avarice, by carnal desire that causes one's thoughts to turn to sensual pleasures, by lack of faith, absence of godly fear, cowardice, spiritual listlessness, grief, argumentativeness, indolence, drowsiness, self-righteousness, pride, boastfulness, covetousness, dissoluteness, gluttony, by despair, which is the worst of them all, and by all the rest of the vices subtly operating.[11]

(6) Even the good works they did or the godly way of life they seemed to lead were done to please people and reap words of praise from them. Even if they had a share in certain spiritual gifts, they sold these divine gifts to the spirits of self-centeredness and flattery. Because they defiled themselves with the other passions, they mixed their good occupations with wicked and carnal thoughts; thus they

[9]*Energoumenon*; see notes 2 and 3.
[10]*Energeiōn.*
[11]*Energēmasin.*

made[12] these occupations unacceptable and unclean, like Cain's sacrifice [Gen 4.5]. Therefore they came to the same end as such a person as Cain, were deprived of the bridegroom's joy, and were shut out from the heavenly bridal chamber [Mt 25.1–12].

5 *The need for guidance and discernment*

(1) So, considering and pondering and testing all these things, let us come to realize and understand the situation we are in, in order that, while we still have time for repentance and conversion, we may correct ourselves so our good works, performed with a pure heart, may in fact be true and good, not mixed with carnal thoughts. If we do not do this, our good works will be rejected, like a blemished sacrifice [Lev 1.3, 22.20], on account of our lack of godly fear and negligence and deficiency in true knowledge. Otherwise, patiently enduring the pains of virginity and abstinence and the toils of fasting and all-night vigils and mortifications, we will somehow waste our time. And, because of the aforementioned passions, our acts of righteousness—which appear to be good—will prove unacceptable to Christ, the heavenly priest, like sacrifices found to be blemished.

(2) Therefore, my son, the person who wishes to take up his cross and follow Christ [Mt 10.38] must especially give heed to knowledge and understanding by unceasingly examining the thoughts he has, and by showing great concern for his salvation and constantly driving ahead towards God. He does this through understanding and by asking questions of like-minded and spiritually compatible servants of God who are fighting the same spiritual fight lest, not knowing where he is going and how to walk in the dark, he make his way without the light from a lantern to guide him.

(3) The person who goes his own way, without some sort of gospel knowledge and discernment and guidance, often stumbles and

---

[12] *Apergazonto.*

falls into numerous pits and snares of the Evil One, frequently goes astray and stumbles into numerous dangers, and has no real sense of purpose. Many have undergone numerous pains and ascetic labors and have endured many mortifications and hardships for God's sake—but their stubbornness in going their own way and their lack of discernment and inability to ask their neighbor for help caused all their many toils and labors to be for nothing.

6   *The remembrance of and proper response to God's benefits*

(1) So then, my beloved son, in accordance with the assurances I gave you at the beginning of this treatise, do not be dragged down by the thievery of vice and laziness and so forget the benefits given to you by God, who loves us and deserves our adoration. Instead, set before your eyes those benefits, whether physical or spiritual, conferred on you from the moment of your birth right down to the present; meditate and reflect on them, in accordance with what was said: "Do not forget all his rewards" [Ps 103.2]. (2) Thus, your heart may be easily moved, in its zeal and love for God, to repay him, to the best of your ability, with a scrupulous life, a virtuous way of living, a godly conscience, and appropriate speech; moved, too, to dedicate your whole being to God, won over by the recollection of all these good things you have received from the good and compassionate Master. When you do this, because your heart recollects the benefits it has received, or rather the cooperative assistance given to you from above, it is spontaneously wounded, as it were, with love and longing: for God has not done such wonders for others, who are much better than you, as he in his ineffable compassion has done for you.

(3) Make every effort, then, to remember continuously all the good things that have come to you from God. In particular, continuously remember that great and wonderful grace and benefit that you told us God bestowed on you when you were sailing with your mother from the Holy Land to Constantinople and that fearful and

uncontrollable storm with its huge waves swept over you at night: (4) Everyone in the ship, along with your mother herself, perished in the depths of the sea, and by a miraculous manifestation of divine power, only you and two others were thrown clear of the ship and were saved. Remember how God providentially provided for you to come to Ancyra, and how you were hospitably welcomed with fatherly compassion by a certain freedman, and by divine dispensation became close friends with his very devout son, Epiphanius, in order that both of you might be guided by a holy man onto the path of salvation and be received by the holy servants of God as true sons.

7   Living for God in purity

(1) What worthy repayment can you make to God for all these good things bestowed on you by him who has called your soul to life? In justice you ought from now on no longer to live for yourself but for him who died and was raised for you [2 Cor 5.15] in order to pursue every righteous virtue, in order to put into practice all the commandments, always seeking "the will of God, what is good and perfect and acceptable" [Rom 12.2], and you ought to zealously pursue this with all your might. Subject your youth, my child, to the word of God, as the word itself demands, in order "to present your body as a living sacrifice, holy, acceptable to God, which is your spiritual worship" [Rom 12.1]. (2) Cool and dry up all the moisture of carnal desire by needing little and drinking little and keeping all-night vigils so that you yourself may also say with a proper attitude, "I have been made to be like a wineskin in the frost, but I have not forgotten your righteous ordinances" [Ps 119.83].[13] Knowing that you

---

[13]Evagrius and Cassian often advise against drinking much water because (they believe) the male body turns surplus water into semen, which must then be emitted from the body, so that too much water is inimical to chastity. See Evagrius, *Praktikos* 17 (A. and C. Guillaumont, eds., *Évagre le Pontique. Traité practique ou le moine*, Sources chrétiennes 170–171 [Paris: Cerf, 1971], 171:542); *Ad monachos* 102 (ed. H. Greßmann, *Nonnenspiegel und Mönchsspiegel des Euagrios Pontikos* [TU 39.4; Leipzig, 1913],

are Christ's, in accordance with the apostolic precept, "crucify your own flesh, together with its passions and desires" [Gal 5.24] and "put to death whatever is earthly in you" [Col 3.5], not only the practice of sexual sin, but also the impurity at work in your flesh on account of evil spirits.

(3) The person who expects the crown of true and undefiled and perfect virginity does not stop the fight here but, following apostolic teaching, struggles to put to death [Col 3.5] any indication or stirring of passion itself. The person who with fiery love expects angelic and undefiled virginity for his own body is still not satisfied even here, but prays to obliterate even conceiving of any possibility of lust by merely thinking about it, which arises as a disturbance in the mind without any movement and activating of bodily passion. This can be achieved only through the power and help and support of the Holy Spirit from above—if, indeed, there are those who are worthy of this grace.

(4) Thus the person who expects the crown of pure and undefiled virginity crucifies the flesh [Gal 5.24] through ascetic labors, puts to death whatever is earthly in himself [Col 3.5] through intense and persistent self-control, doing away with the outer person [2 Cor 4.16], paring him down and reducing him and peeling him to the bone in order that, through faith and ascetic labors and the working of grace,[14] "the inner person is renewed day by day" [2 Cor 4.16]. He advances to what is better, growing in love, being strengthened by hope. Adorned with gentleness, he rejoices with the fervent joy of the Spirit. He is directed by the peace that Christ gives, led by kindness, guarded by goodness, surrounded by the fear of God, enlightened by understanding and knowledge, illumined by wisdom, guided by humility. The mind, renewed by the Spirit through these and similar virtues, comes to recognize within itself the impress of the divine

162); and the words attributed to Evagrius at *Historia Monachorum in Aegypto* 20.16 (A. Festugière, ed., SH 34 [Brussels, 1961], 123); Cassian, *Conference* 12.11, 22.3, 22.6 (M. Petschenig, ed., CSEL 13 [Vienna, 1886], 351–53, 616–19, 621–27).

[14]*Charitos energeia.*

image and perceives the spiritual and ineffable beauty of the Lord's likeness and, self-taught and self-instructed, gains possession of the wealth of the inner law.

(5) Therefore, my son, pare down the youthful desires of the flesh; through the aforementioned labors put flesh on your immortal soul and with the aforementioned virtues renew your mind, with the Spirit offering assistance. The fleshly desires of youth, fattened with different kinds of food and with the drinking of wine, are like a pig ready for slaughter: thus the soul is led to the slaughter by the fires enkindled by bodily pleasures, and the mind is taken prisoner by the seething heat of evil desire and cannot resist the pleasures of the flesh. A profusion of blood leads to an effusion of spirit. (6) Young people should especially avoid drinking wine, or even catching a whiff of it, lest a double conflagration be ignited—I mean one caused when innate heat is combined with cups of wine poured in from outside; when this happens, fleshly pleasure boils over and drives away from itself the spiritual pleasure given by the pain of contrition and causes confusion and a hardening of the heart. (7) No, because of spiritual desire, young people should not be allowed to take their fill even of water, for going without water is especially helpful in assisting moderation. If you try this for yourself, rest assured that experience will show it to be so. In laying down this law, we do not wish to impose it on you as a compulsory yoke; rather, we are advising it out of love, making a suggestion and offering it as a good method for helping with true virginity and strict moderation. In offering our advice, we leave it to your own free will to do what it wishes.

8 *Struggling against anger and pride*

(1) Come, let us now also discuss a little the irrational passion of anger. It completely desolates and confounds and darkens the soul and, when it is active and in motion, makes a person act like wild beasts, especially the person suffering from the passion who is iras-

cible and quick to anger. (2) This passion is especially strengthened by pride and, when it grows strong, becomes indestructible, until the diabolical tree of bitterness and anger and fury, its roots moistened with the foul water of pride, blooms and flowers and produces a great crop of transgressions. In this way the edifice built by the Evil One in the soul becomes indestructible as long as it has for its support and stay foundations made of pride.

(3) So, do you want this tree of transgression (see Gen 3)—I mean the passion of bitterness and anger and rage—to wither away within you and become barren so that, taking up the ax of the Spirit, you may cut it down and (according to the apostolic saying [Mt 3.10]) throw it on the fire and remove it along with every evil? (4) Do you want to tear down the house of transgression? This the Evil One wickedly builds in the soul by gathering together at every opportunity, as though he were collecting stones, various plausible or implausible pretexts in our thoughts; these are made from materials fashioned from our words and deeds, and with them he builds a structure in the soul, laying a foundation whose support and stay are proud thoughts.

The need for keeping the Lord's humility in our hearts

(5) If, then, you want this house to be torn down and razed to the ground, keep the humility of the Lord in your heart at all times. Remember who he was and what he became for our sakes, and from what sort of sublime light of divinity he was revealed (insofar as the essences above can see such revelation) and glorified in the heavens by the whole spiritual realm: angels, archangels, thrones, dominions, principalities, essences, cherubim, seraphim, and the unnameable spiritual essences whose names, according to the mysterious saying of the Apostle, are unknown to us [Eph 1.21; Col 1.16]. (6) Reflect on the depths to which the Lord descended in his ineffable goodness as he in all respects became like us [Heb 2.17], "who were dwelling in

darkness and the shadow of death" [Is 9.2; Mt 4.16] and who had been born as prisoners on account of Adam's transgression and were being lorded over by the Enemy through the activity[15] of the passions.

9 *Christ's humility from incarnation to glorification*

(1) When, moreover, we were being held in such harsh captivity and were being ruled by invisible and bitter death, the Master of all creation, both visible and invisible, was not ashamed, but rather became like us in every way, yet without sin [Heb 4.15] (that is, he was without dishonorable passions), by humbling himself and taking on human nature [2 Cor 11.7; Phil 2.8], which had been condemned to dishonorable passions and was subject to divine judgement. (2) All the punishments[16] imposed upon humankind by divine decree for the sin of transgression [Gen 3]—death, toil, hunger, thirst, and the like—he took upon himself, becoming what we are so that we might become what he is.[17] "The Word became flesh" [Jn 1.14] so that flesh might become Word: "Although he was rich, he became poor for our sakes, so that through his poverty we might become rich" [2 Cor 8.9]. Through his great compassion for humankind, he became like us, so that through every virtue we might become like him.

(3) From the time that Christ came to dwell with us, the new humanity, made "in the image and likeness" [Gen 1.26], is truly made new through the grace and power of the Spirit, reaching the full measure of perfect love which casts out fear [1 Jn 4.18] and is no longer able to fall, "for love never falls" [1 Cor 13.8]. "Love," says John, "is God, and the person who abides in love abides in God" [1 Jn 4.16]. (4) The apostles were deemed worthy of this full measure of love, as were those like them who practiced virtue, and presented

---

[15]*Energeias.*

[16]In Greek "punishments" is *epitimia* and "dishonorable" is *atimia.*

[17]See Athanasius of Alexandria, *On the Incarnation* 54.3 (C. Kannengiesser, ed., Sources chrétiennes 199 [Paris: Cerf, 1973], 458): "He became human, so that we might become divine."

themselves perfect to the Lord, and followed the Savior with perfect desire[18] their whole lives.

(5) If you remember always and reflect upon such profound humility, which the Lord in his ineffable compassion took upon himself because of his love for us—that is, God the Word coming to dwell in his mother's womb; his taking human nature upon himself; his birth from a woman; his gradual growth in physical stature; the dishonor he suffered; the insults, the vilifications, the ridiculing jokes; the revilings, the beatings; being spat upon, mocked, and jeered; the purple robe, the crown of thorns [Jn 19.5]; the judgement against him by those in authority; the outcry against him by the lawless Jews, who were his own people, "Away with him! Away with him! Crucify him!" [Jn 19.15]; the cross; the nails, the spear, the drink of sour wine and gall [Mt 27.34]; the derision of the pagans; the laughter of those passing by and saying, "If you are the Son of God, come down from the cross right now and we will believe in you!" [Mt 27.40, 42]; and the rest of the sufferings that he patiently endured for our sakes: crucifixion, death, three-day burial in the tomb, the descent into hell— (6) then remember the fruits that have come from these sufferings, their nature and number: the resurrection from the dead; the harrowing of hell, by which he stripped death of its weapons for those who are united with the Lord; the ascension into heaven; the seat at the right hand of the Father [Eph 1.20]; the glory and honor "far above all rule and authority, and above every name that is named" [Eph 1.21]; the veneration accorded to the "firstborn from the dead" [Col 1.18] by all the angels on account of the sufferings he endured, (7) in accordance with what the Apostle says: "Let the same mind be in you that was also in Christ Jesus, who, though he was in the form of God, did not regard equality with God as something to be exploited, but emptied himself, taking the form of a slave and, being found

---

[18]Mark has just denounced passions (*pathē*) at 9.1. Here, however, he encourages desire (*pothos*). The difference is clear from the way it is used, for example, by Clement of Alexandria (*Stromateis* 8.1.3; ed. O. Stählin, GCS 17 [Berlin, 1970], 82) to designate the desire to attain virtue.

in human form, he humbled himself and became obedient to the point of death, even to death on the cross. Therefore God also highly exalted him and gave him the name above every name, so that at the name of Jesus Christ every knee shall bend, in heaven and on earth and under the earth," and what follows [Phil 2.5–10]. See to what great glory and heights the Lord's humanity was raised, in accordance with God's justice, because of the aforementioned sufferings!

10 *Remembering Christ's humility, and the consequences of being negligent*

(1) So then, if you keep the remembrance of these things in your heart with unflagging desire and purpose, the passion of bitterness and anger and rage will not master you.[19] When you undercut the foundations of the passion of arrogance by recalling Christ's humility, the whole structure of iniquity, of rage and of anger, easily and automatically collapses. (2) What a sclerotic and stony heart someone has if he continuously keeps in mind this great humility that the Divinity of the Only-begotten One took on for our sake, and recalls the sufferings enumerated and spoken of earlier, and is not crushed and stung into repentance and humbled! Will he not willingly become dust and ashes [Job 42.6], something to be trampled underfoot by people?

So, when your soul is humbled and crushed and you behold the Lord's humility, what sort of rage will be able to seize hold of your soul? What sort of anger, what sort of bitterness will be able to overcome the soul? (3) It seems to me that forgetfulness of these thoughts that are useful and life-giving for us; and laziness, the sibling of forgetfulness; and ignorance, their like-minded co-worker, are the deep-seated and inner passions of the soul. They are hard to discover and difficult to correct. They overrun and overshadow the soul with

---

[19]Once more, Mark contrasts spiritually profitable desire (*pothos*) to spiritually destructive passion (*pathos*).

a harmful curiosity.[20] They prepare the way for the rest of the evil passions to become active and furtively enter the soul, making it lose its fear of God and disregard what is good, which provides quick and easy access and operating room for every sort of passion. (4) When the soul has been overrun by forgetfulness, which is utterly evil; by laziness, which destroys; and by ignorance, the mother and nurturer of all evils, then the wretched and blinded mind is easily shackled by everything it sees or thinks about or hears. (5) For example, if the mind sees a woman's beauty, it is immediately wounded with carnal desire. So from that point on it eagerly and delightedly welcomes memories of what it has seen or heard or touched, and these memories, by forming mental impressions and evil preoccupations within the mind, re-present that beauty to the mind's eye. In this way, through the working of lustful spirits, they defile the wretched mind that is still subject to the passions.

11   *The seriousness of even secret thoughts*

(1) Afterwards, the flesh, too, if it is well-fed and youthful and overly-moist,[21] being easily aroused by such recollections as these, sets into motion[22] the workings of the flesh by means of the passion. Moved to lust, it works uncleanness, sometimes through dreams and sometimes while awake. Even if someone does not in reality have intercourse with a woman and is thought by people to be chaste and virgin and pure, or even has the reputation of being a saint, this person is judged impious and adulterous and dissolute by him who observes what is hidden [Mt 6.6, 8]. He will justly be condemned on the last day if he does not bewail and mourn his sins and with fasting and all-night vigils and unceasing prayers wear down the desires of the flesh and, healing and amending the mind by means

---

[20]At *Melchizedek* 6, Mark also sharply criticizes people for their harmful curiosity (*periergasia*).

[21]See n. 13, above.

[22]*Energei.*

of holy recollections and meditations on the word of God, offer worthy repentance to God, before whom he thought about or did these evils. (2) For the living voice does not lie when it says, "But I say to you that everyone who has looked at a woman lustfully has already committed adultery with her in his heart" [Mt 5.28]. On account of this it is beneficial especially for the young not to meet women at all, if possible, even if these women are considered holy.

The importance of acquiring discernment from a spiritual director

(3) If it is possible for someone to live away from people, it makes the warfare easier to bear, and one recognizes it more clearly. This is especially true for one who pays scrupulous attention to himself and, striving ascetically, has a way of life characterized by needing little and drinking very little water and keeping numerous all-night vigils while praying, and who is especially zealous to associate with those who are experienced in spiritual matters and to live with them and to be guided by them. It is dangerous to live alone, following one's own devices[23] and going unsupervised, and it is dangerous to live with those who are inexperienced in spiritual warfare. For people of that sort become caught up in other kinds of warfare, because the Enemy's machinations for evil and hidden ambushes are numerous, and he has different kinds of traps laid everywhere. (4) On account of this, a person should eagerly make every effort to live with those who possess spiritual knowledge, or at least to constantly meet with them, so that, even if he himself does not possess the lamp of true

[23] According to G. W. H. Lampe (*Patristic Greek Lexicon* [Oxford: Clarendon Press, 1961], 664), this is the first occurrence of *idiorythmia*. Lampe notes that here it has "a bad sense," though in later Greek that is not necessarily the case. Could it be that Mark is explicitly disavowing a particular kind of monastic practice here? If so, he may be following in the footsteps of St Basil, who recommended monastic life in community as something far better than solitary monastic life. Community provides opportunities for guidance and service that are not readily available to the monk in seclusion. See further A. Holmes, *A Life Pleasing to God: The Spirituality of the Rules of St. Basil* (London: Darton, Longman and Todd, 2000).

knowledge because he is still childish and spiritually immature, by walking with someone who does possess one, he does not walk in darkness, and is not in danger from snares and traps, and does not fall into the hands of spiritual beasts that dwell in the darkness and seize and destroy those who are walking in it without the spiritual lamp of God's word.

12 *Combating the three giants: ignorance, forgetfulness, and laziness*

(1) Therefore, my son, if you wish to acquire interiorly your own lamp whose spiritual light shines with the knowledge of the Holy Spirit so you can walk without stumbling in the darkest night of this present age and have your steps guided by the Lord so that, in accordance with the prophetic saying, your whole desire is the way of the gospel [Ps 37.23]—that is, if you wish to embrace the most perfect gospel commandments with fervent faith and share in the sufferings of the Lord by means of longing desire and prayer, then I will show you a wonderful method and plan in order to do so. It requires spiritual effort, using not bodily exertion or struggle but rather toil by the soul and mind and attentive understanding, assisted by fear and love of God. By means of this plan, you can easily rout the enemy's armies, as blessed David did: by means of his faith and trust in God, he killed a single giant sent by the Philistines, and thus with the help of his own people he easily routed thousands of enemy soldiers [1 Sam 17.40–54].

(2) The premise of our discourse here envisions *three* powerful and mighty giants sent by the foreigners; the whole opposing force of the spiritual Holofernes depends on these three.[24] Once they have

---

[24]See Judith 2.4–5. Holofernes, who was Nebuchadnezzar's general and "second only to himself," commanded 120,000 infantry and 12,000 cavalry. Mark makes an abrupt transition from the Philistines to Holofernes, but it is hardly incomprehensible, and there is no reason to emend the text (as some editors have done) or even express surprise at the transition, as though Mark were badly confused (as de Durand's note at this passage might suggest).

been brought down and killed, then the whole force of evil spirits will be weakened and can be destroyed. The three strong giants of the Evil One under consideration here are those that have already been mentioned: ignorance, the mother of all evils; forgetfulness, its brother and co-worker and assistant; and laziness, which weaves the dark cloak and veil that blankets the soul like a dark cloud. (3) Laziness supports and strengthens the other two, providing a foundation for them and shaping persistent evil in the soul that is grossly negligent. The other, supporting, passions are then strengthened and extended by laziness, forgetfulness, and ignorance; because they help one another and without each other are unable to maintain their position, they demonstrate that they are the strong forces of the Adversary and the powerful leaders of the Evil One. Through them the whole army composed of the spirits of evil infiltrates and sets up camp and is able to carry out its objectives. Without these three, the aforementioned spirits are not able to maintain their position.

13   *Defeating the giants*

(1) If, therefore, you wish to gain victory over the aforementioned passions and wish to easily rout the armies of the spiritual Philistines, through prayer and with God's co-operation go deep within and, entering into the depths of your heart, track down these three powerful giants of the Devil—I mean forgetfulness and laziness and ignorance, which prop up the spiritual Philistines. Through these three the rest of the evil passions infiltrate, operate,[25] and live and gain strength in the souls of the pleasure-loving and uninstructed. (2) Through great attentiveness and control of the mind, with assistance from above, find these passions, about which most people are ignorant, not even suspecting their existence, but which, being evil, are more destructive than all the other passions. With the weapons of righteousness [Rom 6.13], which are opposed to them—I mean

[25] *Energei.*

healthy mindfulness, the source of everything good; and enlightened knowledge, through which the soul awakens and drives out from itself the darkness of ignorance; and noble desire,[26] which prepares the soul and urges it on to salvation. Armed with these weapons of virtue, through the power of the Holy Spirit, through prayer and entreaty, you will contend nobly and bravely against the three aforementioned giants of the spiritual Philistines.

Final exhortation

(3) Through noble and healthy mindfulness of God, always reflecting on "whatever is true, whatever is honorable, whatever is just, whatever is pure, whatever is reverent, if something is excellent, and if something is worthy of praise" [Phil 4.8], drive away from yourself forgetfulness, which is wholly evil. Through enlightened and heavenly knowledge, obliterate the destructive darkness of ignorance. Through desire that is wholly virtuous and supremely good, drive away the godless laziness that works evil in the soul. Once you have acquired these virtues, not by a mere act of the will but by the power of God and with the co-operation of the Holy Spirit, with great attentiveness and prayer, you will be able to be saved from the three aforementioned mighty giants of the Evil One. When true knowledge and mindfulness of the word of God and healthy desire work together in concord and through active[27] grace stand together shoulder to shoulder in the soul, carefully protecting it, they obliterate every trace of forgetfulness and ignorance and laziness in the soul, and these are reduced to nothingness. Afterwards, grace reigns in the soul, through Christ Jesus our Lord, to whom be glory for ever and ever. Amen.

---

[26]*Prothymia*, a virtue, which should be contrasted with *epithymia*, "desire" or "lust," mentioned earlier by Mark.

[27]*Energous*.

CHAPTER TWO

Nicholas' Response to Mark

INTRODUCTION

The following brief letter, "Nicholas' Response to Mark," has been transmitted with Mark's works in some of the manuscripts. George de Durand did not edit it for his collection of Mark's works. That is not surprising: Since he did not consider *To Nicholas* an authentic writing by Mark, he would have had no special interest in a putative reply to it. In fact, he dismissed it as "a rather flat rehash of the 'Three Giants' theme" from *To Nicholas*![1] But his claim is not entirely satisfactory. In fact, the "Three Giants" are hardly central to *Nicholas' Response*, even if they are mentioned at two separate points in the response. The response is in no way a simple reduction of that theme from *To Nicholas*.

As for the rest of de Durand's criticism, we would agree that *Nicholas' Response* is "rather flat," but our conclusion is just the opposite of de Durand's: There is no good reason for anyone to have forged *Nicholas' Response*. The letter has no intrinsic merit as a work of theology. It is modestly interesting as a case study of ascetic introspection, but cannot be compared to the masterpieces of monastic self-evaluation written by Evagrius. In short, there are no obvious reasons for someone to have forged this (frankly, rather banal) letter and ascribed it to Mark's otherwise unknown correspondent. If *To Nicholas* is accepted as one of Mark's writings, there is no obvious reason to think that *Nicholas' Response* is anything

---

[1]De Durand, *Marc le Moine*, 1:42.

other than a concise acknowledgment from the grateful recipient of Mark's counsel.

Since no critical edition of Nicholas' reply is available, we have translated the letter from Galland's edition of Mark's works, as reprinted by Abbé Migne (PG 65.1051–53).

Nicholas' Response to Mark²

1 *Thanksgiving to God for Mark's response*

Thanks, thanks be to God, thanks for his unsurpassable and ineffable gift: He showed his love for humanity to a soul captive to terrible passions and almost completely estranged from him; and he watched over and visited it through a will that is compassionate and also utterly dedicated to God—I mean, through your virtuous and holy soul, which is devoted to God. From your soul you have sent me a radiant spark, full of divine light, and a hook with spiritual bait. It drew my miserable soul up from the tempest and from the thickest darkness, by the lamp of words that have been born in labor and longing by a thought that is united to God. So the excellent Lord made my understanding³ reject the three giants whom you revealed to me.⁴ They really are large and savage giants who never cease fighting the human race. And on this earth, whom do they attack as fiercely and terribly as they attack me? For even now I am shamefully but voluntarily ruled by them.

2 *How Mark's letter affected Nicholas*

But he who "never delights in the destruction of the living" [Wis 1.13] had mercy and manifested his longsuffering and compassionate love for humanity: He set in motion that pious thought, and awakened the will that lay in the deepest sleep, and revealed and made known to me the giants whom I have just mentioned. I mean, first, forgetfulness, which drove Adam from Paradise (for if he had not forgotten

---

²Source: PG 65.1051–53.
³*Dianoia.*
⁴The "three giants" of ignorance, forgetfulness, and laziness are mentioned in Mark's letter, *To Nicholas* 12.

the Lord's command, he would not have lost such great glory); then the negligence with which he negligently listened to his companion; then the ignorance through which he ignored who he was and what he was doing. The Lord Jesus made these three spirits manifest to me through the Holy Spirit, who dwells in you. Indeed, he truly sent a two-edged sword, which is the word of God, and cleaved my mind in half with great calm [cf. Heb 4.12]. What is more, he also instilled in my will a kind of spiritual sweetness, so to speak, from your words. How could I have enough mouths and tongues, then, to give appropriate thanks to God my true Lord for the acts of kindness toward me of which you reminded me[5]—or again, for the systematic way you wrote to me in your letter and for your compassionate words? They are stimulants to searching for the truth and keeping God's laws and much else, and are very profitable for those who wish to follow the path of the Lord that leads to eternal life.

3   *Mark's teaching is also profitable for others*

Such profit from your message came not only to me, but to as many as heard it as well. They were greatly enlightened in their thinking and bore much profitable fruit from the words that you have spoken so brilliantly. The words were doubtless strengthened by deeds, and the words were not heard as mere words, but as a visible deed set before our eyes. Your message immediately instilled great vigilance and watchfulness in their wills. Once your message was at work, it did not remain idle but immediately sprouted grain and brought forth ripe fruit. Not only that, but it was also inexhaustible, as God knows. For as often as I happen upon it, my poor soul is never satiated.

---

[5]Perhaps Nicholas is referring to the hospitality he received after the shipwreck in which his mother perished; see *To Nicholas* 6.3–4.

4 *Nicholas expects Mark's prayers to confirm this good beginning*

So by the intercession of Your Holiness, this gift will be steadfast. Thus may the heavenly spark abide in me, may the aforementioned giants be destroyed utterly and absolutely, so that I should never be made to forget and cast myself down into the aforementioned evils by the treachery of my free will and become food for my enemies. But I believe in my Lord Jesus Christ, who dwells in you, that, because of your holiness and the holiness of those who contend like you, he will never overlook me or deliver me to the mouths of those giants. Instead, because his holy servants are forever reminding me of his path, he will come to know poor me through your holy prayers. For this reason, I beseech and entreat your compassionate and holy soul not to condemn me because, inspired by confidence, I have dared to write a letter in response to Your Holiness. But since I know that your paternal affections are open to me, even if it is by shabby letters that I beseech and beg you to remember me at every hour (for the Lord always attends to the one who waits upon and continually honors him, by which I mean the rightly purified mind of your blessed soul), through Your Holiness may even I be delivered from my vices and find a good end to life, through the grace of Christ God. To him be honor and power, with the Father and the Holy Spirit, to ages of ages. Amen.

CHAPTER THREE

On the Spiritual Law

Introduction to Chapters Three and Four

Mark's *On the Spiritual Law* and its companion piece *Concerning Those Who Imagine That They Are Justified by Works* are surely his best-known writings. It is very rare to find instances of Mark's works being read without finding specific mention of *Spiritual Law* (and usually *Works* as well). We have already seen in the general introduction they were known by many Greek, Latin, Syriac, and Slavonic authors. Photius, Paul Evergetinos, Nicodemus the Hagiorite, and Paissy Velichkovsky certainly knew both; Anthony Melissa, Symeon the Pious, and Symeon the New Theologian knew at least *Spiritual Law*. Abraham of Kaskar cites both works in his *Rule*; Thomas of Marga quotes both of them in his *Historia Monastica*; Ebedjesu tells us that Babai and Abraham bar Dasandad wrote commentaries on *Spiritual Law*. A copy of *Spiritual Law* was available at St Gall, c. 850, where an Irish monk began to translate it into Latin; even though the manuscript that survives is incomplete, it is possible that the project was not aborted, since John Scotus Eriugena seems to have drawn on *Spiritual Law* for his *Periphyseon*. We may well ask why these works proved so consistently attractive over the centuries.

Mark's Teaching

1: On the Spiritual Law

Perhaps the main reason is that, between the two of them, they address a fundamental paradox of Christian life. In *Spiritual Law*, Mark insists that Christian freedom necessarily means, not lawlessness, but obedience to Christ's "law of freedom" (see *Spiritual Law* 28, 30). To preclude confusion, he then adds *Works* to stipulate that obedience to the law of Christ in no sense *earns* heaven as a reward. In *To Nicholas*, we have already seen how quickly Mark qualifies his suggestion that a desire for the reward of future blessings ought to motivate Nicholas: He warns that the expectation of a heavenly payoff is insufficient to sustain the spiritual life (*To Nicholas* 2.5, 4.1–6, 11.1–2). A similar dynamic is at work in these two writings. Even as he recommends prayer, reading, vigils, and fasting, Mark requires humility in these undertakings, because anyone who undertakes them in pride will invariably pollute his relationship with God by thinking that, because of his accomplishments, he has justified himself and therefore has a claim on divine rewards.

It is exactly for this reason that, early in *Spiritual Law*, Mark repeatedly warns against conceit (*Spiritual Law* 8–9, 12) and recommends humility (81, 127). Humility is of the utmost importance because it keeps one from self-justification (126). For the sake of acquiring humility, Mark recommends not just accepting, but even *embracing* criticism (73, 129, 152). One who takes criticism seriously is able to identify his faults more readily, and is thus better prepared for those faults to be set right. On a related note, Mark regularly emphasizes the significance of monastic introspection. Anyone who is indifferent to his own thoughts will quickly come to trouble, and the Christian who fails to scrutinize his thoughts is easy prey for Satan (cf. 91, 161–64, 178, 186).

These lessons, and more, are the practical steps that Mark points out, but as he sees it they are all based on Scripture. In fact, Scripture reveals Christ's "law of freedom," which is why Mark tirelessly urges his readers to put the teachings of Scripture into practice. Although it is necessary to study Scripture, merely reading Scripture is insufficient. As he memorably puts it, "Read the words of Scripture by putting them into practice, and do not spin out subtle interpretations, getting puffed up with conceit in the process" (87). The purpose of studying Scripture this way is not to be "puffed up" by knowledge (9); instead, it is to understand the hidden spiritual meaning of Scripture (24). But that spiritual meaning is not an esoteric mystery; rather, the spiritual meaning is Christ crucified:

> The Lord is hidden within his own commandments and is found by those who seek him in proportion to their efforts (191).

> Do not look for this law's being perfected through human virtues; perfection is not found in human virtues. Its perfection is hidden in the cross of Christ (29).

A consideration of the perfection of the law "hidden in the cross of Christ" brings us immediately back to the fundamental importance of humility.[1] Humility, in turn, points the way forward to the second part of Mark's diptych, *Concerning Those Who Imagine That They Are Justified by Works.*

2: Concerning Those Who Imagine That They Are Justified by Works

By now it is clear that Christian freedom, as Mark envisages it, has nothing to do with unrestricted self-expression. His teaching in

---

[1]See further Mark's discussion of acquiring Christ's humility at *Disputation with an Attorney* 1(14).

Works reinforces this point. Mark presents Christ as Master for two reasons—first, because he created humanity, and second, because through his death he created humanity, anew (*Works* 20). The sovereignty of Christ is for Mark the foundation of Christian freedom. Christian freedom is therefore realized in faithfully serving the Lord, who in response freely bestows the gift of sonship (cf. 2). Mark emphasizes that the gift is freely bestowed while he simultaneously stresses that we are God's slaves: "A slave does not demand freedom as a reward, but rather satisfies his master as someone who is indebted to him and who waits for his freedom as a gift" (3; see also 18–21). Even though God ultimately does graciously confer sonship on the faithful, Mark stresses that this is in no sense remuneration. Christian freedom, for him, is voluntary and loving service to God. Works are therefore a necessary, but not sufficient, condition for being adopted by God. Thus, in one of his most memorable sentences, Mark is able to say:

> Some, without keeping the commandments, think they are keeping the faith, while others, keeping the commandments, expect to receive the kingdom as a reward owed to them. Both are deprived of the kingdom (17).

In *Works*, then, Mark encourages a deeper understanding of the importance of Christian works. Good deeds are still essential, but not as a way of winning God's favor (which God freely gives); rather, they are a loving response to God in that they specifically aim at preserving the precious gift of purity already given by God through the "washing of regeneration" (22).

Mark's teachings in *Works* flow from what he has already written in *Spiritual Law*, but run deeper. For example, he retains the strong claim that knowledge must be enacted for it to be genuine (12). Likewise, he calls for introspection, but poses his teaching in a more enigmatic way that calls for greater understanding from the reader (52, 176). He returns to the themes of the hidden meaning of suffering—previously specified as what is hidden in the cross of Christ—by talking about God's mercy being "wonderfully hidden in [the Christian's] unwanted sufferings" (130, cf. 210). He calls once more for the use of one's memory, but whereas before he recommended reflection on God's mercies, now what is to be recalled is God himself (122, 125). Another topic that receives profounder treatment in *Works* is the importance of Christ's commandments; here, Mark places emphasis on how Christ enables the fulfillment of his commandments (85–86). Finally, it is noteworthy that Mark once more endorses prayer, but in *Works* he introduces "contemplative prayer" (28–29)—a higher stage of prayer than the kinds of prayer mentioned in *Spiritual Law*. With these topics, Mark offers advanced instruction that builds on the foundation laid in *Spiritual Law*. The abiding lesson of *Works*, however, is inculcation of that humility that springs from recognizing the all-importance of God's grace. As Mark succinctly puts it, "Humility is not the condemnation of one's conscience but the recognition of God's grace and sympathy" (103).

The Relationship between *Spiritual Law* and *Works*

We have just seen that numerous themes that Mark initially addresses in *Spiritual Law* are taken up again in a more developed way in *Works*. This strengthens the initial impression that leads us to speak of the two as being "companion pieces." Georges de Durand has noted further reasons: the "spiritual law" is mentioned in the conclusion of *Works*, and *Spiritual Law* has an introduction but ends abruptly and lacks the doxology that Mark ordinarily uses to end his works, whereas *Works* lacks an introduction and begins abruptly but has the characteristic doxology.[2] He speculates that an earlier stage of writing may lie behind the text that we now possess, and advances a number of hypotheses (some of them quite attractive) for explain-

[2]De Durand, *Marc le Moine*, 1:61–63.

ing how the two pieces came to be linked so closely.[3] His hypothesis of originally separate treatises notwithstanding, we are inclined to think that Mark probably intended for the works to be taken as a diptych. The integration of the two pieces, especially evident in the intensification of certain key themes (as noted above), is so extensive that it is reasonable to think that they were written—or possibly retouched—to form a single work in two parts.

The Literary Form[4]

Spiritual Law and *Works* are unique among Mark's writings because he wrote them in *kephalaia*, or "chapters," a favored genre for spiritual and monastic authors. The benefit of writing in chapters is that it presents the teaching in concise, memorable form. The author *par excellence* of monastic chapters is surely Evagrius Ponticus, and recent research into his use of the genre has indicated that, in addition to being memorable, chapters have the added benefit of forcing the reader to think about the connections (which are sometimes numerous) that link the different elements together.[5] In this way, the author creates a text that makes demands of the reader; more specifically, the author writes in such a way that the reader's understanding of the material will be at least in part contingent upon enacting the teachings it presents. Even though Mark's chapters do not appear as opaque as Evagrius', both *Spiritual Law* and *Works* still retain the elusiveness that comes from a lack of clear internal structure and connection, so that Mark's writings no less than Evagrius' presuppose that the reader will actively engage the text in order to make sense of it.

---

[3]De Durand, *Marc le Moine*, 1:64–73.

[4]See further "ΚΕΦΑΛΑΙΑ. Eine byzantinische Literaturform und ihre antiken Wurzeln," *Byzantinische Zeitschrift* 47 (1954): 285–91.

[5]See J. Driscoll, *The 'Ad Monachos' of Evagrius Ponticus: Its Structure and a Select Commentary*, Studia Anselmiana 104 (Rome: Sant' Anselmo), 305–84.

This comparison could also be made with an earlier author about whom we know regrettably little: Sextus. Even though the *Sentences of Sextus* originated in a pagan milieu, they were enormously popular and were translated into several Christian languages; Henry Chadwick has detected evidence of Christianization resulting from the process.[6] Sextus' work also made an enormous impact on the development of a Christian monastic ethic. After the *Sentences* spread throughout the Christian world, and after Evagrius further popularized the genre, several other Christian authors embraced it. One thinks particularly of Diadochus of Photike, Maximus the Confessor, Thalassios, Ilias the Presbyter, Symeon the New Theologian, Niketas Stethatos, Gregory of Sinai, and Gregory Palamas. As this roster indicates, the genre is well represented in the *Philokalia*. By choosing the "chapter" as the form in which to set forth his teaching, Mark has placed himself in very distinguished company.

[6] Chadwick, *The Sentences of Sextus.*

On the Spiritual Law[7]

Since you[8] have often desired to know what the Apostle (That is, St Paul.) means when he says that "the law is spiritual" [Rom 7.14], and what knowledge and practice is fitting for those who wish to keep the spiritual law, we have spoken about it to the best of our ability.

1   First of all, we know that God is the beginning and middle and end of everything good,[9] and it is impossible to do or believe anything good except through[10] Christ Jesus and the Holy Spirit.

2   Everything good is given as a gift by the Lord [Jas 1.17], and whoever believes that this is true will not lose the good that he has been given. Steadfast faith is a strong tower [Ps 61.3; Prov 18.10], and Christ becomes everything for the person who has faith.

3   May he who takes the lead in every good thing lead the way for all your intentions, so that what you propose to do may be done in accordance with God.

4   When the person who is humble and does his work in a spiritual manner reads the Holy Scriptures, he will apply everything he reads to himself and not to someone else.

5   Call upon the Lord to open the eyes of your heart, so that you may see the benefit of prayer and reading.

6   The person who has some spiritual gift and feels compassion for those who do not have it will keep the gift because of his

---

[7]Source: de Durand, *Marc le Moine*, 1:74–128.

[8]Second person plural here but second person singular thereafter.

[9]Plato, *Laws* 4.715E–716A (R. G. Bury, ed., LCL 2 vols [London: 1961] 1:292). This passage was quoted by Eusebius (*Preparation for the Gospel* 11.13.5—PG 21:881) and Origen (*Against Celsus* 6.15; ed. M. Borret, Sources chrétiennes 147 [Paris: Cerf, 1969], 214). By Mark's time, the term *telos*, "end," may already have acquired technical resonance for Christian ascetics as referring to the ultimate goal of their struggles. See Evagrius, *Epistula fidei* 7 (ed. J. Gribomont, *Le Lettere*, 98–102) and Cassian, *Conferences* 1.4.3 (CSEL 13:8).

[10]Or "in": *en*.

compassion, but the braggart will lose it when attacked on all sides by temptations to boastfulness.

7 A humble person's mouth will speak the truth, but the person who speaks against the truth is like that servant who hit the Lord in the face [Jn 18.22].

8 Do not be a disciple of someone who praises himself, lest you learn pride instead of humility.

9 Do not let your heart become conceited about your interpretations of Scripture, lest your intellect ever fall afoul of the spirit of blasphemy.[11]

10 Do not try to resolve a tangled situation with contentiousness, but rather with what the spiritual law calls for: patience and prayer and unwavering hope.

11 Blind is the person who cries and says, "Son of David, have mercy on me!" [Lk 18.38], who prays superficially[12] and does not yet possess spiritual knowledge. When the man who was blind recovered his sight and saw the Lord, he no longer venerated him as Son of David but confessed him to be Son of God [Jn 9.38].

12 Do not become conceited because you shed tears when you pray; Christ has touched your eyes, and you have received your sight spiritually.

13 The person who, in imitation of the blind man, throws off his cloak and draws near to the Lord, follows him and becomes a herald of perfect doctrines.

14 When one's thoughts brood on evil, it makes the heart insolent, but when one destroys evil through self-restraint and hope, it breaks the heart and makes it contrite.

15 One way of making the heart contrite is normal and leads it to compunction, while the other way is abnormal and causes it injury.

---

[11]"Interpretations" translates *noēmasi* and "intellect" *nous*; the two words are related etymologically.

[12]*Sōmatikōs*, literally "corporally"; contrasted with "spiritual" later in the saying.

16   Vigil and prayer and patient endurance of what comes one's way bring contrition that does not harm the heart and in fact is beneficial, but only if we do not interfere with the proper balance of these ascetic practices through some kind of excess. The person who perseveres in these practices will be helped with others as well, but the person who is negligent and fritters them away will suffer unbearable pain when he leaves this life.

17   A pleasure-seeking heart is a prison and a chain for the soul at the time a person leaves this life, but the conscientious heart is an open door.[13]

18   A hard heart is the iron gate leading into the city, but for the person who mortifies and afflicts himself, the gate will open of its own accord, just as it also did for Peter [Acts 12.10].

19   There are many ways to pray, and some are more profitable than others. At the same time, there is not a single harmful method of prayer; otherwise it would not be prayer but the work of Satan.

20   A person who wanted to do evil first prayed as usual and, finding himself providentially thwarted, was grateful afterwards.

21   When David wanted to kill Nabal the Carmelite, remembering that divine retribution would follow, he abandoned his intention and was very grateful [1 Sam 25.2–39].

22   Again, we know what sort of things David did when he forgot God, and we know that he did not stop what he was doing until Nathan reminded him [2 Sam 12.1–15].

23   At those times when you think of God, multiply your prayers, so that when you forget him the Lord may remind you.

24   When you read Holy Scripture, apprehend spiritually its hidden meanings, "for whatever was written in former times," the Apostle says, "was written for our instruction" [Rom 15.4].

25   Scripture calls faith "the assurance of things hoped for" [Heb 11.1], and calls those who do not acknowledge the indwelling of Christ "worthless" [2 Cor 13.5].

---

[13]"Pleasure-seeking" translates *philēdonos* and "conscientious" renders *philoponos*, literally "loving toil," hence "industrious" or "conscientious."

26   Just as a thought is made known through actions and words, our future reward is made known through the activities of the heart.[14]

27   Clearly, a compassionate heart will receive compassion, and a merciful heart will likewise receive mercy. It follows that hearts that are the opposite of these will in turn receive the opposite.

28   The law of freedom teaches the whole truth. Many people study this law according to the dictates of knowledge, but few people understand that it is measured by practicing the commandments.

29   Do not look for this law's being perfected through human virtues; perfection is not found in human virtues. Its perfection is hidden in the cross of Christ.

30   The law of freedom is studied by means of true knowledge, is understood through the practice of the commandments, and is brought to fulfillment through the mercies of our Lord Jesus Christ.

31   When we are compelled by conscience to carry out all of God's commandments, then we will understand that the Lord's law is blameless [Ps 19.8 (LXX)], that we practice it by practicing goodness, and that it cannot be perfected in us without God's mercies.

32   Those who do not consider themselves under obligation to all of Christ's commandments study God's law superficially,[15] "understanding neither what they are saying nor what they are asserting" [1 Tim 1.7]. As a result, they think they can fulfill the law through works.

33   There are actions that are clearly good when performed, but the aim of the person performing them is not good; and there are other actions that are clearly evil, but the aim of the person performing them is good.

34   What we have just said applies not only to works that certain people do, but also to the words they say. Some pervert their actions through inexperience or ignorance, while others do so through evil intentions, and still others do so through pious aims.

---

[14]"Actions" translates *ergōn* and "activities" *energēmatôn*.
[15]*Sōmatikôs*, literally "corporally"; see n. 12 above.

35   It is difficult for those who are naive to detect the person who is slandering someone while masking it under the pretext of praise. They have the same difficulty with an arrogant person cloaked in humility.

36   Once those who long misrepresent the truth by using falsehood give up their act, they are condemned by their actions.

37   One person clearly does a good deed by standing up for his neighbor, while another person benefits by deliberately not doing so.

38   There is rebuke that comes from evil and vindictiveness, and there is another kind of rebuke that comes from fear of God and respect for the truth.

39   No longer rebuke a person who has stopped sinning and who repents. If you say that you are rebuking him in accordance with God's will, first reveal your own evil deeds.

40   God is the source of every virtue, just as the sun is the source of daylight.

41   When you have done something virtuous, remember him who says, "Without me you can do nothing" [Jn 15.5].

42   Affliction prepares people for good, just as self-conceit and pleasure prepare them for evil.

43   The person who is wronged by people escapes sinning and finds succor equal to the affliction he suffers.

44   The person who has faith that Christ will reward him endures every wrong in proportion to the faith he has [Rom. 12.6].

45   The person who prays for those who wrong him overthrows demons. The person who opposes the leaders of the demons becomes wounded by their subordinates.

46   It is better to have difficulties with people and not with demons. The person who is pleasing to the Lord defeats both.

47   Every good thing comes from the Lord in a secret and sacred way, but in a secret and sacred way flees from the unthankful and ungrateful.

48   Every vice ends in forbidden pleasure, and every virtue ends in spiritual consolation. The former, when it prevails, exacerbates its properties, while the latter, likewise, cultivates what is akin to it.

49 Reproach from people causes the heart affliction, but becomes a source of purity for the person who patiently endures it.

50 Ignorance makes us ready to oppose what is beneficial, and when it becomes emboldened, it strengthens evil's foremost attributes.

51 Without doing damage, be ready for affliction, and, since you will have to give an account of yourself, rid yourself of greed.

52 When you sin secretly, do not try to keep it a secret, for "all things are naked and lie exposed before the eyes of the one to whom we must render an account" [Heb 4.13].

53 Reveal yourself by revealing your thoughts to the Master, for "a person will judge by appearances, but God sees into the heart" [1 Sam 16.7].

54 Do not think or do anything without having some aim in sight; the person who journeys aimlessly will have labored in vain.

55 Because God's justice is inescapable, repentance comes with difficulty for the person who sins needlessly.

56 Painful calamity reminds the wise person of God and correspondingly afflicts the person who keeps forgetting the Lord.

57 Let all unwanted suffering teach you to remember God, and you will not lack an opportunity for repentance.

58 Forgetfulness has no power in and of itself, but gains strength the more we are negligent and careless.

59 Do not say, "What can I do? I don't want to be forgetful, but it happens anyway," since when you do remember, you miscalculate your obligation anyway.

60 Do what you remember to do, and what you do not remember to do will be revealed to you. Only do not surrender yourself thoughtlessly to forgetfulness.

61 Scripture says, "Hell and perdition are obvious to the Lord" [Prov 15.11 (LXX)]. By these words, Scripture means ignorance of the heart and forgetfulness.

62   Hell is ignorance, because both are murky; perdition is forgetfulness, because both destroy what exists.[16]

63   Concern yourself with your own evils and not with those of your neighbor, and there is no way that your spiritual workshop will be ransacked.[17]

64   Complete disregard for all the good that we have within our power is unthinkable, but almsgiving and prayer calls back those who show such disregard.

65   To accept every affliction as God's will is the very embodiment of piety, for true love is tested by hostile forces.

66   Do not say you have acquired virtue unless you have suffered affliction, for virtue is not tested through ease and comfort.

67   Think about the outcome of every unwanted affliction, and you will find that it has been the destruction of sin.

68   Our neighbors will offer much advice about what is useful and beneficial for us, but nothing is better qualified than our own judgement.

69   If you are looking for spiritual healing, pay attention to your conscience; do whatever it tells you, and you will benefit.

70   God knows the secrets each of us has [Ps 44.21], as does our conscience; from these, then, let each of us accept correction.

71   The person who unwillingly toils completely impoverishes himself, while the person who runs with hope is doubly rich.[18]

72   Each person applies himself as much as he can in accordance with his own wishes, but God decides the outcome of these desires in accordance with justice.

73   If you want to receive praise from people without being condemned for it, first welcome criticism for your sins.

---

[16]In Greek "destroy" (*apōlonto*) and "perdition" (*apōleia*) are cognate. For the first part of §62, cf. Evagrius, *Thirty-three Chapters* §25 (PG 40.1268): "'Hell' is the rational nature's ignorance that occurs because of deprivation of the contemplation of God."

[17]There may be a play on words here: "ransacked" translates *sylēthē*, whereas "forgetfulness" in §58 is *lēthē*, though the words are not related etymologically.

[18]With "runs with hope," Mark seems to be bringing together two Pauline words.

74 Whenever someone accepts any kind of reproach for the sake of Christ's truth, he will be glorified a hundred times more by the multitude of the faithful.[19]

75 But it is better to do each and every good work on account of the good things to come.

76 Whenever one person helps another by word or deed, let both understand that this is the grace of God at work. The person who does not realize this will be under the authority of the person who does.

77 The person who hypocritically praises his neighbor will in time reproach him, and will himself bring shame upon himself.

78 The person who is ignorant of his enemies' ambush is readily slain, and the person who does not know the causes of the passions easily falls.

79 From pleasure-seeking comes indifference, and from indifference comes forgetfulness, for God has given everyone the knowledge of what is useful and beneficial.

80 A person advises his neighbor in accordance with his own understanding, but God works in the listener in accordance with that person's faith.

81 I have seen ignorant people work with humility, and they became wiser than those who are wise. Another ignorant person, when he heard these people being praised, did not imitate their humility, but rather prided himself on being ignorant and was gripped by arrogance.

82 The person who disparages understanding and boasts of being uneducated not only speaks ignorantly, but also lacks knowledge [2 Cor 11.6].

83 Just as proficiency in speaking is one thing and sound judgement another, so ignorance with speech is one thing and foolishness another.[20]

---

[19]"By the multitude (of the faithful)," *hypo plēthous*, may also be translated "in measure," "in quantity."

[20]"Sound judgement" translates *phronēsis* and "foolishness" *aphrosunē*.

84   Being inept at speaking will not harm someone who is very devout, just as proficiency with words will not harm someone who is humble.

85   Do not say, "I don't know what I should do, so I'm not responsible for not doing it." If you did every good thing you have knowledge of, then everything else would in turn become clear to you, as though they were being observed by you as you went from one room to another.

86   There is no point in knowing what work you should do later before you have done what you should do first, for "knowledge puffs up" when it is lazy, but "love builds up" when it "endures all things" [1 Cor 8.1, 13.7].

87   Read the words of Scripture by putting them into practice, and do not spin out subtle interpretations, becoming puffed up with conceit in the process.

88   The person who neglects practice and leans on mere knowledge holds, not a two-edged sword [Heb 4.12], but a staff made of reeds; this, when he goes into battle, "will pierce his hand," Scripture says [2 Kings 18.21], and, entering his flesh, will inject its natural poison into him in front of his enemies.

89   Every thought has its weight and measure in God's presence, for a person may consider the same matter either passionately or moderately.[21]

90   After keeping a commandment, expect temptation on account of it, for love for Christ is tested by hostile forces.

91   Never take your thoughts lightly by disregarding them, for no thought escapes God's notice.[22]

---

[21]Mark is here enjoining moderation in the affective coloration of one's thoughts, and it may be significant that he prefers to contrast thinking passionately (*empathōs*) to thinking moderately (*mesotropōs*)—rather than contrasting it with thinking dispassionately (*apathōs*). In fact, dispassion—a not entirely satisfying calque for the much more complicated Greek term *apatheia*—is an ideal that Mark invokes only rarely.

[22]See §55.

92   When you see a thought suggesting that you seek people's acclaim, you can be sure that it is setting you up to be humiliated.

93   The Enemy understands the justice of the spiritual law and seeks only the mind's assent. By doing this, he either subjects the person under his thumb to penitential sufferings or, if the person does not repent, afflicts him by heaping unwanted misfortunes upon him.

94   Sometimes the Enemy also readies a person to fight against these misfortunes so that here, too, he increases suffering and, when the person dies, adduces this lack of patient endurance to a lack of faith.

95   Many people have squarely confronted the many circumstances that happen to them, but without prayer and repentance no one has escaped fear.

96   One evil reinforces another; likewise, good things also increase because of each other and urge the person who shares in them on to better things.

97   The Devil downplays minor sins; otherwise he cannot lead a person on to greater evil.

98   People's approval is the root of shameful desire, just as being reproached for one's evil ways is the root of moderation—not when we hear reproach, but when we accept it.

99   The person who has renounced the world and still lives in luxury has gained nothing, for what he used to do by means of money and property he still does now, although he possesses nothing.

100   Moreover, if the person who practices ascetic self-restraint possesses money and property, he is a brother in spirit to the first fellow. Because both take satisfaction in spiritual pleasure, they have the same mother; but they have a different father, because each has a different passion.

101   Sometimes a person reduces one passion by living another even more luxuriously, and then is praised by those unaware of his intentions. Perhaps even he himself is unaware of what he is doing as he toils without hope of profit.

102   The source of all evil is self-conceit and pleasure. Unless a person hates them, there is no way that he will defeat the passions.

103   "A root of all evils," it is said, "is the love of money" [1 Tim 6.10], but it is clear that even the love of money is founded on self-conceit and pleasure.

104   The intellect is blinded by these three passions: namely, love of money and self-conceit and pleasure. These, according to Scripture, are "three daughters of the horseleech" [Prov 30.15], dearly loved by their mother, folly.

105   Nothing can blunt and dull knowledge and faith, the twin sisters of our being, like these three.

106   Anger and rage and war and murders and the whole remaining catalogue of evils have such great control over humankind because of these three.

107   Thus we must hate love of money and self-conceit and pleasure as mothers of the evils and stepmothers of the virtues.

108   On account of these three we have been commanded "not to love the world and the things in the world" [1 Jn 2.15], not so we uncritically hate God's creatures, but so we reduce the opportunities that these three passions have.

109   "No one going to war," it says, "gets entangled in day-to-day matters" [2 Tim 2.4]. The person who entangles himself with the passions while desiring to defeat them is like the person who puts out a fire with dried corn stalks.

110   The person who becomes angry with his neighbor on account of riches or acclaim or pleasure does not yet realize that God manages all things with justice.

111   When you hear the Lord saying, "If someone does not renounce all his possessions, he is not worthy of me" [Lk 14.33; Mt 10.38], do not think that what he says applies only to money and property, but rather that it also applies to all things concerning evil.

112   The person who does not know the truth cannot truly believe, for knowledge naturally precedes faith.

113   Just as God assigns to everything visible what is appropriate to each, so it is with human thoughts also, whether we like it or not.

114   If some obvious sinner who has not repented has suffered nothing before leaving this life, you may be sure that judgement for this person will be merciless [Jas 2.13].

115   The person who sensibly prays patiently endures whatever happens to him, whereas the person who remembers the wrongs done to him has not yet offered pure prayer.

116   When harmed or insulted or persecuted by someone, do not think about the present, but wait for the future, and you will find that he has been the agent for bringing about a number of good things for you, not only in the present, but also in the age to come.

117   Just as wormwood's bitterness helps those with a bad appetite, so suffering evils benefits those with bad dispositions. Such medicine helps the former to convalesce and the latter to repent.

118   If you do not want to suffer evil, do no evil, since the one inevitably follows upon the other, "for whatever each person sows he also reaps" [Gal 6.7].

119   Since we sow injuries willingly and reap them unwillingly, we ought to marvel at God's justice. Because a certain amount of time intervenes between sowing and reaping, we refuse to believe that there will be retribution.

120   After you have sinned, do not blame your action but rather your thought; had your intellect not run ahead, your body would not have followed right behind it.

121   The person who secretly does evil is more evil than those who do wrong openly. Therefore that person is also punished more evilly.

122   The person who lays traps and does evil surreptitiously "is a snake," according to Scripture, "lying in wait on the road and biting beneath the horse's hoof" [Gen 49.17 (LXX)].

123   The person who praises his neighbor to someone for something and criticizes him to someone else for the same thing becomes enslaved by self-conceit and jealousy. By praising his neighbor, he tries to hide his jealousy, and by criticizing him, he sets himself up as having a better reputation than his neighbor.

124   Just as sheep and wolves cannot feed in the same place, so a person cannot obtain mercy if he treacherously deceives his neighbor.

125   The person who secretly mixes in his own desires while giving instruction is an adulterer, as is made clear in Wisdom [Prov 6.32–33], and because of his stupidity he suffers grief and dishonor.

126   Just as water and fire are opposites and do not mix, so self-justification and humility oppose one another.

127   Let the person who seeks forgiveness for his sins love humility; the person who condemns someone else puts the seal on his own wickedness.

128   Do not leave any sin, even the most insignificant, unexpunged, lest later on it drag you down into greater evil [Lk 12.58].

129   If you wish to be saved, love what is spoken to you in truth, and never heedlessly turn away from criticism.

130   What was spoken in truth converted "a brood of vipers" and showed them how "to flee from the coming wrath" [Mt 3.7].

131   The person who welcomes words of truth will receive God the Word, for the Lord says, "The person who welcomes you welcomes me" [Mt 10.40].

132   The paralytic lowered down into the house [Mark 2.4] signifies a sinner who is being reprimanded by the faithful in accordance with God's will, and who receives forgiveness because of the faith of these people.

133   It is better to pray devoutly for your neighbor than to reprimand him every time he sins.

134   The person who truly repents is jeered at by the foolish. This is a sure sign for him that he is well-pleasing to God.

135   "The athlete practices self-control in everything" [1 Cor 9.25] and will not let up until the Lord completely destroys the Babylonian people [Jer 27.16 (LXX)].[23]

---

[23]"Athlete" (*agōnizomenos*) is literally "the person who contends," and who, in monastic parlance, engages in spiritual warfare (*agon*).

136   Consider with me that there are twelve passions that lead to sin. If you willingly cherish one of them, that one passion will come to occupy the place of the other eleven.[24]

137   Sin is a blazing fire. The less wood you put on it, the faster it dies out; conversely, the more wood you put on it, the more it blazes up.[25]

138   When you are elated by praise, expect disgrace to follow, for the Lord says, "The person who exalts himself will be humbled" [Lk 14.11].

139   When we cast off every voluntary evil from our thinking, then we battle against passions that we have by predisposition.[26]

140   "Predisposition" is the involuntary remembrance of former evils. It is prevented by the combatant from developing into a passion, and is repulsed by the victor while it is still a provocation.

141   A provocation is something that moves the heart without mental images.[27] It is held in check by those who are experienced, as soldiers control a fortified mountain pass.

142   Once our thoughts are accompanied by images, we have given them our assent. Something that moves the heart but is without images is a provocation that does not incur guilt. There are those who flee even from these as they would a "blazing stick plucked from the fire" [Zech 3.2], and there are those who do not recoil until the flame burns them.[28]

---

[24]De Durand (*Marc le Moine*, 1:108 n. 1) notes that the tradition of identifying eleven sinful passions can be traced to Aristotle's *Nicomachaean Ethics* and voices his suspicion that the two numbers at §136 may result from Aristotle's influence.

[25]See §163.

[26]*Prolēpsin*; see §152 and §182.

[27]*Aneidōlon*; see Evagrius, *Praktikos* 55 (SC 171:628), and §183 for *eidōla*.

[28]Mark's discussion of the psychological and spiritual implications of thinking with images was foreshadowed by Evagrius' *On the thoughts* 25 (SC 438:240–44). The Syriac tradition has further material at the end of this chapter: "The light of the soul is the knowledge of truth which, when it enters the soul, drives away from it all the shadows of falsehood. Then the soul can distinguish good things from bad and things foreign to it from things natural to it. For just as someone who is committing adultery in a house not his own flees in fear and trembling when he hears the voice of the master of the house, so too Satan, once he has drawn near to the temple of Christ

143   Do not say, "What I don't want to happen, happens." Even though you may not want the results themselves, you love what brings them about.[29]

144   The person who looks for praise is addicted to a passion, and the person who bitterly laments misfortune that befalls him loves pleasure.

145   The thinking of a pleasure-seeking person teeters as though on a balance beam: Sometimes such a person weeps and wails on account of his sins, and sometimes he contradicts and fights his neighbor, championing a life of luxury.

146   The person who tests everything and holds fast to what is good [1 Thess 5.21] will as a result abstain from all evil.

147   "Whoever is slow to anger possesses great understanding" [Prov 14.29], as does the person who lends his ear to words of wisdom.

148   Without remembrance of God, there can be no true knowledge; without the former, the latter is illegitimate.[30]

149   Speech that utilizes subtle distinctions will [(not)][31] help the hard-hearted person, because without fear he will not accept the sufferings that lead one to repentance.

150   Assured speech befits a gentle person insofar as he does not try God's patience and is not hit with frequent transgressions.

151   Do not rebuke a powerful man for being arrogant; rather, point out to him that he will be assailed by dishonor in the future. If he has any sense, he will readily accept this kind of criticism.

152   The person who hates criticism is by inclination caught up in his passion, but the person who welcomes[32] criticism is clearly carried along by a prior disposition.[33]

the Lord which we are, flees in fear and trembling, vile and hiding himself, when he hears the voice of the Master of the house."

    [29]See Rom 7:15 and §59 and §85.

    [30]On "remembrance of God," see §56.

    [31]In including *ouk*, we follow the reading of MS Athens National Library 549 and Obsopaeus' edition.

    [32]Literally "loves," *agapōn*.

    [33] *Prolēpsin*; see §139 and §184.

153   Have no wish to listen to other people's offenses. Through a wish like this the forms of those offenses are imprinted in you.

154   When you become caught up in evil talk, be angry with yourself and not with the person talking. Listening to evil also makes the messenger evil.

155   If someone finds himself among people idly gossiping, let him consider himself responsible for such words, if not on account of a recent debt then because of an old one.

156   If you hear someone hypocritically praising you, accept the blame that will come from him in due course.

157   Make peace with present afflictions for the sake of future blessings, and missteps will not weaken your resolve to keep fighting.

158   Whenever someone supplies your bodily needs and you praise him and call him good without taking God into consideration, this same person will later seem to you to be evil.

159   Every good thing comes from the Lord providentially, and those who bring them are servants of the good.

160   Accept with equanimity the fact that good and evil are intertwined; this way God will reverse all inequities.

161   Inequities in our thoughts cause changes in our condition, for God appropriately assigns unintended consequences to our voluntary actions.

162   What is perceptible is offspring of what is intelligible, by God's righteous decree providing us with what we need.

163   Thoughts spring up where there is a pleasure-loving heart, and from a fire's smoke we recognize the type of wood that is laid upon it.[34]

164   Take care of your thoughts, and you will not be wearied with temptations; but if you stop doing this, patiently endure whatever happens to you.

165   Pray that temptation not come to you [Lk 11.4], but whatever comes, accept it as your own and not as something foreign.

[34]See §137.

166   Remove all thought of greed, and then you will be able to see the Devil's wiles.

167   Whoever claims to know all the wiles of the Devil but does not, presents himself as perfect.

168   The more the intellect leaves bodily concerns behind, the more it sees the cunning tricks of its enemies.

169   The person who is led astray by his thoughts is blinded by them; he sees the results of sin but cannot see its causes.

170   There are people who seem to be keeping a commandment when in reality they are slaves to passion, and through evil thoughts are utterly destroying whatever good they were doing.

171   When you first become involved with evil, do not say, "There is no way that it will defeat me." To the extent that you are involved with it, you have already been defeated.

172   Everything that happens starts out small and, nourished little by little, grows large.

173   The wiles that evil uses make up a tightly woven net; if the person who is partially caught in it becomes careless, he will be completely entangled.

174   Do not desire to hear about the misfortunes of your human enemies. Those who like to hear such reports will reap the fruits of what they themselves have sown.

175   Do not think that every affliction befalls people on account of sin, because there are some who are pleasing to God who are still tempted. It is written that the impious and lawless will be persecuted [Ps 36.28 (LXX)]; it says as well that "all who want to live a godly life in Christ will be persecuted" [2 Tim 3.12].[35]

176   When you are feeling afflicted, look for the origin of the affliction; since knowledge of the source mitigates the distress, it becomes easy to bear.[36]

[35]The connection is closer in Greek: "impious" translates *asebeis* and "godly" *eusebōs*.

[36]An alternate reading for "affliction" is "pleasure," and thus the saying would be translated: When you are feeling afflicted, look for an onslaught of pleasure. This onslaught of pleasure mitigates the affliction and thus is welcomed.

177   Some call people intelligent because they are discerning about everyday[37] matters, but the intelligent are those who control their own desires.

178   Until you have eradicated the evils in your heart, do not obey it, because the heart seeks to increase what it already has stored inside.

179   Just as some kinds of snakes are found in wooded areas and others lurk in houses, some passions take shape in our thoughts while others inhere to actions (although they can change from one type to another).

180   When you see concerns troubling you to the very core of your being and enticing your intellect, which was at peace, into succumbing to the passions, know that your intellect has already taken the lead in these matters, gone into action, and made your heart aware of the situation.

181   No cloud is formed without the wind's efforts, and no passion is born without a thought.

182   If we no longer carry out "the desires of the flesh" (as Scripture puts it) [Eph 2.3], the desires that are latent within us will, with the Lord's help, readily come to an end.

183   Idols[38] that have become well-established in the mind are more evil and dominating, but those that are associated with thought precede them and are their source.

184   One kind of evil takes possession of the heart through long predisposition;[39] another kind wages war against our thoughts through everyday activities.

185   God weighs our actions according to our intentions. "May the Lord," it says, "reward you according to your heart" [Ps 20.4].

186   The person who does not persevere in investigating his conscience will not consent to bodily suffering out of devotion to God.

[37]*Aisthētōn*—that is, perceptible matters, things belonging to the senses rather than to the imperceptible or spiritual realm.

[38]*Eidōla*; see §141.

[39]*Prolēpsin*; see §139 and §152.

187 The conscience is nature's book. The person who actively reads it experiences divine help.

188 The person who does not willingly choose to suffer for the sake of the truth will be disciplined.

189 The person who knows God's will and does it to the best of his ability will, by suffering a little, escape greater sufferings.

190 The person who wants to defeat temptations without prayer and patient endurance will not shove temptations away from himself, but will instead become tangled up in them even more.

191 The Lord is hidden within his own commandments, and is found by those who seek him in proportion to their efforts.

192 Do not say, "I have kept the commandments but have not found the Lord"—for you have often found "knowledge with righteousness," as Scripture says. "Those who rightly seek him will find peace" [Prov 16.8 (LXX)].

193 Peace is deliverance from the passions. Peace, as the holy Apostle says, is not found except through the workings of the Holy Spirit [Rom 8.2, 6].

194 Fulfilling a commandment is one thing, and virtue is another, although each receives incentive from the other to do good.

195 Fulfilling a commandment means doing what you are commanded to do, but virtue means becoming someone who is pleasing to the truth.

196 Just as all material wealth is one and the same but is acquired in a number of different ways, so is virtue one thing, being multifaceted in its operations.

197 The person who makes a display of wisdom, giving speeches without following up his words with action, gets wealthy through wrongdoing and, according to Scripture, "the fruits of his labors will end up in the homes of strangers" [Prov 5.10].

198 It is said that everything will do gold's bidding, and spiritual matters will be governed by the grace of God.

199 A good conscience is found through prayer and pure prayer through the conscience. Each by nature needs the other.

200   Jacob made for Joseph a coat of many colors [Gen 37.3], and the Lord made the knowledge of the truth for the gentle, as it is written: "He will teach the gentle his ways" [Ps 25.9].

201   Always do as much good as you can, and when you have the opportunity to do more than good, do not do less, for "the person who turns back," it says, "is not fit for the kingdom of heaven" [Lk 9.62].

CHAPTER FOUR

Concerning Those Who Imagine That They Are Justified by Works[1]

1 In the texts that follow, the erroneous beliefs of those outside the faith will be refuted by those who are well grounded in the faith and who fully recognize the truth.

2 The Lord, wishing to show that every commandment is obligatory but that sonship[2] is a gift bestowed on human beings by means of his own blood, says, "When you have done everything that you were ordered to do, say, 'We are worthless slaves, we have done only what we ought to have done'" [Lk 17.10]. Thus the kingdom of heaven is not a reward for works but is rather a master's gift prepared for his faithful servants.[3]

3 A slave does not demand freedom as a reward, but rather satisfies his master as someone who is indebted to him and who waits for his freedom as a gift.

4 "Christ died for our sins in accordance with the Scriptures" [1 Cor 15.3], and to those who serve him well he gives[4] freedom as a gift, for he says, "Well done, good and faithful servant; since you have been trustworthy in a few things, I will put you in charge of many things. Come share in your master's joy" [Lk 25.21].

5 The person who relies on mere knowledge is not yet a faithful servant; no, the faithful servant is the person who puts his faith in Christ by obeying what he commands.

[1]Source: de Durand, *Marc le Moine*, 1:130–200.
[2]"Sonship," *huiothesia*, is a Pauline concept; see Rom 8.15, 23; 9.4; Gal 4.5; Eph 1.5. See §19.
[3]"Gift" in §2–4 translates *charis*, which also means "grace." On the kingdom of God or of heaven being "prepared," see Mt 20.23, 25.34, 25.41.
[4]"Gives," *charizetai*, has at its root *charis*, "gift/grace."

6 The person who honors his master does what the master orders; when he makes a mistake or disobeys, he patiently accepts what is coming to him as something he deserves.

7 If you have a zeal for learning, also have a zeal for toil and suffering; mere knowledge only puffs up a person [1 Cor 8.1].

8 Trials and temptations that come upon us unexpectedly teach us, by divine dispensation, to love toil and suffering, and lead us to repentance even when we are unwilling.

9 Afflictions that come upon people are the offspring of their own evil doings, but if we patiently accept them through prayer, we will once again find ourselves with an abundance of good things.

10 Some people, when they are praised for their virtuous behavior, are delighted and think that their delightful self-regard is some sort of spiritual consolation. Others, rebuked for their sins, are aggrieved, and consider this beneficial suffering to be the result of some kind of evil done to them.

11 All those who, using the pretext of their own spiritual struggles, disparage those who are more neglectful, think they are justified by corporal works, but all of us who, relying on mere knowledge, look down upon the ignorant are much more foolish than they.

12 Knowledge, even if it is true knowledge, is not yet firmly grounded apart from works done in accordance with it, because everything is grounded by being put into practice.

13 Oftentimes knowledge is thrown into shadow because we neglect to put it into practice; those who completely neglect their practices will also, little by little, forget how to do them. Scripture therefore advises us to know God in accordance with knowledge in order that through our works we may correctly serve him in the future.

14 When we clearly fulfill the commandments, we receive from the Lord in return what is appropriate to our own circumstances, but the benefits we receive depend on our goals and intentions.

15 The person who wants to do something but is unable to do so stands before God, who knows the heart, as though the person had done it. One must understand that this applies to both good and bad actions.

16   The mind carries out many good and bad things without the body, whereas the body can accomplish none of these things without the mind, since the law of freedom goes into effect before a person does something.

17   Some, without keeping the commandments, think they are keeping the faith, while others, keeping the commandments, expect to receive the kingdom as a reward owed to them. Both are deprived of the kingdom.

18   A master has no obligation to reward his slaves, nor, on the other hand, will those who are not faithful servants receive their freedom.

19   If "Christ died for us in accordance with the Scriptures" [1 Cor 15.3] and "we do not live for ourselves but for him who died and was raised for us" [2 Cor 5.15], it is clear that we are obligated to serve him until our deaths. How then can we consider sonship something owed to us?

20   Christ is Master by essence and is Master by divine dispensation, because he has brought into being those who did not exist, and with his own blood has redeemed those who were dead in sin [Jn 1.3] and has given the gift of grace to those who thus believe [Rom 5.9; Rev 5.9].

21   When, therefore, you hear Scripture say, "He will reward each person according to his works" [Ps 62.12; Mt 16.27], it does not say that works deserve hell or the kingdom, but rather that works are done out of faith or lack of faith in him. Christ repays each person not as a businessman fulfilling his contracts but as God, our Creator and Redeemer.

22   We who have been considered worthy to receive the washing of regeneration[5] offer[6] good works not as repayment, but as a means of preserving the purity that has been given to us.

[5]That is, Baptism.
[6]*Prospherein* was used especially of offerings to a benefactor and of sacrificial offerings to God, then was used for the offering of eucharistic gifts and the offering

23 Every good work that we do through our own nature causes us to abstain from its opposing evil, but without grace it cannot increase our holiness.

24 The person who practices self-control[7] avoids gluttony; the person without possessions, greed; the person who keeps silence, talking much; the person who is pure, hedonism; the chaste person, sexual sin; the person who is satisfied with little, avarice; the person who is calm, getting upset; the person who is humble, self-centeredness; the person who is obedient, contentiousness; the person who practices self-examination, hypocrisy.

Similarly, the person who prays avoids despair; the person who is poor, the need for numerous possessions; the person who confesses the faith, denying the faith; the martyr, idolatry. Do you see how every virtue that is carried out even at the risk of death is nothing other than the avoidance of sin? Avoiding sin is something that comes naturally; it is not something done in exchange for the kingdom. A person can barely maintain what comes to him naturally, while Christ, through the cross, gives sonship as a gift.[8]

25 One commandment is specific while another is comprehensive. Thus somewhere he specifically orders us to share with the person who does not have anything [Lk 3.11], while somewhere else he commands us to give up all our possessions [Lk 14.33].

26 Grace possesses an energy[9] unknown to the immature; evil also possesses another kind of energy that resembles the truth. It is advisable not to examine such energies too closely because of the possibility of wandering off into error; nor is it advisable to condemn them, because they may contain the truth. Instead, it is advisable to bring everything before God in hope, for he knows what is useful in both energies.

---

of the consecrated elements by the eucharistic celebrant. For references see Lampe, *Patristic Greek Lexicon*, 1183B, *s.v.* (L).

   [7]*Enkratēs. Enkrateia* is a central monastic concept and practice; the word also suggests "continence, abstinence," an ascetic life.

   [8]*Charizetai*; see §4.

   [9]Mark discusses "both energies" at length in *Baptism*; see especially *Baptism* 5.

27   The person who wishes to cross the spiritual sea is one who is patient, humble, vigilant, and abstinent. If he impetuously sets out without these four, he will only trouble his heart and will not be able to cross.

28   Contemplative quiet is helpful because it nullifies evils. If it also takes on the four virtues[10] in prayer as a means of assistance, there is no quicker way to passionlessness.[11]

29   It is not possible for the mind to be quiet unless the body is quiet also, nor is it possible to tear down the wall between them without contemplative quiet and prayer.

30   The flesh desires in opposition to the Spirit and the Spirit desires in opposition to the flesh [Gal 5.17]. Those who live in the Spirit will never carry out the desires of the flesh.

31   There is no perfect prayer unless the mind calls upon God; the Lord listens when our thoughts cry out without distraction.

32   When the mind is praying without distraction, it afflicts the heart, and "a broken and contrite heart God will not despise" [Ps 51.17].

33   Prayer is also called a virtue, but in fact it is the mother of the virtues: It gives birth to them through union with Christ.

34   Whatever we do without prayer and without good hope will turn out later to be faulty and harmful.

35   When you hear "the last will be first and the first last" [Mt 19.30, 20.16], know that it means those who participate in the virtues and those who participate in love. Love is the last of the virtues by birth but is first of all in value. Those virtues born "before" it show themselves to be "last."

36   If you are discouraged because you are afflicted by numerous evils, call to mind your departure from this world and the grievous punishments that await you.

37   It is better to join oneself to God through hope and prayer than to call to mind external things, even if such thoughts are helpful.

---

[10]Patience, humility, vigilance, and abstinence, listed in §27.
[11]*Apatheia.*

38   No single virtue in and of itself will open the door of our nature unless all the virtues are linked together one after another.

39   The person who indulges in idle thoughts cannot say he practices self-control; even when thoughts are helpful, they are not more helpful than hope.

40   "There is sin that is mortal" [1 Jn 5.16]: every sin that goes unrepented. Even if a holy person prays on behalf of another regarding such a sin, he will not be heard.

41   The person who properly repents does not try to compensate for his past sins by toiling now, but rather through such toil makes peace with God.

42   If our nature obligates us to do each day whatever good is in our power, what will we have left to repay God with for our past evil deeds?

43   Whatever outstanding achievements in virtue we manage today do not compensate for our past negligence, but rather condemn us for it.

44   The person who is afflicted mentally and yet relaxes his physical regimen is like the person who is afflicted physically and so allows his mind to become dissipated. Voluntary affliction of either mind or body benefits the other: Mental affliction benefits the body, and physical affliction benefits the mind. When the two of them are not united, things become worse for both of them.

45   It is a great virtue to accept patiently whatever comes and to love those who hate you, in accordance with what the Lord said [Mt 5.44]. The sign of genuine love is that you forgive wrongs done to you.[12]

46   It is not possible to forgive someone with all your heart for his misdeeds unless you possess true knowledge. Such knowledge demonstrates that each person deserves what comes to him.

47   You will lose nothing that you have given up for the Lord's sake, because it will return to you many times over at the appropriate time [Mt 13.18–23].

---

[12]Some manuscripts add, "for thus the Lord also loved the world."

48   When the mind forgets the object of godliness, then any visible act of virtue becomes pointless.

49   If evil intentions are harmful for every person, they are especially so for those who undertake an exacting way of life.

50   Philosophically investigate human will and God's retribution by working, for words are not wiser[13] than work.

51   Help follows closely behind sufferings undertaken out of devotion to God. This must be learned through obeying God's law and following our own conscience.

52   A thought came to one person and he seized on it without reflection, while a thought came to another person and he tested its truth. Think about which of them acted in a more godly manner.

53   The hallmark of true knowledge is the patient endurance of afflictions and not blaming people for our own misfortunes.

54   The person who does good and looks for a reward is not serving God but his own will. It is not possible for a sinner to escape retribution[14] except through repentance commensurate with what he has done.

55   Some people say, "We cannot be good unless we clearly receive the grace of the Spirit," but those who are inherently disposed to seek pleasures always decline to do what lies within their power, because they say they are helpless to do differently.

56   Grace has been mystically bestowed on those who have been baptized in Christ and becomes active in them to the extent that they keep the commandments. Grace never ceases to secretly help us but it is up to us, as far as it lies within our own power, to do good or not to do good. Grace first rouses the conscience in a manner that conforms to God's wishes; that is how even evildoers have repented and come to please God. Again, grace may be hidden in a neighbor's advice. There are times when it also accompanies one's thoughts when one is reading and, as a natural consequence, teaches

---

[13]Since "wiser" and "philosophically" both contain the root *sophos*, "wise," there is a dig at philosophy here.

[14]In Greek, "retribution" and "reward" are the same word: *antapodosis*.

the mind the truth about itself. If, therefore, we do not hide the talent that has in consequence been given to us [Mt 25.20–25], we shall without a doubt enter into the Lord's joy.

57   The person who seeks out the activities of the Spirit before he keeps the commandments is like someone who sells himself into slavery: As soon as he is bought, he seeks to be given his writ of freedom—along with his purchase price!

58   The person who discovers that external events have happened to him through God's justice is the person who in seeking the Lord has found knowledge along with justice [Prov 16.8 (LXX)].

59   If you come to realize that, in accordance with Scripture, "the Lord's judgments are in all the earth" [1 Chr 16.14; Ps 105.7], every misfortune that happens to you will teach you knowledge of God.

60   Each person gets what he is due in accordance with his own way of thinking, but only God understands the variety of ways such things happen and how they all fit together.

61   When you suffer some dishonor at the hands of people, immediately consider the glory that God will give you in addition [Jn 5.44], and you will not be saddened and upset by the dishonor but will be found faithful and blameless when glory comes.

62   When a multitude praise you in accordance with God's good pleasure, do not adulterate the Lord's management of things by ostentatiously parading about, lest the situation be reversed and you fall into dishonor.

63   A seed will not grow without earth and water, and a person will not gain anything without voluntary suffering and God's help.

64   Rain cannot fall without a cloud, nor can we please God without a good conscience.

65   Do not reject learning, even if you are very wise, for what God provides through divine dispensation is more valuable than our own wisdom.

66   When, through some kind of sensual pleasure, the heart is moved away from where it practices industriousness and diligence, then, like a very heavy rock that has come loose and is rolling downhill, it becomes hard to control.

67   Just as an inexperienced calf eagerly searching out grass for grazing finds itself in a precipitous spot, the soul finds itself little by little being led astray by its thoughts.

68   When the mind, having grown to full maturity in the Lord, releases the soul from its long-held preoccupations, then the heart, since the mind and the passions pull it in opposite directions, is tortured as though it were on the rack in the hands of public executioners.

69   Just as sailors on the open sea gladly endure the burning sun,[15] those who hate evil love rebuke. The former withstand winds and the latter the passions.

70   Just as fleeing in winter or on the Sabbath [Mt 24.20] distresses the body and desecrates the soul, a resurgence of the passions distresses an aged body and desecrates a consecrated soul.

71   No one is as good and compassionate as God,[16] but even he does not forgive the unrepentant.

72   Many of us feel remorse for our sins, yet we welcome what caused them.

73   A mole burrowing underground is blind and cannot see the stars, and the person who does not have faith with regard to temporal things cannot have faith with regard to eternal things either.

74   Grace upon grace [Jn 1.16], true knowledge has been given to human beings as a gift by God; above all else, it teaches those who have been given the gift to have faith in the one who has bestowed the gift on them.

75   When a sinful soul does not accept the afflictions that come upon it, then the angels say about it, "We tried to heal Babylon, but she could not be healed" [Jer 51.9].

76   When the mind forgets true knowledge, it fights with people over things contrary to it as though such things were useful.

---

[15]Some manuscripts add "in the hope of gain."
[16]Some manuscripts read "as the Lord."

77 Just as fire cannot last long in water, a shameful thought cannot last long in a heart that loves God, because each person who loves God is also a person who loves suffering. Voluntary suffering is by nature the enemy of pleasure.

78 A passion that someone willingly allows to dominate his activity will later violently stir up the person who is under its influence, even against his will.

79 We love the causes of involuntary thoughts, and that is why they come. It is clear that this is true also for our deeds as well as for our voluntary thoughts.

80 Haughtiness and boastfulness are causes of blasphemy. Avarice and self-conceit are causes of cruelty and hypocrisy.

81 When the Devil sees that the mind has prayed from the heart, then he attacks with great and evilly devised temptations, for he refuses to destroy the minor virtues with elaborate attacks.

82 When a thought lingers, the person is clearly attached to it, but when it is quickly destroyed, this shows that he opposes it and wages war against it.

83 There are three mental states into which the mind by changing enters: that according to nature, that contrary to nature, and that above nature.[17]

When the mind enters the state according to nature, it finds that it itself is the cause of evil thoughts and confesses its sins to God, fully acknowledging the causes of the passions.

When the mind is in the state contrary to nature, it forgets God's justice and fights with people as though they were wronging it.

When the mind is admitted into the state above nature, it finds the fruits of the Holy Spirit, which the Apostle enumerated: "love, joy, peace," etc. [Gal 5.22], and it knows that if it gives preference to bodily concerns, it cannot remain there.

The mind that withdraws from that state falls into sin and into all the terrible calamities that are the consequences of sin, if not immediately, then in due time, as God's justice allows.

[17]Cf. Evagrius Ponticus, *Kephalaia Gnostica* 2.31, version S1 (PO 28:72).

84 Each person's knowledge is genuine to the extent that it is grounded in gentleness, humility, and love.

85 Each person baptized in an orthodox manner has mystically received the fullness of grace, but each person is fully assured of grace afterwards to the extent that he keeps the commandments.

86 When someone in good conscience fulfills Christ's commandment, he is given consolation and comfort in proportion to the multitude of sufferings that his heart has endured. But each of these will come at the appropriate time.

87 Maintain constant prayer about everything so that you accomplish nothing without God's help.

88 Nothing is better able to offer assistance than prayer, and nothing is more helpful than prayer in procuring God's favor.

89 Prayer includes the ability to keep all the commandments, for nothing is said to be superior to love for God.

90 Undistracted prayer for the person who persists in it is a sign of his love for God, but careless and distracted prayer is a sign of his love of pleasure.

91 The person who keeps vigil and shows patience and prays without being worn down clearly partakes of the Holy Spirit, while the person who becomes worn down while doing these things, and yet willingly endures them, quickly receives help also.

92 That one commandment is superior to another goes without saying; consequently, one kind of faith will be found to be more firmly grounded than another. There is "faith that comes from what is heard," in accordance with what the Apostle says [Rom 10.17], and there is faith that is "the assurance of things hoped for" [Heb 11.1].

93 It is good to help inquirers by talking with them, but it is better to assist them through prayer and the excellence of one's character. The person who offers himself to God through these helps his neighbor by helping himself.

94 If you want to help the person who is eager to learn by keeping things short and sweet, show him prayer and right faith and the patient endurance of whatever comes, for everything good follows from these.

95   Once someone has placed his hope in God concerning any matter, he no longer quarrels about it with his neighbor.

96   If, according to Scripture, everything involuntary has its cause in things that are voluntary, no one has an enemy greater than himself. By "voluntary" one understands "thoughts," and by "involuntary," "circumstances."

97   Pre-eminent among all the evils is ignorance; next comes lack of faith.

98   Flee temptation by means of patience and prayer. If you resist temptation without these, it only attacks more forcefully.

99   The person who is gentle in God's sight is wiser than the wise, and the person who is humble in heart is more powerful than the powerful, since he bears the yoke of Christ with knowledge [Mt 11.29].

100   Whatever we say or do without prayer turns out later to be dangerous or harmful, and what we do rebukes us without our knowing it.

101   One person is righteous through works and words and thoughts, but many are righteous through faith and grace and repentance.

102   Just as prideful thinking is foreign to the person who repents, humble thinking is impossible for the person who sins willingly.

103   Humility is not the condemnation of one's conscience, but the recognition of God's grace and sympathy.[18]

104   Ordinary air has the same relationship to a house as God's grace has to the spiritual mind.

105   The more you remove what is material, the more the air enters of its own accord, and the more you add what is material, the more the air stays outside.

---

[18]In Greek, "recognition" is *epignōsis* and "condemnation" is *katagnōsis*.

106   What is material for a house consists of pots and pans and the food you cook in them, while what is material for the mind is self-conceit and sensual pleasure.

107   When there is room in the heart, one has hope in God, and when the heart is stuffed full, one has bodily concerns.

108   One and unchanging is the grace bestowed by the Spirit, and it performs its activities within each person as it wishes [1 Cor 12.11].

109   Just as rain, when it waters the earth, supplies each plant with the quality that characterizes it—sweetness to plants that are sweet, bitterness to plants that are bitter—when grace steadfastly inserts itself into the hearts of the faithful, it bestows activities appropriate to each of the virtues: For the person who hungers for Christ's sake, grace becomes food; and for the person who thirsts, grace becomes the sweetest of drinks; for the person who shivers, grace becomes a coat; and for the person who is weary, grace becomes rest; for the person who prays, grace becomes heartfelt hope; and for the person who mourns, grace becomes comfort and consolation.

110   Thus when you hear divine Scripture say about the Holy Spirit that "it settled upon each of the apostles" [Acts 2.3], or "sprang upon the prophet" [1 Sam 11.6], or "operates" [1 Cor 12.11], or "is grieved" [Eph 4.30], or "is quenched" [1 Thess 5.19], or "is exasperated" [Is 63.10], and again, that "some have the firstfruits" [Ro 8.23], while others are "filled with the Holy Spirit" [Acts 2.4], do not suppose that the Spirit suffers any kind of division or variation or change, but believe that, just as we have said, the Spirit is unvarying and unchanging and all-powerful. Thus in its energies it both remains what it is, and in a divine way keeps in reserve what each person needs: Upon those who have been baptized, it pours itself out fully, like the sun. Each of us, insofar as we hate the passions that cast their shadow over us and remove them, is correspondingly illumined by the Spirit, but insofar as each of us loves the passions and dwells on them, we likewise remain in darkness.

111 The person who hates the passions removes their causes, while the person who is addicted to those things that cause the passions is attacked by the passions, even though he may not wish it.

112 When we are influenced by evil thoughts, let us hold ourselves responsible, not ancestral sin.

113 The roots of thoughts are the obvious vices, whose cause we champion with our hands and feet and mouths every chance we get.

114 It is not possible to be friends with a passion and mull it over unless we love its causes. Who shows no concern for being shamed while being friends with self-esteem? Or who loves being humiliated and becomes upset at being dishonored? Who has "a broken and contrite heart" [Ps 51.17] and still welcomes sexual pleasure? Or who puts complete faith in Christ [Heb 12.2] and worries about quarrels or transitory things?

115 If a person is treated with contempt by someone and yet does not dispute in word or thought the person who has heaped contempt on him, he has acquired true knowledge and is demonstrating a solid faith in the Lord.

116 People are liars and practice wrongdoing with their scales [Ps 61.10 (LXX)], but God reserves what is just for each person.

117 If neither the wrongdoer keeps his gains nor the person wronged remains in want, then "a person passes away like a phantom and troubles himself in vain" [Ps 39.6 (LXX)].

118 When you see someone suffering greatly from infamy and disgrace, you may be assured that, once pleasurably filled with thoughts of self-esteem, he is now harvesting by the handful what has sprung from the seeds he sowed in his heart.

119 The person who enjoys bodily pleasures more than he should will pay for his excessive behavior a hundred times over in sufferings.

120 A leader should tell a subordinate what his duties are and, if he is disobeyed, should warn him of the evil consequences.

121 The person who is wronged by someone and who does not seek recompense from the person who has wronged him has, by his actions, put his faith in Christ, and will receive a hundredfold in this age, and will inherit eternal life [Mark 10.30].

122   Recollection of God is the pain that a person suffers in his heart for the sake of godliness, but everyone who forgets God becomes self-indulgent and unfeeling.

123   Do not say that someone who has defeated the passions cannot suffer afflictions; even if he does not suffer them on his own behalf, he ought to do so on behalf of his neighbor.

124   When the Enemy succeeds in recording numerous forgotten sins in his "accounts due" book, at that time he also forces the debtor to remember these same sins, rightly taking full advantage of "the law of sin" [Rom 8.2].

125   If you want to continually remember God, do not shun misfortunes that happen to you, as though they were unjust, but patiently accept what happens to you as being just. The patient acceptance of each misfortune activates one's memory, whereas refusing to do so weakens the heart's efforts and, as a result of this weakening, causes forgetfulness.

126   If you want your sins to be "covered" by the Lord [Ps 32.1], do not parade your virtues before others. God will treat our sins the same way that we treat our virtues.

127   Having hidden your virtue, do not exalt yourself as though you had arrived at righteousness; righteousness is not just hiding your good deeds, but also never thinking about anything forbidden.

128   Do not rejoice when you do good for someone, but rather when you patiently endure and forgive the opposition that accompanies such an act. Just as night follows day, spiteful acts follow in return for acts of kindness.

129   Self-centeredness and greed and pleasure do not allow acts of charity to remain undefiled, unless these first fall before the fear of God.

130   God's mercy is wonderfully hidden in unwanted sufferings, drawing the person who patiently endures them to repentance and deliverance from eternal punishment.

131   Some who keep the commandments expect them to balance out their sins, while others, in keeping the commandments, reconcile with him who died for our sins. We should consider which of these views is correct.

132   Fear of hell and a desire for paradise[19] allow us to patiently endure afflictions, and they do this not of their own accord but because of him who knows our thoughts.

133   The person who has faith in the things to come abstains without prompting from the pleasures of this world, while the person without faith becomes unfeeling and pleasure-loving.

134   Do not say, "How can someone who is poor be a pleasure-seeker, since he does not have the means to do so?" Someone merely by his thoughts can be an even more wretched pleasure-seeker.

135   Knowledge about things is one thing, and knowledge of the truth is another. As the sun excels the moon, so too is knowledge of the truth more beneficial than knowledge about things. Knowledge about things increases proportionately to the way we keep the commandments, while knowledge of the truth increases to the extent that we put our hope in Christ. If you want "to be saved and come to the knowledge of the truth" [1 Tim 2.4], therefore, always try to go beyond sensible things and through hope alone cling to God. At that point, being deflected from the truth against your will, you will find the principalities and powers [Col 1.16] attacking you and waging war against you, but if you defeat them through prayer and remain hopeful, you will enter into the grace of God that will deliver you from the wrath to come [Mt 3.7].

136   The person who understands what was mystically said by blessed Paul, "Our struggle is against the spiritual forces of evil" [Eph 6.12], will also understand the Lord's parable in which he spoke about "the need to pray always and not to lose heart" [Lk 18.1].

137   The Law figuratively commands us to work six days and to rest on the seventh [Ex 20.9–10; Deut 5.13–14]. Thus, doing good by means of one's possessions or through one's actions is properly

---

[19]Some manuscripts have "love of the kingdom" instead of "a desire for paradise."

the soul's work, but the soul's "rest" and "repose" is to sell everything and to give to the poor, in accordance with what the Lord says [Mt 19.21]. Through poverty the soul rests and has the leisure for spiritual hope. Paul urges us to enter eagerly into this rest when he says, "Let us make every effort to enter into that rest" [Heb 4.11].

Having said this, we are not excluding the things to come, nor are we limiting the general reward to life here on earth. No, we are saying that we must first have the grace of the Holy Spirit working in our hearts; to the extent that this is so, we will enter the kingdom of heaven. The Lord made this clear when he said, "The kingdom of God is within you" [Lk 17.21]. The Apostle said this also: "Faith is the assurance of things hoped for" [Heb 11.1], and again, "Run in such a way that you may take [the prize]" [cf. 1 Cor 9.24], and again, "Examine yourselves to see whether you are living in the faith. [Test yourselves.] Do you not realize that Christ Jesus dwells in you?—unless, of course, you fail to meet the test!" [2 Cor 13.5]

138   The person who has come to know the truth does not oppose the afflictions that befall him, because he knows that they lead a person to the fear of God.

139   Old sins, when recalled in detail, harm the person who hopes in God, because they give way to sorrow and deprive him of hope, and if he pictures them without sorrow they bring back the old pollution.

140   When the mind through renunciation achieves unwavering hope, then the Enemy causes it to picture past evils on the pretext that it is confessing them to God; he does this in order to rekindle passions that by God's grace have been forgotten, and to secretly harm the person. Then, even if that person is filled with joy and despises the passions, he will eventually become anxious and troubled over his past actions. If his mind remains befogged and self-indulgent, he will without a doubt dally with the Enemy's advances, and, swayed by the passions, will familiarize himself with them, with the result that such recalling of past evils will prove to be not a confession, but a predisposition to sin again. If you wish to offer blameless confession to God, do not recall your past errors in detail, but courageously stand firm against their assaults.

141   Afflictions come upon us because of sins we have accrued, bringing what is appropriate to each trespass.

142   The person who possesses knowledge[20] and knows the truth confesses to God not by reminding himself of things he has done, but by patiently enduring what happens to him.

143   If you refuse suffering and dishonor, do not claim that your other virtues count as repentance. Self-centeredness and indifference, by their very nature, are servants of sin, even when they are doing what is right.

144   Just as suffering and dishonor give birth to the virtues, pleasure and praise are accustomed to give birth to evils.

145   All bodily pleasure is the result of prior laxity, and lack of faith engenders laxity.

146   The person who is under the sway of sin cannot by himself prevail against what the flesh desires, because he is providing every part of his body with incessant and addictive stimulation.

147   Those who are under the sway of the passions must pray and be obedient, because even with help they can barely fight against their predispositions.

148   The person who wrestles his own will by means of obedience and prayer is a well-disciplined athlete, clearly demonstrating his spiritual struggles through his renunciation of perceptible things.

149   The person who does not conform his will to God gets tripped up by his own efforts and falls into the hands of his opponents.

150   When you see two evil persons befriending one another, you may be sure that each is working in cooperation with the other's will.

---

[20]"Person who possesses knowledge": *gnōstikos*, a term employed by Evagrius Ponticus to describe the person who has arrived at the second level of spiritual proficiency.

151   The arrogant and the self-centered gladly work with one another, because the arrogant person praises the self-centered person who servilely prostrates himself before him, while the self-centered person extols the arrogant person who praises him.

152   The person who loves the truth and learns from it acquires the truth in two ways: When he is praised for his good works, he becomes even more eager to do them, and when he is rebuked for his sins, he is compelled to repent.

153   Our life should correspond to our progress in the faith, and we ought to offer our prayers to God in accordance with the way we live our life.

154   It is good to hold fast to the most central commandment, and not worry about particular things or pray for them in particular, but only "seek the kingdom," as the Lord says [Mt 6.33]. If we are still concerned about each of our needs, however, we should pray about each of them. The person who plans or does anything without prayer will not accomplish anything in the end; this is what the Lord meant when he said, "You can do nothing without me" [Jn 15.5].

155   Even more unreasonable acts of disobedience follow hard upon the person who senselessly disregards the commandment about prayer, each act of disobedience handing him over to the next like a prisoner.

156   The person who welcomes afflictions in the present in expectation of future rewards has found knowledge of the truth and will be readily delivered from anger and sorrow.

157   The person who chooses mistreatment and dishonor for the sake of the truth is walking the apostolic path, having taken up his cross [Mt 16.24] and being bound in chains [Acts 28.20], but the person who tries to be attentive to his heart without these two will find his mind wandering from the path and will fall into temptation and the Devil's snare.

158   It is not possible for someone ever to do battle against evil thoughts without taking their causes into consideration, nor to do battle against the causes without considering the thoughts. When we rid ourselves of one without the other, before long the one that remains has us all caught up in both.

159   The person who fights people out of fear of being mistreated or reproached, will either suffer even more on account of what happens to him here, or will be punished mercilessly in the age to come.

160   The person who wishes to avoid all misfortune should take everything to God in prayer, and with his mind hold fast to hope in him, while excluding, as far as possible, all concern about perceptible things.

161   When the Devil finds a person needlessly occupied with bodily concerns, he first snatches away from him the spoils that this person has acquired with knowledge, and then cuts off his hope in God as he would cut off his head.

162   If you ever reach the stronghold of pure prayer, do not accept the knowledge about things offered to you at that time by the Enemy, lest you lose what is greater. It is better to rain arrows down on him through prayer, since he is, as it were, cooped up down below, rather than to negotiate with him as he offers us his loot and tries to lure us away from our prayer opposing him.

163   Knowledge about things helps a person during times of temptation and spiritual listlessness, but at a time of pure prayer such knowledge is usually harmful.

164   If it is your position to teach in the Lord and you are disobeyed, grieve inwardly but do not become visibly upset; if you grieve, you will not be condemned along with the person who disobeyed you, but if you become upset you will be tempted in the same way as he is.

165   When you are teaching, do not conceal what is appropriate for those present, openly explaining whatever is decent and fitting but cryptically expounding on difficult matters.

166   If someone is not under obedience to you, do not accuse him of some fault to his face; this would suggest that you have authority over him and are not just giving advice.

167   Things that are said that apply to everyone help everyone because they apply to each person in accordance with the dictates of his own conscience.

168   The person who speaks correctly also ought to use his words as though he himself had received them from God; the truth comes not from the person who is speaking, but from God who is working in him [Col 1.29].

169   Do not argue with those who do not profess obedience to you when they oppose the truth, lest you arouse their hatred against Holy Scripture [Prov 10.12].

170   The person who gives way to someone under obedience to him when the latter contradicts him is leading that other person astray on that matter and is preparing him to renounce his vows of obedience.

171   The person who, with the fear of God in his heart, admonishes or rebukes a sinner acquires for himself the virtue opposed to that sin, but the person who holds a grudge and utters reproaches with ill will succumbs to a similar passion, in accordance with the spiritual law.

172   The person who has learned the law well fears the Lawgiver and, putting his hope in him, turns away from every kind of evil.

173   Do not speak out of both sides of your mouth, accustomed to saying one thing while your conscience is saying something else, for Scripture places such a person under a curse [Sir 28.13].

174   One person speaks the truth and is hated for it by the foolish, as were the apostles, while another person speaks hypocritically and is loved for it. Neither of these waits long to receive his reward, because the Lord, in his own good time, will give each his due.

175   The person who wishes to do away with future evil hardships ought to gladly bear present difficulties. Thus mentally exchanging one situation for another, through small sufferings he will escape greater ones.

176   Safeguard your speech from boasting and your thoughts from presumptuousness, lest you yield to them and do things inimical to your nature. A person cannot accomplish anything good by himself but only through God, who sees everything.

177   God, who sees everything, assigns a proper value to the things we do and does the same with our thoughts and voluntary imaginings.

178   Involuntary thoughts spring from previous sin while voluntary thoughts come from free will. Thus the latter will be found to be the cause of the former.

179   Sorrow follows close behind evil thoughts that arise against our will; thus they immediately disappear. Joy follows close behind freely chosen thoughts; thus it becomes difficult to get rid of them.

180   The person who loves pleasure is saddened by criticism and hardships, while the person who loves God is saddened by praise and abundance.

181   The person who does not understand God's judgments intellectually walks a trail with precipitous cliffs on both sides and is easily knocked off balance by every gust of wind: when he is praised, he prides himself on it, and when he is criticized, he takes such criticism bitterly; when he feasts, he makes a pig out of himself, and when he suffers hardships, he whines and complains; when he understands something, he makes sure everyone knows it, and when he does not understand something, he pretends that he does; when he is rich, he boasts about it, and when he is poor, he acts like he isn't; having gotten his fill, he audaciously asks for more, and when he fasts, he does so by calling attention to himself; he quarrels with those who criticize him, and those who make excuses for him he considers fools. Thus, unless someone acquires, by the grace of Christ, knowledge of the truth and fear of God, he is severely wounded, not only by the passions, but also by chance occurrences.

182   When you want to resolve a complicated matter, look for what will please God in the situation, and you will find his solution to be to your benefit.

183   Whenever God is pleased about matters, all creation joins in serving them, but when God repudiates things, creation likewise opposes them.

184   The person who resists lowering happenstances sets himself against God's commandment without knowing it, but the person who accepts them with true knowledge acts in accordance with what Scripture says: "Wait patiently on the Lord" [Ps 27.14].

185   When some trial or temptation comes upon you, do not ask why or through whom it has come, but rather how you can patiently endure it with thanksgiving and an attitude of forgiveness.

186   Another person's evil does not add to our own sins unless we welcome it by means of our own evil thoughts.

187   If it is not easy to find someone pleasing to God who has not suffered temptation, we should thank God for everything that happens to us.

188   If Peter had not failed to catch anything while fishing at night, he would not have caught anything during the day [Lk 5.4–6]; and if Paul had not experienced being blinded, he would not have been given spiritual sight [Acts 9.8]; and if Stephen had not been calumniated as a blasphemer [Acts 6.11], he would not have seen the heavens opened and looked upon the Lord [Acts 7.55–56].

189   Just as work that accords with God's wishes is called "virtue," unexpected affliction is termed "temptation."

190   God tested Abraham [Heb 11.17; Gen 22.1–14]l that is, God afflicted him for his own benefit, not in order to learn what kind of person Abraham was—for he who knows all things before they come into existence already knew him—but in order to provide him with opportunities for demonstrating perfect faith.

191   Every affliction tests which way the will is tipped, whether it is inclining toward the right or to the left. This is why chance afflictions are called "temptations": they provide the person who experiences them the opportunity to test his hidden desires.

192   Fear of God forces us to fight against evil, and when we do, the Lord's grace destroys it.

193   Wisdom is not only knowing the truth about natural consequences, but is also patiently enduring the wickedness of those who harm us as though we deserved it. Those who are content with the former become proud and arrogant, while those who attain the latter acquire humility.

194   If you do not want to be influenced by evil thoughts, welcome humiliation for your soul and affliction for your body, not occasionally, but always, everywhere, and in every situation.

195   The person who is willingly disciplined by afflictions is not held against his will in the grips of thoughts, whereas the person who does not accept such disciplining is taken prisoner by thoughts, even against his will.

196   When you are wronged and your heart and feelings have become hardened, do not be sad; what lay dormant has been roused by divine dispensation. Instead be glad and repel the thoughts that have risen up against you, knowing that if they are destroyed as they are attacking, the evil they bring with them is naturally destroyed along with their movements. If the thoughts persist, however, the evil that accompanies them customarily increases.

197   Unless the heart is shattered by contrition, it is absolutely impossible to free oneself of evil. Three-part self-control shatters the heart and makes it contrite—I mean the controlling of one's sleep and food and bodily relaxation. Too much food and sleep and relaxation lead to overindulgence in sensual pleasures, and over-indulgence makes one liable to have evil thoughts, which is inimical both to prayer and to carrying out one's assigned ministry.

198   If it is your duty to give orders to the brothers, carry out these duties, and do not hesitate to tell those who oppose your orders what they ought to do. When they obey you, you will be rewarded for their virtue, and when they disobey you, you will forgive them nevertheless and will receive equal forgiveness from him who said, "Forgive and you will be forgiven" [Lk 6.37].

199   Every happenstance is like a market day: The person who knows how to do business will make much money, while the person who does not know how to do business will suffer losses.

200   When someone does not obey you after you have given him orders once, do not try to force him to obey by arguing with him, but rather keep for yourself the profit he has thrown away. Your own forbearance will do you more good than correcting him.

201   When one person's harmful behavior begins to affect a number of other people, that is not the time to show patience nor to look out for your own benefit; instead, you should look for what benefits the majority so that they may be saved. Virtue that benefits a multitude is better than virtue that benefits a single person.

202   If a person falls into some kind of sin and does not show contrition proportionate to his mistake, he will easily be caught again in the same net.

203   Just as a lioness does not approach a calf in friendship, shamelessness does not look with kindness on contrition that accords with God's will [2 Cor 7.10].

204   Just as a sheep does not produce offspring with a wolf, neither does the heart's suffering mate with satiety in order to conceive virtues.

205   No one can experience suffering and contrition that accord with God's will unless he first loves what causes them.

206   Fear of God and criticism lead to contrition; self-control and keeping vigil keep company with suffering.

207   The person who is not instructed by scriptural commandments and admonitions will be spurred on by the horse's whip and the ass's goad [Prov 26.3 (LXX)], and if he resists these as well, he will be led with a bit and bridle in his mouth [Ps 32.9].

208   The person who is easily defeated by small things is also inevitably enslaved to major things, but the person who pays no attention to the former also, with the Lord's help, resists the latter.

209   Do not try to help the person who boasts about his virtues by criticizing him; the same person cannot both love showing off and be a lover of the truth.

210   Every word of Christ demonstrates God's mercy and justice and wisdom, and their power penetrates those who willingly listen to his words. That is why the unmerciful and the unjust, who listened unwillingly to the wisdom of God [1 Cor 2.7–8], were not able to understand it but even crucified Christ for speaking it. Therefore let us also see whether we listen to him willingly, for he said, "The person who loves me will keep my commandments and will be loved by my Father, and I too will love him and will reveal myself to him" [Jn 14.21]. Do you see how he has hidden his self-revelation in the commandments?

211   The most comprehensive of all the commandments is the love of God and of one's neighbor [Mark 12.30–31], which is maintained[21] by abstaining from material things and through stilling one's thoughts. Knowing this, the Lord commands us, saying, "Do not worry about tomorrow" [Mt 6.34]—and rightly so. How can the person who has not freed himself from material things and from worrying about them ever be freed from evil thoughts? How can the person who is caught up in thoughts see the subsistent sin hidden beneath them? This sin darkens the soul and envelops it in gloom, attacking it by means of evil thoughts and words and deeds. The Devil tempts a person with an assault that he is able to ward off and thus secretly initiates matters, and such a person, on account of his love of pleasure and self-centeredness, willingly comes along. Even if his powers of discernment cause him to hesitate, he takes delight in the workings of temptation and thus welcomes it.

How will the person who has not contemplated the all-embracing nature of such sin ever pray about it and be cleansed of it? And if he has not been purified, how will he find that place where his natural condition remains clean and pure? And if he has not discovered this, how will he ever see the inner dwelling-place of Christ [Heb 3.6], since we are indeed the dwelling-places of God, as the Prophet, the Gospel, and the Apostle say [Zech 2.10; Jn 14.23; 1 Cor 3.16]? Thus we

---

[21]*Sunistatai*, an important word here, also suggests "supported," "confirmed," "attested," "evinced."

should, following the path just laid out, seek out this dwelling-place and should, with prayer, stand knocking at the door, so that either here and now or at our death, the Master of the house will open the door to us and will not say, because of our negligence, "I do not know where you are from" [Lk 13.25].

Not only should we ask and receive [Jn 16.24], but we should also keep safe what we have been given, for there are those who lose what they have received. Thus both those who are young and those who are late learners may perhaps come to possess a rudimentary understanding or chance experience of these matters about which we have spoken, which even godly and very experienced elders, with constant and patient practice, can scarcely attain; through carelessness these elders have often lost their way, and then through voluntary suffering have renewed their search and found what they were looking for. So let us also not cease doing the same until, following their lead, we have acquired such a firm and inalienable practice.

We have come to a place where we now understand, out of many, these few ordinances of the spiritual law. The Great Psalm [Ps 119] constantly instructs us to learn them and to sing psalms without ceasing to the Lord. To him be the glory, forever and ever. Amen.

CHAPTER FIVE

On Repentance

INTRODUCTION

What does "repentance" mean?

Mark's emphasis is on an attitude toward God, rather than on particular actions. His call for repentance (Greek, *metanoia*) is programmatic:

> Repentance, I think, is not limited to either certain occasions or acts, but rather is practiced by keeping Christ's commandments proportionately to their nature. Certain commandments are comprehensive, incorporating within themselves numerous individual commandments and circumscribing numerous evils in one stroke (*Repentance* 6).

So even though he mentions the Novatianists, his focus does not seem to be the sort of repentance that was central to the Novatianist controversy (that is, the repentance needed for sacramental reconciliation with the Church). His diatribe is better understood as an echo of the Lord, crying out, "Repent, for the kingdom of heaven is at hand!" (Mt 4.17). The tone of *Repentance* is exhortatory.

What Mark is doing, at its most basic level, is calling for renewed and intensified responsiveness to God, by prodding his readers out of spiritual complacency. In Mark's treatise, the Lord's call for repentance is not so much aimed at an impending eschatological crisis;

instead, the call—in fact, the proximity and address of the Lord himself—is already the moment of truth: "The word of the Lord contains
within it the power of the kingdom: it is, for the faithful, 'the assurance of things hoped for,' 'the pledge of the inheritance to come,' the
first fruits of eternal good things, while for the faithless and impious
it is a fully realized reproach for their disbelief" (2).

De Durand eloquently summarizes what repentance means for
Mark:

> It [consists] in a permanent conviction of *not* having attained
> perfection, a regret for the faults and inadequacies that we
> find in every moment of our life; in brief, in a feeling that is
> rather near to what one would call "compunction," if that
> word did not have a rather old-fashioned, even slightly
> ridiculous, ring to it and if Mark had not used (albeit rarely)
> the Greek word that is its precise equivalent: *katanuxis*.[1]

As de Durand rightly points out, Mark adopts two voices in the
work. He speaks both as a moralist (when he rouses his readers to
repentance) and as a theologian (when he explains why repentance
is permanently a necessary component of the Christian life).[2] The
voice of the moralist is heard loud and clear in these pages. As for the
theological premises of *Repentance*, the reader will find that Mark
has already adumbrated them in *Spiritual Law* and *Works*.

In *Repentance*, he presupposes adherence to Christ's commandments and the inadequacy of unaided human effort. Indeed, it is
precisely human inadequacy that necessitates constant repentance,
in keeping with de Durand's summary ("regret for the faults and
inadequacies that we find in every moment of our life"). So repentance is a key element of the spiritual life. As Mark claims at the

---

[1]De Durand, *Marc le Moine*, 1:206–07. The precise words he uses in qualifying
the term "compunction" are "si le terme français n'avait un cachet quelque peu vieillot
. . ."; but since the English word has the same sort of resonance, we have translated "le
terme français" as "that word" out of solidarity.

[2]See de Durand, *Marc le Moine*, 1:207–11.

beginning of *Repentance*: "all the various laws have as their goal one end: repentance" (1).

Whom is Mark addressing?

The tone of *Repentance* in some points verges on polemical. But even so, it is unlikely that Mark is engaging with adversaries who are rejecting the possibility of repentance on principle. His some-what imprecise reference to one "who embraces the tenets of the Novatianists" (7) should not mislead us. Mark writes aggressively from time to time, but this is best understood as a rhetorical device that is well suited to stirring up a complacent reader. All the evidence points to a reader who is part of the Catholic Church, but who has become dangerously indifferent to his shortcomings.

Another important question about Mark's audience is whether he is writing for monks or for Christians at large. A definitive answer to that question is not available. A reasonable case can be made, however, for thinking that Mark is addressing himself to Christians at large.

Georges de Durand has noted that the word *monachos* is not found in *Repentance*. Absence of proof is not proof of absence, of course, but still the possibility that Mark was addressing himself to a general Christian readership (rather than restricting himself to "professional ascetics") must be taken seriously. As Mark himself specifies, "repentance is an appropriate concern for everyone, at all times, both sinners and righteous, if they wish to obtain salvation" (7). Furthermore, de Durand has pointed out that the only peniten-tial "acts" that Mark recommends in the work are prayer and fast-ing (*Repentance* 7, 11). (To this list, we should add examining one's thoughts and patience.) This can be contrasted to John Climacus' description of penitential acts like sitting in sackcloth and ashes, gnashing one's teeth, weeping, and the like.[3]

[3]For further discussion of all of these points, see de Durand, *Marc le Moine*,

Also noteworthy is Mark's concern for social hierarchy: He specifically describes how one acts toward one's social inferiors, equals, and superiors (3–5). Even though monastic life during that age did not preclude such ranking,[4] the fact that he dedicates several paragraphs to this theme may provide further corroboration for the claim that he wrote for a general Christian audience. His description of the wealthy who use their possessions in a godly way—because they know that "one receives in order to share with someone else who has nothing" (5)—seems to refer to Christians who manage their own property; it would be very surprising for him to speak of monks in that way. It is true that Mark goes on to talk about ways of being "wealthy" that do not involve material possessions (as when he writes that "most of us possess wealth even without having money"), but he never retracts or modifies his position with respect to those who actually do have money.

It is reasonable to conclude, therefore, that Mark intended for his advice to be generally applicable for everyone who is willing to take seriously the Lord's call for repentance. In other words, Mark wrote *Repentance* for all Christians.

1:205. The descriptions by John Climacus are found in the *Ladder of Divine Ascent*, Rung 5.

[4]For example, Evagrius' *To a Virgin* 12 (ed. H. Greßmann, *Nonnenspiegel*, [TU 39.4], 147) specifically addresses how she should behave toward her servant. Similar evidence is found in Western sources. Augustine's monastic rule envisages monks from different backgrounds and indicates that traces of social order are acceptable within the monastery: see *Praeceptum* 3.3 (ed. L. Verheijen, *La Règle de Saint Augustin* [Paris: Études Augustiniennes, 1967], 1:421). For Augustine, monastic equality is based on having everything in common, not necessarily on having identical provisions.

On Repentance[5]

Repentance as the foundation of the Christian life

1 Since our Lord Jesus Christ, the power and wisdom of God [1 Cor 1.24], himself as God knows and foresees the salvation of everyone, he set down the law of freedom by means of a variety of ordinances and ordained one goal appropriate for everyone when he said, "Repent" [Mt 4.17]. Because of this, it is possible for us to know that all the various laws have as their goal one end: repentance. He summed this up when he commanded the apostles, "Say to them, 'Repent, the kingdom of heaven has come near'" [Mt 10.7, 4.17]. By no means was he speaking of the nearness of the kingdom in temporal terms, as though he were talking about its present immanence in the world, for the Truth would not seek to define what is indefinable with dates and times. It is obvious that those who were alive at that time and those who followed them have gone to their rest without taking part in a universal consummation, but the Lord knew that his words held the power of both "kingdom" and "repentance": "Repent," he says, "for the kingdom of heaven has come near" [Mt 4.17].

If one does not grant this, how then is "the kingdom of heaven like yeast that a woman took and mixed in with three measures of flour until all of it was leavened" [Mt 13.33]? To put it another way: The intellect, once it has received the word of the Lord, takes the word and mixes it within the threefold substance (I mean that of the body and soul and spirit, in accordance with what the Apostle says [1 Thess 5.23]), and adds everything immaterial that body and soul and spirit manifest in thoughts to the one leaven of faith, like so much flour, until these thoughts have been completely assimilated to the word acting on them. In the same way, he compared the word of truth and a mustard seed, a small seed that is sown in the heart of

[5]Source: de Durand, *Marc le Moine*, 2:214–58.

those who listen [Mt 13.31–32]. Because of the way it naturally works, it grows into a very large tree whose high branches birds nest in; thus it becomes a house of refuge for errant thoughts.

The power of the word

The Lord showed that this is true when he said that the apostles were pure because of the word they had heard [Jn 15.3]. They made full use of the active power that comes with the word and thus became pure: "Indeed the word of God is living and active" [Heb 4.12]. Therefore the Lord condemned as faithless those who do not make full use of such power as is supplied: "If I had not come and spoken to them, they would not have sin. But now they have no excuse for their sin" [Jn 15.22].

2　We have said these things not as though we did not believe[6] in the coming kingdom, which will come without fail in its own, undetermined, time, but because the word of the Lord contains within it the power of the kingdom: It is, for the faithful, "the assurance of things hoped for" [Heb 11.1], "the pledge of the inheritance to come" [Eph 1.14], the first fruits of eternal good things, while for the faithless and impious, it is a fully realized reproach for their disbelief.[7] Therefore he says, "Repent. The kingdom of heaven has come near" [Mt 4.17].

---

[6]*Apistountes*; "faithless" in the previous paragraph translates the related word *apistous*. Mark next speaks of "the faithful" (*tois pistois*) and "the faithless" (*tois apistois*).

[7]The faithful have "assurance" (*hypostasis*), while the faithless have a "fully realized" (*enhypostasis*) reproach.

Those who do not heed the warning are worse than irrational animals

Thus if the word, by supplying the heart with the power to do what it is being told, shows those who only stop to hear it the work that they as debtors are obligated to do, how will we be persuaded to make full use with our bodies of the benefits that the Lord offers us? We have rejected the power not only of words, but also of the numerous great benefits that have accompanied those words. Not only have we hidden the one talent in the ground, we have also hidden the five talents and the two [Mt 25.14–30]! Do not even brute animals, as far as their nature allows, quite naturally obey the handler who shows them kindness, so that even the savagery of wild beasts is turned into obedience as they obey the words of their benefactor? How profoundly are we—with our free will, honored above all living things—shown to be more savage than wild beasts and more irrational than animals that lack reason! They are happy to be neighbors with one another: Each animal is satisfied with sharing pasturage with the animal that happens to be grazing near it, and without jealousy it leaves to the other the pasturage at its feet. We, however, who have been put in charge of the irrational animals and are their masters, prefer evil over nature. As a result, without any force or constraint making us do otherwise, we behave mercilessly and jealously towards our own kind.[8]

Such persons as these, I believe, John characterized as "snakes and broods of vipers" [Mt 23.33]; he orders them "to flee from the wrath to come" and "to be found bearing fruit worthy of repentance" [Mt 3.7–8], and commands the person with two coats to share with

---

[8]"Our own kind" translates *homophylos*. Mark writes in a tradition in which this term has acquired distinct notes of religious solidarity. Examples are found in Philo, *On the Special Laws of the Jews* 4.159 (Colson, *Philo*, 8:106–8); Clement, *Stromateis* 7.3.18.3 (GCS 17:14); Evagrius, *On Prayer* 40 (Tugwell, *Evagrius*, 9); and especially Gregory of Nyssa, *Life of Moses* 2.15 and 2.310.1–311.4; also significant is Gregory's description of Moses delivering "his own kind," taken to refer to progress in the spiritual life, at 2.89–101 and 2.227–231 (SC 1*bis*:36, 130; 56–57, 105–6).

the person who has none, and to do likewise with regard to food [Lk 3.11]. If he compared to snakes those who lived before the faith took hold and who, on account of their lack of feeling for their fellows, were ignorant of their responsibilities, he would have no comparison for the evil that we do, we who live with faith and knowledge and who have received so much, we who sin without restraint!

Relating to other people: Our social inferiors

3   I will therefore pass over those hidden thoughts that each person can bring under control, as far as he is able, and will speak only of those practices that we pursue when we are hateful with one another, especially with those we think have wronged us. We treat neither the insignificant nor the important as God wants.

It is obvious that we behave arrogantly with those who are beneath our notice or who are poorer than we, as if wishing to exercise authority over wage-earners or slaves, claiming that excellence is no longer defined by being "in Christ" but is defined rather by physical appearance and wealth. And when we see someone sin who is particularly haughty and arrogant, we do not dare rebuke him, and we say to those who happen to be present, "It is written: 'Do not pronounce judgement about anything before the appropriate time—until the Lord comes'" [1 Cor 4.5]. But when we find some small cause for complaint about those who are less well off, immediately we ostentatiously go on the attack, saying, "It is written: 'Rebuke the sinner in the presence of everyone'" [1 Tim 5.20]! In this way we perversely cover up our own hypocrisy—our evil-doing—with scriptural witnesses, all the while fully convinced that we are doing what God wants when we rebuke others.

Relating to other people: Our social equals

This, then, is the way we treat inferiors. With regard to those of the same social standing as ourselves, at the smallest sorts of pretexts we immediately turn our backs on them, devising every kind of machination to seek revenge. And we do not make up with them until we have brought them around to our way of seeing things. Seizing such a pretext, rejoicing at our good fortune, we display our wickedness and, after we have gained our revenge and gotten our fill of evil-doing, then we declare that we are once again friends with them, laying the foundation, for a second "friendship" by means of the evil victory that we have gained beforehand.

A corresponding structure will in every instance necessarily be built on such a foundation and the builder will by necessity be looking for strife, since, for the person who wants to win, "friendship" can never last without contentiousness. On the contrary, hatred always accompanies "victory," just as Holy Scripture says: "Hatred stirs up strife" [Prov 10.12]. Such sickness comes to those who pursue the highest positions of rank and wealth, just as dysentery afflicted "the leading man of the island" [Acts 28.7–8]. Even now Blessed Paul is curing this very malady, saying, "In humility regard others as better than yourselves" [Phil 2.3].

Relating to other people: Our social superiors

Thus are we disposed towards those of more humble rank than ourselves or those of equal standing. As for our wickedness towards those more powerful than ourselves, it is so varied and well-hidden that it is difficult to speak about it or even conceive of it. We do not submit to our superiors as though we were keeping a commandment. No, we flatter those whom we are unable to harm, and with a jealous eye we bitterly look down on their prosperity; we do not happily listen when their good fortune is trumpeted about. By our outward show and with eirenic speech we flatter such persons as these, but our thoughts are disposed against them, so that what was said is fulfilled about us: "Those who speak peace with their neighbors while evil is in their hearts" [Ps 28.3].

Sin and the will

4   We have spoken thus far about those who are carried to and fro willy-nilly by their desires. We now wish to show that those who sin willingly are further removed from God and are only with difficulty inclined to repent. How do those who refuse to do what Daniel said and find forgiveness not do so willingly? He said, "Redeem your sins with acts of mercy and your iniquities with acts of compassion for the poor and needy" [Dan 4.27]. But you will say, "I don't have any money. How will I perform acts of compassion for the poor and needy?" You don't have money, but you do have free will and the will to act.[9] Renounce your own will and with your money do good. Are you unable to do good with your corporal hand? Do good with the right hand of free will: "When your brother sins against you, forgive him" [Lk 17.3], in accordance with the word of the Lord, and that will be your great act of mercy. If we seek forgiveness from God, we must forgive each person every offense, so that what was said may be realized: "Forgive, and it will be forgiven you" [Lk 6.37].

It is a great thing for a person with money to give it away to the poor and needy, but to show compassion to a neighbor for the purpose of forgiving him is an even greater thing, to the same degree that the soul is naturally of more value than the body. Those of us who have sought forgiveness from God have often received it; on account of this forgiveness, evil no longer abides with us. But we do not consent to offer the same forgiveness to our neighbors. We are like that evil slave who, forgiven a debt of ten thousand talents

---

[9]In Greek "money" (*chrēmata*) and "acts of will," translated as "free will and the will to act" (*thelēmata*), have a closer sound association than in English.

by his master, would not forgive his fellow slave who owed him one hundred denarii.[10] Did not that slave's master lawfully respond when he said to him, "'You wicked slave! I forgave you all that debt because you pleaded with me. Should you not also have had mercy on your fellow slave?' And in anger," it says, "his master handed the slave over to the torturers until he paid everything he owed." Then the Lord adds, "So my heavenly Father will do to you if each of you does not from your heart forgive your brother his transgressions" [Mt 18.23–35].

The need for mercy and compassion

Thus Scripture also denounces elsewhere those who have been enriched by God with various benefits and advantages, but who are without mercy and compassion; it says, "Woe to you who are rich, because you have received your consolation" [Lk 6.24]. Truly, for us wealth consists of the various gifts that we have received from God. Woe to us, however, because we have implored God and have often been shown mercy, but when we ourselves have been implored, we have shown no one mercy, but have withheld our consolation.[11]

5 What we have said about the wealthy was not meant as an accusation against everyone who is well off, for there are those among the wealthy who manage their wealth properly and who observe the will of God, who has given them their wealth. They have received a hundredfold in this age, as it is written [Mark 10.30], as did blessed Abraham and righteous Job; because these latter were merciful, they became even wealthier, both here and in the age to come. But, as we have already said, we do reproach those of avaricious character who turn their backs on God's gifts, whether these take the form of money or of various acts of compassion, and who refuse

---

[10] A talent was more than fifteen years' wages for a laborer, and a denarius was a day's pay.

[11] In Greek "implore" (*parakalein*) and "consolation" (*paraklēsis*) share the same root; *parakalein* means "implore, entreat, beseech" as well as "exhort" and "console."

to show mercy towards their neighbor. It is not possessions given by the Lord that harm the possessor; rather, it is the greed that comes with possessions that brings harm, and heartlessness is the mother of such greed. Those who are well grounded in the faith entirely avoid heartlessness and greed because they have completely renounced present things, not because they thoughtlessly hate God's creation but because they have put their faith in Christ, who commands their renunciation. From him they receive what they need each day.

A person can, then, even without wealth, be a rich person, whether in speech or understanding or any sort of attachment, if he greedily hangs on to those things that are freely granted in common to everyone. One receives in order to share with someone else who has nothing. If someone is disposed to act unmercifully towards his neighbor, he will receive in addition the "woe" that the Lord pronounced because he has already received his consolation [Lk 6.24]. Saint James the Apostle also says something similar to this when he says to rich people of this sort: "Come now, you rich people, weep and wail for the miseries that you have coming" [Jas 5.1]. When he commands us to weep and wail, he is urging us to repent. Aware that we have little control over the passion for riches, he says, "Your riches have rotted away" [Jas 5.2], that is to say, "Your riches are useless since you have not shared them with others."

That it is possible to be greedy even without possessions

Most of us possess wealth even without having money: We have buried covetousness in our mental strongboxes as if it were gold. The prophet explicitly says about this, "My wounds grow foul and fester" [Ps 38.6]. He calls a loveless and greedy character "wounds"; with the phrase "grow foul and fester" he indicates a careless disregard that lasts until death, and considers this to be putrefaction and stench. Some of us, to be sure, choose to leave their fortune buried underground rather than share it with someone in need. But then, when death overtakes us, such a wound as the prophet speaks about attaches itself to our soul like putrefaction and as an accusation of our thoughtlessness. An eternal wound attached to the soul like this does not allow it to enter the heavenly Church of the firstborn [Heb 12.22–23], as the law concerning those who have a disgraceful defilement clearly states.

6   Perhaps there would be an appropriate time to lay bare our most grievous wounds and show them to the physician of souls. Saint Paul said, "your present abundance to meet their needs" [2 Cor 8.14], but we do the opposite: We snatch even what the poor lack and add it to our abundance. And this we often do even when there is no money involved! When we sin against our brother over some matter, not only do we leave him untreated, but we even imperiously demand from him an apology—one that we owed him! By doing this, we are doing nothing other than what was said earlier, adding even what the poor lack to our abundance, that is to say, putting ourselves in opposition to Scripture.

But this is no reason for us to despair. God forbid! We are not judged on account of the multitude of evils we do, but rather because we refuse to repent and acknowledge Christ's wonderful deeds, as the truth itself testifies: "Do you think," it says, "that those whose blood Pilate mixed with their sacrifices were worse sinners than everybody else? No, I tell you; but unless you repent, you will perish as they did. And what about those eighteen whom the tower of Siloam fell on and killed? Do you think they were worse sinners than all the other people living in Jerusalem? No, I tell you; but unless all of you repent, you will perish just as they did" [Lk 13.1–5]. Do you see that we are condemned because we stop repenting?

That repentance is appropriate at all times

Repentance, I think, is not limited to either certain occasions or certain acts, but rather is practiced by keeping Christ's commandments proportionately to their nature. Certain commandments are comprehensive, incorporating within themselves numerous individual commandments and circumscribing numerous evils in one stroke. For example, it is written, "Give to everyone who asks you for something" [Lk 6.30], and "Do not stop the person who is taking your possessions" [Lk 6.30], and "Do not turn away someone who wants to borrow something from you" [Mt 5.42]. Those cover particulars, but these are comprehensive: "Sell your possessions and give the money to the poor" [Mt 19.21], and "Take up your cross and come follow me" [Mt 16.24, 19.21]. By "cross" I mean the patient endurance of afflictions that occur. Thus the person who has distributed everything he owns to the poor and has taken up his cross has at once kept all the aforesaid commandments. And again: "I want the men," it says, "to pray in every place, lifting up holy hands" [1 Tim 2.8], and, in addition, "Go into your bedroom and pray in secret" [Mt 6.6], and again, "Pray without ceasing" [1 Thess 5.17]. The person who goes into his bedroom and prays without ceasing has included "prayer in every place." Again it says, "Do not sin sexually, do not commit adultery, do not murder" [Rom 13.9], and similar things, and in addition, "We destroy arguments and every proud obstacle raised up [against the knowledge of God]" [2 Cor 10.5]. The person who destroys arguments has excluded all of the aforementioned evils. On account of this, those who love God and are firmly grounded in the comprehensive commandments also make every effort with regard to particular commandments and do not overlook opportunities to keep them when they arise.

The virtues that especially promote repentance

7   On account of this, I think that the work of repentance is woven together by means of these three virtues: subjugating[12] thoughts, praying without ceasing [1 Thess 5.17], and patiently enduring afflic-

[12]*Kathairein* also means "destroy."

tions that occur. These things ought to have not only exterior but also interior action so as to make passionless those who persevere in them. Since, therefore, without the three aforementioned virtues the work of repentance cannot be perfected, as our discourse has pointed out, I think that repentance is an appropriate concern for everyone, at all times, both sinners and righteous, if they wish to obtain salvation. Thus there is no definition of perfection that does not have need of action arising from the aforementioned virtues. For beginners, the virtues are an introduction to godliness, while for the more advanced they represent progress, and for the perfect they reinforce the firm foundation built by means of them.

Neither times and seasons nor works of righteousness can hinder the virtues, only the erroneous beliefs caused by ignorance. This condition comes about when a person slides all too easily into pleasures and, under the pretext of despair, becomes solely a pleasure-seeker and embraces the tenets of the Novatianists[13] and rejects repentance. These are also the ones who rely on the Apostle when he preaches to the Hebrews,[14] who are sinning willingly and being baptized daily. He says, "not laying again the foundation: repentance from dead works, faith in God, and instruction about Baptism" [Heb 6.1–2]. He said this not because, as those people say, he rejects repentance—God forbid!—but because he is teaching that in every act of repentance there is one foundation—one Baptism in Christ—in order that those who put their faith in circumcision will

---

[13]The Novatianist schism takes its name from Novatian, the third-century Roman presbyter and antipope who opposed the re-entry into the Church of those who lapsed during the Decian persecution (249–51). Mark refers to them to evoke the belief that a Christian who has once fallen cannot be restored to the Church—an imprecise, but basically accurate view of Novatian's position. Initially it is surprising to find Mark writing about this movement, but in fact Novatianist communities are attested in the East until c. 600 (when Eulogius of Alexandria wrote against them). George Synkellos' *Chronography* (ninth century) is a sympathetic source for Novatianism in Constantinople. De Durand doubts whether Mark is writing from first-hand knowledge of Novatianists (1:204–05).

[14]Most writers in late antiquity believed that Hebrews was written by Saint Paul.

not be baptized daily. And he adds, "For it is impossible to restore again to repentance those who have once been enlightened,[15] and have tasted the heavenly gift, and have shared in the Holy Spirit, and have tasted the goodness of the word of God and the powers of the age to come, and then have fallen away" [Heb 6.4–6]. He knows that there is only one restoration and foundation prescribed for all repentance: holy Baptism. So a little later he adds, "If we willingly sin after having received the knowledge of the truth, there no longer remains a sacrifice for sin" [Heb 10.26].

The example of Esau

8   Since what the Apostle so appropriately said applies wherever such conditions as these exist, it is clear that he is speaking not only to the Jews but also to all those who willingly sin. First among these are those who say that there is no repentance after Baptism and who, on account of this, are subsequently carried off on their own accord and continue to commit transgressions. They also offer as testimony what was said about Esau, contradicting themselves at every turn. Holy Scripture, in fact, reproaches Esau because he did not repent his sin when he profaned his birthright [Gen 25.29–34] and when he had sexual intercourse with pagans [Gen 26.34, 28.6–9]: "There is no one as sacrilegious and sexually impure as Esau, who sold his birthright for a single meal. You know that later, when he wanted to inherit the blessing, he was rejected, even though with tears he sought the blessing, for he found no chance to repent" [Heb 12.16–17; Gen 27.30–40].

Concerning the blessing, then, it says in the letter to the Hebrews that "with tears he sought it," not "on account of repentance." This is true, since we also find in the Story of Creation[16] that Esau "wept for the blessing and with tears sought it"; while for his sins, it adds,

---

[15]"Enlightenment" (*phōtismos*) means "baptism."
[16]That is, Genesis.

he nowhere repented, but said rather, "The days [of mourning] for my father are coming, and then I will kill my brother Jacob" [Gen 27.41]. Saint Paul has inverted the order of these words, and he did so deliberately, I believe, so that his thought would be clear for those who are more devout as they search the Scriptures, while for those who are more negligent and inattentive his thought would be difficult to discern, lest, under the pretext of some future repentance, they sin now without fear.

Some, then, make a pretense of repentance while intentionally becoming addicted to evils, while others, because they do not believe that repentance really exists, become hardened and hand themselves over to the Devil; but for both groups the malady[17] is dreadful and incurable. For this reason the Truth offers a suitable remedy for everyone when he[18] says, "Repent, for the kingdom of heaven has drawn near" [Mt 4.17], so that those who are spiritual and those who are advanced in the spiritual life will not neglect this precept as they fortify themselves with what others tell them are insignificant and small matters, for, it says, "The person who despises small things will fail little by little" [Sir 19.1].

The shortcomings of the spiritual person

And do not say, "How can the spiritual person fail?" If such a person persists in little things, he will not fail. When, however, he welcomes some small thing from among those things that are hostile to the spiritual life and persists in it without repenting, that thing, insignificant in and of itself, once it has settled in and grown, refuses to live any longer as an orphan with him; rather, with a small show of friendship, it violently drags him, as though he were bound and gagged, to its parents. If, after waging battle through prayer, the

[17]*Pathos*, which also means "passion." Forms of *pathos*—"evil desire" (*prospatheia*), "passionlessness" (*apatheia*)—occur several times in this section. In §7 passionlessness (*apatheia*) is a much-desired virtue.

[18]The Truth is Christ; see §1; see Jn 14.6.

spiritual person manages to cut himself free of this evil desire, he will hold his ground by maintaining his standards (although he will lose something of his former passionlessness insofar as the desire for some evil separates him from it). If in the end he accommodates himself to the tighter grip of what has hold of him, giving up on his efforts at battle and prayer, it is inevitable that he will also be hooked like a fish by other passions, and thus, as one passion succeeds another, little by little he is led astray by force of habit. To the extent that he is led away, he is cut off from God's help and afterwards is carried along into even greater evils, perhaps even against his will, by the force of what had first got hold of him.

9   Undoubtedly you will say to me, "Couldn't he have called on God when the evil first appeared and not fallen in the end?" And I will say to you that he could have but, thinking that something so small was a matter of no importance and willingly welcoming it as if it were nothing, he no longer called on God about it, not realizing that that small thing was the beginning and source of something larger, as much for good as for evil. When the passion had grown in size and, through his own free will, gained a foothold, it afterwards crowed over him by forcing him, against his will, to do what it wanted.

Only then did this spiritual person come to his senses and call on God, waging war against the enemy whom he had at first unwittingly championed when he fought against people on behalf of his enemy. Even when he was heard by the Lord, he did not receive help, because things did not turn out as people expected but as the Lord arranged them for this person's benefit. The Lord, knowing how easily swayed and inattentive we are, provides people with great help through afflictions, lest we be saved without suffering afflictions and return once again to our accustomed sins. Thus we must counsel patience with the things that happen to us and advise complete devotion to repentance.

Repentance is needed even as we draw near to perfection

10   But you will undoubtedly say to me, "What need do those who are truly pleasing to God and who are drawing near to perfection still have for repentance?" That there have been—and are—such people, I fully agree, but be wise and listen, and you will understand how even such persons as these have need of repentance. Lying comes from the Devil, says the Lord [Jn 8.44], and he considered looking at a woman with lust to be adultery [Mt 5.28], and likened anger towards one's neighbor to murder [Mt 5. 21–22], and made it clear that we would have to give an account for a careless word [Mt 12.36]. Who, then, is so virtuous that he is not tempted even to lie, and is innocent of ever having looked at a woman with lust, and has never been rashly angry with his neighbor nor been found guilty of a careless word, so as not to need repentance?[19] Even if no such person exists now, at some point he existed, and he had need of repentance until the day he died.

Let us posit, however, that some people are found without these faults and are strangers to every evil engendered by them—but this is impossible, since Saint Paul says, "All have sinned and fall short of the glory of God, being justified by his grace as a gift" [Rom 3.23–24]. Even if there were such virtuous people, even they are children of Adam and undoubtedly were born under the sin of transgression [Gen 3], and thus have been condemned and sentenced to death, unable to be saved without the Lord.[20] The Lord was crucified and with his own blood redeemed everyone [Eph 1.7], and at that time they were also delivered [from sin]. And so the Redeemer set a single standard for everyone that encompasses every situation, and he said to the apostles, "Say to them, 'Repent, for the kingdom of heaven has drawn near'" [Mt 4.17]. At the same time, he gave the

---

[19]For a comparable discussion of this theme, see John Cassian, *Conference* 23 (CSEL 13:638–71).

[20]Here Mark offers his view of ancestral sin, which bears a striking resemblance to Augustine's view. See the discussion entitled, "*The Fall and its consequences,*" in the general introduction, above.

commandments that fulfill repentance and ordained that they were to be carried out to the point of death: "The person who loses his life for my sake and the sake of the gospel will keep it for eternal life" [Mt 10.39; Mark 8.35; Jn 12.25]. Again, when he ordered us to repudiate everything, he added, "and even his own life" [Lk 14.26]. And he seals it by saying, "The person who breaks one of these commandments, even the least of them, and teaches people to do likewise will be called least in the kingdom of heaven" [Mt 5.19]. If the Redeemer ordained repentance even to the point of death, then, as has been demonstrated, the person who says that he has achieved repentance before he dies breaks the commandment by removing death [from the Lord's injunctions].

Repentance is required up to the point of death

11   It follows that for both those who are great and those who are not, repentance is unfinished until death. Even if we are unable to achieve it in practice until then, we ought to practice it as an aim, lest by our intentions we break the commandment and be subject to condemnation and judgement and be called "least in the kingdom of heaven" [Mt 5.19]. Consider those who from the beginning of time have passed through this life, and you will find that it has been through repentance that those who have pleased God have achieved the mystery of godliness. No one has been condemned unless he disregarded repentance, and no one has been justified unless he has paid careful attention to repentance. Samson and Saul and Eli, with his sons, shared partially in holiness: First, they disregarded repentance, to their destruction, and finally, when the time limit had expired for them to repent, they succumbed to a terrible death [Jdg 16.23–31; 1 Sam 31; 1 Chr 10; 1 Sam 4.11–22]. If the Devil does not cease waging war against us, neither should repentance ever be idle. The saints are also compelled to offer it on behalf of their neighbors. Without active love, the saints are unable to reach perfection.

Learn how nature teaches us not to give up repenting until we die. The mind, source of thinking, cannot remain idle; even if it were perfect, it would do well to continue working for what is right.[21] If, under the pretext that it has reached perfection, the mind stops doing good works, it undoubtedly nods off in the opposite direction.[22] As soon as it rights itself, it once again is naturally pulled to doing what is right. Doing what is right, for beginners and the advanced and the perfect, means praying and purifying one's thoughts and patiently enduring whatever comes.[23] Without these, it is not possible to achieve the other virtues that make repentance acceptable. If repentance consists of asking for mercy, the person who has what he needs, needs to take special care not to hear, "You already have everything you need!" [1 Cor 4.8]. Even more, the person who does not yet have what he needs, needs to ask, "because everyone who asks receives" [Mt 7.8]. If the person who is merciful receives mercy [Mt 5.7], then it is repentance, I believe, that holds together the whole cosmos. By divine dispensation, the one is helped by the other. Because of repentance, God saved the Ninevites [Jon 3.5–10], and God consumed the Sodomites with fire because they neglected it [Gen 18.20–22, 19.24–25].

12   If we struggle and fight by repenting, even to the point of death, we do not thereby fulfill our obligation, for such struggle does not entitle us to the kingdom of heaven. Just as we eat and drink and speak and hear, so too by nature ought we to repent. The person who is worthy of dying once[24] has died in accordance with the law [Heb 9.27], and the person who lives by faith [Gal 2.20] lives on account of repentance. Even if it is not on account of *our* sin but rather the sin of the transgression [Gen 3], we are cleansed when we are baptized

---

[21]See Evagrius Ponticus, *Chapters of Exhortation* 70 (PG 79:1256): "The mind does not stop giving birth [to thoughts]; so you extirpate the bad ones, and cultivate the good ones."

[22]Literally "to the left." In this paragraph Mark plays on the Greek words for "right" and "left."

[23]These are the three virtues that Mark discusses in §7.

[24]That is, in Baptism.

and, once we are cleansed, we receive commandments.[25] The person who does not do the latter has profaned the former and "is forgetful of the cleansing of his past sins" [2 Pet 1.9]. No one is found without sins every day lest he ever neglect any of the commandments.

How repentance is beneficial for other spiritual efforts

Repentance should therefore be a requirement for everyone. Because of repentance, those things that at one time had to be done by an act of will are now done instinctively because one hates the passion and avoids its consequences. The person who circumscribes repentance turns back [Lk 9.62] and repeats his old transgressions. The person who has knowledge of the truth [1 Tim 2.4] knows that he also needs repentance, for each of them is guided by the other. Christ has made himself the guarantor of our repentance; the person who neglects it rejects him who made the guarantee. As for works, we are unable to do anything worthy, but have great mercy shown us on account of our intentions. The person who acts forcefully until the day of his death and grabs hold of repentance will be saved, even if he sins in certain matters, because of his forceful action [Mt 11.12]. The Lord has promised this in the Gospels.

The person who says he does not need repentance judges himself to be righteous and is called an "evil grandchild" by Scripture [Prov 30.12 (LXX)]. The person who conceitedly assumes that he is in a state of righteousness, as though he had perfected repentance and finished with it, has, on the contrary, in my opinion joined forces with the pleasures, if self-conceit and arrogance are indeed pleasures.[26] The person who is self-conceited cannot be saved, for, it is written,

---

[25]Mark is referring here to Baptism for infants who have inherited "the sin of transgression" but have no personal sins. For the "sin of transgression" from birth, see §10.

[26]*Hêdonai*, "pleasures," has mostly negative connotations in early monastic literature; the pleasures are linked with the passions, both of which distract the faithful from God.

"the conceited and contemptuous braggart will never accomplish anything" [Hab 2.5]. If humility in no way harms the perfect, even the braggart himself cannot get rid of its source, repentance!

Faithful Abraham and righteous Job called themselves "earth and ashes" [Gen 18.27; Job 42.6]. These words are the mark of humility. The person who satisfies himself that he has had his fill of repentance cannot be humble. The three children, who were truly great witnesses, confessed in the midst of burning flames that they had both sinned and broken the law, saying that they had repented their past evils, and were perfect thereafter, and almost their whole song of praise demonstrates the power of repentance [Dan 3.26–45].

13   If then both those who have been very pleasing to God and those who through their works have been shown to be perfect have made use of this resource until the day of their death, who, under the pretext of righteousness, will afterwards place his confidence in himself and disregard repentance? It is my belief that even if someone were as holy as Paul or Peter, not even then would he undertake abandoning the source of humility. For this reason Peter likened himself to Cornelius; by doing this, he downplayed what was divine and manifested his own character by saying, "Stand up; I too am only a mortal" [Acts 10.26], and confessed that he had been taught by God to say that no one was profane or unclean [Acts 10.28].

Paul, after having grace given to him by Christ [Acts 26.12–18], believing that he would nowhere find rest until the day he died, [27] spoke thus: "But I press on to make it my own because Christ has made me his own" [Phil 3.12]. By "making it his own" he means "persevering until his death," just as, when he wrote to faithful Timothy, he made it clear that his death was near, saying, "I have fought the

---

[27]The verb *hypolēgein* in this clause is unusual, meaning "to desist gradually." But this does not make a great deal of sense. The word perplexed ancient readers, too. We have followed the conjecture of one copyist by adding *oudamou*, "never," and taking *hypolēgein* to mean "to find rest." But since the root of the verb, *lēgein,* refers to the waning of the moon in the *Apocalypse of Barnabas* 9 (see Lampe, *Patristic Greek Lexicon,* 799A), it might be taken here to mean "to disappear gradually." If so, the sense of Mark's claim is that Paul believed he would gradually be worn down until he died.

good fight, I have finished the race, I have kept the faith" [2 Tim 4.7]. He did not provide for himself a way out or a time limit, as though he had given up the race because he had finished it and no longer needed to fight on behalf of the body of Christ (which is the Church) [Col 1.24]—he did not ever give up the race while he was on the earth; he said, rather, that his death would mark the end of the race and the end of the fight. Thus he says, "I am already being poured out as a libation, and the time of my departure has come" [2 Tim 4.6].

Do you see that he did not say, "I am stopping," but rather, "I am already being poured out as a libation." Both these words and these actions demonstrate to everyone that our obligation to repentance ends with sacrifice and death, on behalf of Christ, the heavenly King, to whom be glory forever. Amen.

CHAPTER SIX

Concerning Fasting

INTRODUCTION

In recent years, several scholars have claimed this treatise was not written by Mark and have attributed it instead to Marcian of Jerusalem. Without wishing to mount a case against their claims, we are including *Concerning Fasting* in this translation. For more on this, the reader is referred to the "Postscript" to the General Introduction.

Concerning Fasting is Mark's only writing in which he focuses on a specific ascetic discipline. As we shall see, he most probably wrote *Fasting* for the benefit of other monks; but the advice he offers certainly has a potentially broader application, since it is general in scope and moderate in execution. He calls for balance in fasting. What is desirable is that bodily desires should be subjected to the mind, but excessively abstaining from food can result in weakness of the body ("torpor"), which in turn becomes a distraction when one tries to pray. Bodily desires are relevant not only to how much food one should eat, but also to what kind of food one should eat. Mark opposes the desire for variety with the same strength that he opposes the desire for satiety. The reason for eating, he implies, is to maintain good health (see *Fasting* 1), and for that neither selection nor abundance is needed.

Throughout this brief work, Mark maintains his characteristically introspective approach to asceticism. For Mark, reflecting upon what one is doing—and why one is doing it—is an important part of appropriate Christian behavior, without which a wholesome activity can easily become detrimental:

> Just as fasting helps those who submit to it with some thought and consideration, so too it harms those who apply themselves to it without reflection. Those who worry about the efficacy of fasting ought also to be on guard against the harm it can cause—that is, the self-conceit it can bring about (3).

The great danger in fasting, according to Mark, is not nutritional deficiency. It is not even being unable to concentrate during a service because of a rumbling in the belly. Instead, it is conceitedness that comes from being proud of an accomplishment.

Once more, Mark is echoing his stern warnings about not being justified through works. The likely recipients of *Fasting* were probably monks. This conclusion is based on Mark's denunciation of a competitive spirit amongst ascetics ("We begin to think we are better than our fellow ascetics" [2]). One can certainly imagine a zealous clutch of Christians "in the world" vying for the distinction of being champion faster, but it is more plausible to suppose that Mark is addressing a problem that arose in a monastery. Further support for this claim occurs in the passage where Mark contrasts the lives of his readers to the lives of the biblical patriarchs: "We, on the other hand, *have withdrawn from the world and have looked down on wealth and forsaken our homes and think we are devoted to God*—and are still mocked by demons, all on account of our pride" (4). The sharp contrast between, on the one hand, the godly patriarchs who ruled their households and provided for them and, on the other, Mark's readers indicates that he is writing to fellow monks.

Concerning Fasting[1]

The importance of moderation in eating

1　It is appropriate for those setting out on a course of ascetic discipline, both young and old, also to have a goal in sight, keeping their bodies in good health, fearing neither weariness nor ill-treatment. They should give their complete attention, willingly and eagerly, to fasting, which is the most useful and trustworthy discipline. They should eat their bread by weight and drink water by measure, and do so at fixed times [Ez 4.10–11]. Such a regimen will ensure that they leave the afternoon meal hungry and thirsty and not hinder the appointed worship offered to God because of the delight taken in various foods.

　　If we wish to eat until we are stuffed, we will quickly lapse into spiritual torpor and turn our attention to some other desire, and if we gain possession of this desire and completely satisfy ourselves, we will in turn reject this one and abandon it just as we did the previous one. It is not possible for us, whether we imagine ourselves fasting or fulfilling our desires, to remain satisfied once we have gotten our fill. What food is more truly perfect than manna? Israel ate this and was satisfied [Is 44.16]. When they had nothing better to desire, they desired what was inferior, garlic and onions [Num 11.5–6]; as a result, the desire for other things became implanted in them along with satiety. Thus, if we desire something else when we fill ourselves with bread, let us not fill ourselves when we eat bread, so that when we are hungry we always desire to be filled with that.[2] In this way

---

[1]Source: de Durand, *Marc le Moine*, 2:158–66
[2]The author is chiefly warning against variety in one's diet, but the specific meaning of this advice is somewhat vague. In the phrase the "desire to be filled with that," the Greek word "that" (*touton*) can refer either to "bread" (*arton*) or "something else" (*heteron*). If we take it to mean "bread," the advice is that we should keep ourselves content with bread so that, even when we want more food, all we want is bread; but

we will both avoid the harm that comes with desire and produce the righteousness that comes with abstinence.

It is hard work to get the shameless belly under control

2   But perhaps one of those who are hesitant to fast will say, "It isn't a sin for a person to partake of food, is it?" We, however, are not offering our advice because partaking of food is a sin, but because of the sin that follows *after* eating. Israel did not sin because of its desire, but because of its desire it slandered God and acted impiously, for Israel said, "Will God be able to spread a table in the wilderness?" [Ps 78.19]. After God spread a table for them, then the anger of God was kindled against them [Ps 78.31], and he bound their elect hand and foot so they would not desire other food as long as they lived and utter words against the Most High, and those remaining be completely destroyed.

It is hard work to get the shameless belly under control. It is a god to those defeated by it [see Phil 3.9], and it is not possible for the person who places his trust in it to escape punishment. Not only is there the danger of satiety; there is also the danger of not having enough food. When we spend a prolonged period of time without eating anything, spiritual torpor seizes the opportunity to rise up and wage war against us: At night it takes our keeping vigil and turns it into sleep, and during the day it takes our prayer and turns it into carnal thoughts; as a result, sleep does us no good and our carnal thoughts cause us the greatest harm. We begin to think we are better than our fellow ascetics, ‹jealously commenting on our superiors› while denigrating those inferior to us.[3] This is the worst kind of offense. If a stupid farmer works his land with great expenditure yet

---

if we take it to mean "something else," the advice is that we should not eat too much bread, because this will lead us to want something more than bread.

[3] The text appears to be corrupt. We have followed de Durand's suggestion, which is based on the Syriac version.

leaves it unsown, he has labored for nothing. So too with us: If with great diligence we make a slave of our flesh without laying a good foundation built on prayer,[4] rather than working for our benefit we have zealously worked to our detriment.

The need for fasting; safeguarding against self-conceit

3   But perhaps someone will say, "If righteousness comes through prayer, what is the need for fasting?" There is always a need for fasting!

If some poor farmer sows on dry land without first composting the earth, he will reap thorns instead of wheat. So too with us: If we do not mortify our flesh with fasting before we lay a foundation of prayer, we will reap sin for ourselves instead of righteousness. This flesh of ours comes from that same earth as the farmer plows, and if the former does not receive as much care and attention as the latter, it will never bear fruit of righteousness.

We say these things not to hinder those who want to be helped by fasting, but to encourage those who do not want to be harmed by fasting. Just as fasting helps those who submit to it with some thought and consideration, so too it harms those who apply themselves to it without reflection. Those who worry about the efficacy of fasting ought also to be on guard against the harm it can cause—that is, the self-conceit it can bring about. In addition, the bread that we eat after completing the fast that we have set for ourselves should be portioned out on those days when we are not eating[5] in order that,

---

[4] The "good foundation built on prayer" has a depth of meaning that is not immediately obvious in translation. *Logon tēs proseuchēs* also means "rationale of prayer," but the Greek verb *katabalō* means "to put down," and in English we do not talk about "putting down" a rationale.

[5] The precise meaning of this advice is obscure, but it could mean that the readers ought to eat a little after a long period of fasting, even on days when they would ordinarily abstain from eating (on Wednesdays and Fridays). This can be compared to the practice observed in the Orthodox Church of not fasting during Bright Week, even on days when the Orthodox ordinarily fast.

taking a little bit each day, we may muzzle the presumptions of our flesh and acquire a heart strengthened for even more helpful prayer. In this way, safeguarded from pride through the power of God, we may spend all the days of our lives in humility [Lk 1.75]. Without humility, no one can please God [Heb 12.14, 11.6].

The humility that fasting brings and its fruits

4   If we have applied ourselves to practicing humility, we have no need of education, for all the evil and terrible things that happen to us happen because of our pride. If a messenger from Satan was given to the Apostle to keep him from being proud [2 Cor 12.7], how much more will Satan himself be given to us who are proud so as to trample us down until we become humble! Our forefathers were the lords and masters of their homes and had great wealth and provided for their women and children—and still conversed with God, all because of their sincere humility. We, on the other hand, have withdrawn from the world, and have looked down on wealth and forsaken our homes, and think we are devoted to God—and are still mocked by demons, all on account of our pride.

The proud person does not know himself; if he knew himself and his own folly and weakness, he would not be proud. How will the person who does not know himself be able to know God? If he is not capable of understanding his own folly, by which he is turned upside down, how will he be able to understand the wisdom of God, from which he is estranged and distant? The person who knows God contemplates God's greatness and deprecates himself, like blessed Job, and says, "I first heard of you as something reported to my ear, but now I see you with my very own eyes. Therefore I deprecate myself and waste away; I consider myself dust and ashes" [Job 42.5–6].

Those who imitate Job, therefore, are the ones who see God, and those who see God are the ones who know him. So, if we too want to see God, let us deprecate and humble ourselves, not merely to see him standing opposite us but also, with him dwelling and resting within us, to delight in him and enjoy him. In this way our foolishness will be made wise in his wisdom, and our weakness will be made strong in his might [see 2 Cor 12.9], which strengthens us in our Lord Jesus Christ. Christ has deemed us worthy of this gift. Even more extravagantly, he deigned to be glorified in us and, for our sake, prevailed over Satan, our enemy and adversary, and put him to shame. In our Lord Jesus Christ himself, because to him belong glory, grandeur, and majesty forever. Amen.

CHAPTER SEVEN

The Mind's Advice to Its Own Soul

INTRODUCTION

With *The Mind's Advice to its Own Soul*, Mark offers up an example of the kind of introspection that he has repeatedly urged his readers to undertake (cf. *Spiritual Law* 91, 161–64, 178, 186; *Works* 52, 176; *Fasting* 3). He does this by personifying the Mind and the Soul. The work is not a dialogue; instead, the Mind takes the lead (which is much as one would expect, since the mind is the highest element of the person and ought to direct the soul, according to the conventions of Greek ascetic literature). Even though this imaginative technique does not give us much insight into how Mark conceives of human anthropology, it must be admitted that Mark uses it successfully to model how the mind ought to direct the impulsive, vital force of the soul.

The Mind is the leading principle and is making progress in the spiritual life, but it is still far from perfect. "Both you and I, naturally influenced by ignorance, are prone to error," it says to the Soul, "and on account of this blame others for our sins, saying that the evil lies outside us" (*Advice* 1). This attempt at deflecting responsibility for sins to someone else (whether Adam, Satan, or anyone—or anything!—else) is a great cause for concern to the Mind. As the Mind is only too well aware, such efforts are detrimental to spiritual progress. Blaming one's sins on an external cause merely serves to bolster conceit.[1] For this reason the Mind says,

[1] Cf. *Advice* 5: "Two evils are obstacles to attaining this virtue: self-conceit and love of pleasure."

we imagine that we are waging war against others while we are really waging war against ourselves. Thinking that we are protecting one another, you and I are in reality fighting against each other; believing that we are benefiting one another, we are really harming each other (ibid.).

When successful, blaming others leads to a break between one's inner state and one's public appearance. This is undoubtedly an example of the hypocrisy Mark warned Nicholas about (see *Nicholas* 4.1–6).

In keeping with this call for responsibility, Mark boldly claims that, after Baptism, free will is able to opt for God or for Satan without compulsion. In consequence of this freedom, the baptized Christian alone bears responsibility for his decisions. But at this point we need to remember the lessons Mark has taught in other writings. He must not be misunderstood as wavering in his belief that virtuous works cannot merit God's favor. In fact, he reiterates the claim that God's gracious forgiveness is more important than our efforts, regardless of how necessary the latter are. As the Mind remarks, "We know that the wages of forgiveness are greater than every virtue" (4).

The Mind particularly warns the Soul against being susceptible to "unreasoning impulses" (2). This is of course consistent with Mark's approach to fasting, but of greater immediate relevance is the fact that complicity with these impulses has dramatic consequences for one's will. They "take over" the will by confirming us in our inclinations toward God or Satan. So even though the impulses in themselves are a matter of indifference, they must be taken very seriously, because each time we submit to one of them makes it more likely that we will submit to it again in the future. The Mind speaks trenchantly on this point: "Battle your own will—and do not take the battle lightly, for this is civil war" (5).

One might expect from the introspective nature of *Advice* that it would focus chiefly on internal states, and yet most of the examples that the Mind cites to illustrate the effects of submitting to "unreasoning impulses" are about interpersonal relations. It is typical of this attention to the social aspects of life that the Mind says, "Death comes not from God, but from people hating their neighbors" (3). Even when neighbors are abusive, however, they are to be loved. In fact, they are to be loved *especially* when they are abusive:

> We ought to have one end in sight at all times and places and at every opportunity: to rejoice and not be saddened when we are wronged in various ways by people—to rejoice; that is, not simple-mindedly, nor purposelessly, but because we have found the cause for forgiving the person who has sinned against us and for receiving forgiveness for our sins (4).

This attitude activates the "hidden" grace of Baptism, thus making both asceticism and forgiveness possible (ibid.).

The Mind's Advice to Its Own Soul[2]

The conflict between the mind and the soul

1   Listen, rational soul, partner in all my deliberations, I wish to explain to you a certain mysterious and ordinary matter. I have undertaken this without having been cleansed of passions, but I am, by the grace of Christ, nevertheless, devoting myself to it for a short while. I am fully aware, dear soul, that both you and I, naturally influenced by ignorance, are prone to error and on account of this blame others for our sins, saying that the evil lies outside us. Sometimes we lay the blame on Adam, while at other times Satan, and other times other people. In doing so we imagine that we are waging war against others, while we are really waging war against ourselves. Thinking that we are protecting one another, you and I are in reality fighting against each other; believing that we are benefiting one another, we are really harming each other, like a madman with his self-inflicted wounds, rightly enduring useless afflictions and reproaches. We appear to love the commandments, but because of error we hate what informs them. Because of this, I clearly see now that we are not drawn wrongfully into either evil or good by some sort of power; on the contrary, from the time we are baptized, when we undertake any kind of endeavor using our free will we serve either God or the Devil, and one or the other quite rightly compels us to take his side.

Two unreasoning impulses

2   We undertake everything that we do because of two unreasoning[3] impulses: a desire for people's praises and a desire for creature

[2]Source: De Durand, *Marc le Moine*, 1:398–414.

[3]*Adialogistoi*; at the beginning of the discourse the mind addresses the soul as "rational," *logikē*.

comforts. These impulses, which, without our willing it, take control over our will, are neither evils nor virtues but are rather proofs of our inclinations. The Lord wishes us to patiently endure reproaches and ill-treatment, whereas the Devil wishes the opposite. So whenever we take delight in these impulses, it is clear that, having disobeyed the Lord, we have given in to the pleasure-seeking spirit; and whenever we are afflicted by the aforesaid impulses, because we have loved the narrow way [Mt 7.13–14], it is clear that we have given ourselves over to God.

Because of this, then, these two impulses have been allowed to have unreasoning control over human beings, so that those who love the commandment and who show their disgust for these impulses will incline their will to Christ, and Christ, gaining access, will lead the mind into the truth. Since this is so, grant me the opposite point, too: Whoever once again loves human fame and physical comfort grants access to the Devil, and the Devil, once he has gained access for himself, from then on insinuates his own evils. Insofar as we take pleasure in thinking about these evils, the Devil does not stop making advances until we can come to hate the aforesaid impulses with all our heart.

But we love these impulses so much that not only do we abandon virtue for them, we also trade them in for one another whenever we have the opportunity: Sometimes we mistreat the body through vanity, while at other times we bring dishonor upon ourselves through our love of pleasure. When we make a pact with these things without any regret, from then on we go around looking for stuff to increase their abilities. The "stuff" of vanity and bodily pleasure is, according to Holy Scripture, "the love of money, the root of all kinds of evil" [1 Tim 6.10].

Problems come from abusing possessions, not from possessions
as such

3   No doubt, my dear soul, you will say to me, "We are neither storing up gold nor do we have any possessions," and I will tell you that neither gold nor possessions in and of themselves cause harm, but, as I said earlier, abusing them makes one subject to the passions. Look, some of those who were rich without becoming subject to the passions were able to please God, as, for example, holy Abraham and Job and David. Meanwhile, some of us, even without wealth, have nourished the passion of coveting the cheapest material things. Thus we are more wretched than those with great possessions: Having given up [worldly] hardships in general, we cunningly live in the lap of luxury, as though we were escaping God's notice. Fleeing the love of money, we do not escape the pursuit of pleasure; we do not store up gold, and yet we accumulate insignificant stuff; we do not seize hold of authority and preeminence, but in every way possible we chase after the praise and prestige that come with them; we have abandoned possessions and yet do not renounce the pleasures that accompany them, and even when we think we are renouncing things, it is not because we are fleeing covetousness, but because we abhor God's creatures: "Do not handle, do not taste, do not touch" [Col 2.21], [we say].

Everyone recapitulates the original transgression

Thus when you hear about the transgression of Adam and Eve, my dear soul, know for a fact that the transgression first took place personally in them, and then you will discover that the transgression occurs in you and me and can be apprehended by the intellect—for "these things happened to them as an example, and they were written down as an admonition to us, on whom the final times of the age have come" [1 Cor 10.11]. Look, having been given new birth through Baptism and placed in the paradise of the Church, we have transgressed the commandment given by him who gave us new birth. The Lord has ordered us to love all those of the same faith and to eat with patience the fruit that each of them bears, as it was said, "Eat from every tree in paradise" [Gen 2.16]. But we, utilizing the thoughts[4] of the serpent, have loved some as good and have hated others as evil, which is equivalent to "the tree of the knowledge of good and evil" [Gen 2.17]. Having tasted it with our intellect, have we not condemned ourselves to death?

The importance of loving others

Death comes not from God, but from people hating their neighbors, "for God did not make death, nor does he delight in the destruction of the living" [Wis 1.13]. He is neither moved by the passion of anger, nor plans revenge, nor changes his mind about what each person deserves; rather, he "has made everything in wisdom" [Ps 104.24] and has predetermined that each person will be judged according to the spiritual law. Therefore he does not say to Adam, "On the day that the two of you eat [of the tree], I will put you to death," but rather, safeguarding the law of justice, he tells them in advance, "On the day that you eat [of the tree], you shall die" [Gen 2.17]. Always and in every case, both for the good and the bad, he has portioned out what follows naturally and has not just invented something, as some people imagine, those who are ignorant of the spiritual law.

Those of us who know this, at least in part, ought to know that if we hate one of our fellow believers because he is evil, we too will be hated by God because we are evil; and if we reject someone's repentance because he is a sinner, we too will be refused repentance because we are sinners; and if we do not forgive our neighbor his

---

[4]Although the word "thoughts," *logismoi*, is etymologically related to "reason" (*logos*) and "rational" (*logikos*), in early monastic thinking "thoughts" are usually bad—that is, they represent perverted, fallen rationality.

sins, our sins will not be forgiven us. This law Christ the lawgiver made very clear when he said, "Do not judge, and you will not be judged; do not condemn, and you will not be condemned; forgive, and you will be forgiven" [Lk 6.37]. This law Saint Paul understood, which he made very clear by saying, "The person who passes judgement on another condemns himself" [Rom 2.1]. And the prophet, who was not ignorant of this law, cried out to God, saying, "Because you will repay each person according to their [sic] work" [Ps 62.12]. And another prophet, speaking for God, says, "'Vengeance is mine; I will repay,' says the Lord" [Rom 12.19; Deut 32.35].

4   But why go verse by verse, when all of Holy Scripture, both Old and New Testaments, and especially the Great Song,[5] very clearly illustrate this law for us? When we discover that this law is spiritual and that it has mystically predetermined all the twists and turns of our life, we, filled with the fear of God, hasten to love our brothers, not only openly but also privately, for this Mosaic law is not one that judges outward events, but is a spiritual law that also verifies what is hidden. God himself, at the appropriate time, laid down that law, suitable for us, and he has fulfilled that law through the grace of our Lord Jesus Christ, who said, "I have not come to abolish the law but rather to fulfill it" [Mt 5.17].

"Rejoice when we are wronged"

It is necessary, therefore, to speak only once about any matter and after that to forgive the person who seems to have done wrong, whether he has committed the wrong rationally or irrationally, because we know that the wages of forgiveness are greater than every virtue. Since we are not able to do this on account of prior sin, we ought to entreat God with vigils and every kind of mortification until

---

[5] As de Durand notes, Mark is probably referring to Moses' final song of instruction (Deut 32.1–42) and of blessing (Deut 33.1–29). The previous quotation is ultimately derived from Moses' song, and the fact that Mark refers to the Mosaic law in the lines that follow makes the conjecture seem plausible.

we find forgiveness and receive this great power. To do this, dear soul, we ought to have one end in sight at all times and places and at every opportunity: to rejoice and not be saddened when we are wronged in various ways by people—to rejoice; that is, not simple-mindedly, nor purposelessly, but because we have found the cause for forgiving the person who has sinned against us and for receiving forgiveness for our sins.

This is the true knowledge of God, one that comprehends all knowledge, through which we are able to call upon God and be heard. This is the harvest that prayer brings in; through this, faith in Christ is demonstrated; through this, we are able to take up the cross and follow the Lord [Mt 16.24]. This is the mother of the first and greatest commandments [Mt 22.38];[6] through this, we are able to love God with all our heart and our neighbor as ourselves [Lk 10.27]. On account of this, we ought to fast and keep vigils and practice mortifications so that our heart, being opened to compassion, may welcome this true knowledge and not reject it. Then we will also find that the grace that has been given to us secretly through holy Baptism will no longer be hidden and unknown, but will be working openly and with complete confidence because we are forgiving our neighbor his sins.

Civil war with one's own will

5   Two evils are obstacles to attaining this virtue: self-conceit and love of pleasure. One must first renounce these with the mind; by doing so, one can lay hold of the virtue. Thus, dear soul, when you willingly abandon yourself to these two evils, do not blame anyone, neither Adam nor Satan nor other people, but rather battle your own will—and do not take the battle lightly, for this is civil war. It is

---

[6]Mark is alluding to Mt 22.37–40, where the Lord says that the two greatest commandments are to love the Lord and to love one's neighbor. In this way, Mark links forgiveness to love.

not external, that we may do battle with the aid of our brothers; it is internal, and no human being will fight by our side with us. We have one ally, Christ, who is mysteriously hidden in us through Baptism, invincible and infallible. He will fight by our side with us, if we keep his commandments to the best of our ability. Those that wage war against us, as I said earlier, are the love of pleasure, which is wrapped up with the body, and self-conceit, which even gets the better of me [i.e., the mind].

These two led Eve astray and deceived Adam. The love of pleasure made the tree seem to be good for food and beautiful[7] to behold [Gen 3.6], while self-conceit said, "You will be like gods, knowing good and evil" [Gen 3.5]. Thus, just as Adam, who was first to be formed, and Eve became ashamed of one another, so too have we cast innocence far from the eyes of reason, and, when we see ourselves naked, our consciences make us ashamed of one another, so we sew together fig leaves for ourselves and clothe ourselves with external words and appearances and rationalizations. The Lord provides us with garments made of skin [Gen 3.21] and says, "By enduring you will gain your souls" [Lk 21.19], and exhorts us with the following: "The person who finds his soul"—that is, by remembering injury or by some sin—"will lose it" [Mt 10.39], and "the person who loses it" in this [life][8] "will keep it for eternal life" [Jn 12.25].[9] To him be glory now and for ever. Amen.

---

[7]Taking *horaion* as *hōraion*.

[8]In Jn 12.25, Jesus talks about those who will lose their life "in this world," but since in Greek "this" is feminine, Mark may have been thinking of *zoē*, "life," which is feminine.

[9]*Psuchē* means both "soul" and "life." The RSV translates *psuchas* in Lk 21.19 with "souls" and *psuchēn* in Mt 10.39 with "life," but we need to remember that Mark has the Mind giving advice here to the Soul (*psuchē*), so the Soul would hear itself (or herself) addressed in both these passages of Scripture.

Select Bibliography

Mark's works

Marc le Moine. *Traités I*. Georges de Durand, O.P., ed. Sources chrétiennes 445. Paris: Cerf, 1999.

Marc le Moine. *Traités II*. Georges de Durand, O.P., ed. Sources chrétiennes 455. Paris: Cerf, 2000.

Other primary sources and translations

Abraham of Kaskar. *Rule*. Arthur Vööbus, ed. *Syriac and Arabic Documents Regarding Legislation Relative to Syrian Asceticism*. Papers of the Estonian Theological Society in Exile 11. Stockholm: ETSE, 1960: 150–62.

Anthony Melissa. *Loci Communes*. PG 136.765–1334.

Apophthegmata Patrum, alphabetic collection. PG 65.71–440.

Athanasius of Alexandria. *On the Incarnation*. Charles Kannengiesser, ed. *Athanase d'Alexandrie: Sur l'Incarnation de la Verbe*. Sources chrétiennes 199. Paris: Cerf, 1973.

Augustine. *Praeceptum*. Luc Verheijen, ed. *La Règle de Saint Augustin*. Paris: Études Augustiniennes, 1967.

Augustine. *Retractationes*. P. Knöll, ed. *Sancti Aureli Augustini: Opera* I.ii, CSEL 36. Vienna: Tempsky, 1902.

Babai. *Commentary on Evagrius' Gnostic Chapters*. Wilhelm von Frankenberg, ed. *Euagrius Ponticus: Abhandlungen der Königlichen Gesellschaft der Wissenschaften zu Göttingen, Philologisch-historische Klasse*, N.F. 13.2. Berlin: Weidmannssche Buchhandlung, 1912: 8–471.

Book of the Cave of Treasures. Su-Min Ri, ed. *La Caverne des Trésors: Les deux recensions syriaques*. CSCO 486–87, Scrip. Syri, 207–8. Louvain: Peeters, 1987.

John Cassian. *Conferences*. Michael Petschenig, ed. *Iohannis Cassiani Opera* I. CSEL 13. Vienna: Tempsky, 1886.

Clement of Alexandria. *Stromateis*. Otto Stählin, ed. *Clemens Alexandrinus: Werke*. GCS 12, 15, 17, 39. Leipzig: Hinrichs, 1909–1936.

Cyril of Alexandria. *Epistula altera ad Nestorium*. Edward Schwarz, ed. ACO
    I.1.i: 26–28. Berlin and Leipzig: Walter de Gruyter, 1927.
Cyril of Alexandria. *Glaphyra in Genesim*. PG 69.1–386.
Diadochus of Photike. *Century*. Janet Rutherford, ed. & trans. *One Hundred
    Practical Texts of Perception and Spiritual Discernment from Diadochos
    of Photike*. Belfast Byzantine Texts and Translations 8. Belfast: Belfast
    Byzantine Enterprises, 2000.
Doctrina Patrum de Incarnatione Verbi. F. Diekamp, ed. Münster in West-
    fallen: Aschendorffsche Verlagsbuchhandlung, 1907.
Dorotheus of Gaza. *Doctrines*. Lucien Regnault and J de Préville, eds.
    Œuvres spirituelles. Sources chrétiennes 92. Paris: Cerf, 1963.
Ekkehard IV. *Casus S. Galli*. Ildefons von Arx, ed. *Scriptores rerum San-
    gallensiu*. Monumenta Germaniae Historica, Scriptorum 2. Hanover:
    Hahn, 1828.
Epiphanius. *Panarion*. K. Holl and J. Dummer, eds. *Ancoratus und Panarion*.
    GCS 31. Leipzig: Hinrichs, 1980.
Eusebius. *Preparation for the Gospel*. PG 21.21–1408.
Evagrius Ponticus. *Ad monachos*. Hugo Greßmann, ed. *Nonnenspiegel und
    Mönchsspiegel des Euagrios Pontikos*. TU 39.4:1152–65. Leipzig: Hin-
    richs, 1913.
Evagrius Ponticus. *Ad Virginem*. Hugo Greßmann, ed. *Nonnenspiegel und
    Mönchsspiegel des Euagrios Pontiko*. TU 39.4:1146–51. Leipzig: Hinrichs,
    1913.
Evagrius Ponticus. *Chapters of Exhortation*. PG 79.1249–1264.
Evagrius Ponticus. *Epistula fidei*. (= [ps-]Basil, "Epistula 8.") Jean Gribo-
    mont, ed. Marcella Forlin-Patrucco, ed. *Basilio di Cesarea, Le Lettere,*
    84–112. Torino: Società Editrice Internazionale, 1983.
Evagrius Ponticus. *Kephalaia Gnostica*. Syriac versions, Antoine Guillau-
    mont, ed. *Les Six Centuries des "Kephalaia Gnostica" d'Évagre le Pon-
    tique*. PO 28. Paris: Firmin-Didot, 1958.
Evagrius Ponticus. *On the Thoughts*. Paul Géhin et al., eds. *Évagre le Pon-
    tique: Sur les pensées*. Sources chrétiennes 438. Paris: Cerf, 1998.
Evagrius Ponticus. *Praktikos*. Antoine and Claire Guillaumont, eds. *Évagre
    le Pontique: Traité pratique ou le moine*. Sources chrétiennes 170–171.
    Paris: Cerf, 1971.
Evagrius Ponticus. *On Prayer*. Simon Tugwell, O.P., ed. *Evagrius Ponticus:
    De oratione*. Oxford: Faculty of Theology, 1981.

Evagrius Ponticus. *Thirty-three Chapters*. PG 40.1264–68.

George Hamartilos. *Chronicon*. PG 110.

Gregory of Nyssa. *Catechetical Orations*. PG 45.11–106.

Gregory of Nyssa. *Life of Moses*. Jean Daniélou, ed. *Grégoire de Nysse: La vie de Moïse*. Sources chrétiennes 1*bis*. Paris: Cerf, 1955.

Gregory of Sinai. *De quiete et oratione*. PG 150.1303–1312.

Hesychius. *Centuriae*. PG 93.1480–1544.

Historia Monachorum in Aegypto. A.-J. Festugière, O.P., ed. *Historia Monachorum in Aegypto*. Subsidia Hagiographica 34. Brussels: Société des Bollandistes, 1961.

"Iambs on the Words of the Holy Fathers, or On the Ascetic Saints." G.C. Amaduzzi, ed. *Anecdota litteraria ex MSS. codicibus eruta* 2:23–32. Rome: A. Fulgonio, 1773.

John IV of Antioch. *De monasteriis laicis non tradendis*. PG 132.1117–1149.

John of Apamea. *Dialogues*. René Levanant, S.J., trans. *Jean d'Apamée: Dialogues et traités*. Sources chrétiennes 311. Paris: Cerf, 1984.

John of Apamea. *Dialogues*. Werner Strothmann, ed. *Johannes von Apamea: Sechs Gespräche mit Thomasios: Der Briefwechsel zwischen Thomasios und Johannes und Drei an Thomasios gerichtete Abhandlungen*. PTS 11. Berlin: Walter de Gruyter, 1972.

John Scottus Eriugena. *Periphyseon*. Edouard Jeauneau, ed. *Johannis Scotti seu Eriugenae: Periphyseon, Liber III*. CCCM 163. Turnholt: Brepols, 1999.

Kallistos and Ignatius Xanthopoulos. *Methodus et regula*. PG 147.635–812.

Liber Graduum. M. Kmosko, ed. PS I.iii. Paris: Firmin-Didot, 1926.

Mark the Monk. *On the Spiritual Law*. G. E. H. Palmer, Philip Sherrard, and Kallistos Ware, trans. *The Philokalia: The Complete Text*, 1:110–24. London: Faber and Faber, 1979.

Mark the Monk. *No Righteousness by Works*. G. E. H. Palmer, Philip Sherrard, and Kallistos Ware, trans. *The Philokalia: The Complete Text,* 1:110–24. London: Faber and Faber, 1979.

Mark the Monk. *Letter to Nicolas the Solitary*. G. E. H. Palmer, Philip Sherrard, and Kallistos Ware, trans. *The Philokalia: The Complete Text* 1:147–60. London: Faber and Faber, 1979.

Mark the Monk. *Traités*. C.-A. Zirnheld, trans. *Marc le Moine: Traités spirituels et théologiques*. Spiritualité Orientale 41. Bégrolles-en-Mauges: Abbaye de Bellefontaine, 1985.

"Melchizedek." Birger Pearson and Søren Giversen, eds. *Nag Hammadi codices IX and X*. Nag Hammadi Studies 15. Leiden: Brill, 1981.

Nicholas. *Rescriptum ad Marcum*. PG 65.1051–54.

Nicephorus. *Historia Ecclesiastica*. PG 145.549–1332; 146; 147.9–448.

Nicetas Stethatos. *Life of St Symeon the New Theologian*. Irénée Hausherr, ed. *Un grand mystique byzantin: Vie de Syméon le Nouveau Théologien (949–1022)*. Orientalia Christiana 12 no. 45. Rome: Pontifical Institute of Oriental Studies, 1928.

Nicodemus the Hagiorite. Peter Chamberas, trans. *Nicodemos of the Holy Mountain: A Handbook of Spiritual Counsels*. Classics of Western Spirituality. New York: Paulist, 1989.

Origen. *Against Celsus*. M. Borret, ed. *Origène: Contre Celse*. Sources chrétiennes 132, 136, 147, 158, 227. Paris: Cerf, 1967–76.

Paissy Velichkovsky. *Dobrotolyubiya*. Dan Zamfiresco, ed. *Dobrotolyubiya, La Philocalie slavonne de Païssy Velichkovsky: Reproduction anastatique intégral de l'édition princeps, Moscou, 1793*. Monuments de la Culture Mondiale. Bucharest: Editions Roza Vînturilor, 1990.

Palladius. *Historia Lausiaca*. C. Butler, OSB, ed.. *The Lausiac History of Palladius*. Texts and Studies 5. Cambridge University Press, 1898–1904.

Philo. *On the Special Laws of the Jews*. F. H. Colson and G. H. Whitaker, eds. *Philo, Works*, 7:100–607, 8:6–154. Loeb Classical Library. London: Heinneman, 1929–1943.

Philokalia. Nicodemus the Hagiorite and Macarius of Corinth, eds. Venice: A. Bortoli, 1782.

Photius. *Bibliotheka*. René Henry, ed. *Photios: Bibliothèque*. Paris: Belles Lettres, 1962.

Plato. *Laws*. R. G. Bury, ed. *Plato: The Laws*, 2 vols. Loeb Classical Library. London: Heinemann, 1961.

Sentences of Sextus. Henry Chadwick, ed. *The Sentences of Sextus: A Contribution to the History of Early Christian Ethics*. Texts and Studies 5. Cambridge University Press, 1959.

Solomon of Basra. *Book of the Bee*. E.A. Wallis Budge, ed. *The Book of the Bee: The Syriac Text*. Anecdota Oxoniensia, Semitic series 1.1. Oxford: Clarendon Press, 1886.

Sozomen. *Historia Ecclesiastica*. PG 67.843–1630.

Symeon the New Theologian. *Catecheses*. Basil Krivocheine, ed. *Syméon le Nouveau Théologien: Catecheses*. Sources chrétiennes 104. Paris: Cerf, 1964.

Theodore the Studite. *Testamentum*. PG 99.1813–1824.

Thomas of Marga. *Historia Monastica*. E. A. Wallis Budge, ed. *The Book of Governors: The Historia Monastica of Thomas Bishop of Margâ A.D. 840*. London: Kegan Paul, 1898.

Timothy of Constantinople. *De receptione Haereticorum*. PG 86.11–68.

Secondary studies

Argles, M. F. "Marcus" (14). *A Dictionary of Christian Biography* 3:827. William Smith and Henry Wace, eds. London: John Murray, 1882.

Assemani, J. S. *Bibliotheca orientalis*. Rome: Typis Sacrae Congregationis de Propaganda Fide, 1725.

Casiday, Augustine. "Gabriel Bunge and the Study of Evagrius Ponticus." *St Vladimir's Theological Quarterly* 48:2 (2004): 249–97.

Chadwick, Henry. "The Identity and Date of Mark the Monk." *Eastern Churches Review* 4 (1972): 125–130.

Cunningham, Mary B. "Creative Selection? Paul of Evergetis's Use of Mark the Monk in the *Synagoge*." *Work and Worship at the Theotokos Evergetis*, 131–142. M. Mullett and A. Kirby, eds. Belfast Byzantine Texts and Translations 6.2. Belfast: Belfast Byzantine Enterprises, 1997.

Driscoll, Jeremy, OSB. *The 'Ad Monachos' of Evagrius Ponticus: Its Structure and a Select Commentary*. Studia Anselmiana 104. Rome: Sant' Anselmo, 1991.

Durand, Georges de, O.P. "Études sur Marc le Moine: I, l'Épître à Nicolas." *Bulletin de Littérature Ecclésiastique* 84 (1984): 259–78.

Durand, Georges de, O.P. "Études sur Marc le Moine, III: Marc et les controverses occidentales." *Bulletin de Littérature Ecclésiastique* 87 (1986): 163–88.

Durand, Georges de, O.P. "Une ancienne stichométrie des Œuvres de Marc l'Ascète." *Revue d'Histoire des Textes* 12–13 (1982–1983): 371–80.

Fessler, Joseph. *Institutiones patrologiae*. Oeniponte: Felician Rauch, 1850. Fessler's comments on Mark were reprinted in PG 65.897–900.

Gallandi, Andreas. *Bibliotheca veterum patrum antiquorumque scriptorum ecclesiasticorum*. Venice: J. B. Albritii Hieron, fil, 1765–1781. Gallandi's comments on Mark were reprinted in PG 65.893–896.

Gribomont, Jean. "Marc le Moine." *Dictionnaire de Spiritualité* 10:274–83. Paris, 1932–.

Gribomont, Jean. "Marc l'Ermite et la christologie évagrienne." *Cristianesimo nella Storia* 3 (1982): 73–81.

Grillmeier, Alois. "Marco Eremita e l'origenismo: Saggio di reinterpretazione di Op. XI." *Cristianesimo nella Storia* 1 (1980): 9–58.

Halleux, André de. "La christologie de Jean le Solitaire." *Le Muséon* 94 (1981): 5–36.

Harris, J. R. "Stichometry." *American Journal of Philology* 4 (1883): 133–57, 309–31.

Hausherr, Irénée. "Dogme et spiritualité orientale." *Revue d'Ascétique et de Mystique* 23 (1947): 3–37. Repr. in his *Études de spiritualité orientale*, 14–79. Orientalia Christiana Analecta 183. Rome: Pontificium Institutum orientalium studiorum, 1969.

Hausherr, Irénée. "Un grand auteur spirituel retrouvé: Jean d'Apamée." *Orientalia Christiana Periodica* 14 (1948): 3–42.

Hesse, Otmar. "Markus Eremita in der syrischen Literatur." W. Voigt, ed. *XVII. Deutscher Orientalistentag 1968 in Würzburg*, 2:450–57. Zeitschrift der deutschen morgenländischen Gesellschaft, Supplementa 1. Wiesbaden: Steiner, 1969.

Hesse, Otmar. "Markus Eremita und seine Schrift 'De Melchisedech.'" *Oriens Christianus* 51 (1967): 72–77.

Holmes, Augustine, OSB. *A Life Pleasing to God: The Spirituality of the Rules of St. Basil.* London: Darton, Longman and Todd, 2000.

Hombergen, Daniël. *The Second Origenist Controversy: A New Perspective on Cyril of Scythopolis' Monastic Biographies as Historical Sources for Sixth-Century Origenism.* Studia Anselmiana 132. Rome: Sant'Anselmo, 2001.

von Ivánka, E. "ΚΕΦΑΛΑΙΑ. Eine byzantinische Literaturform und ihre antiken Wurzeln." *Byzantinische Zeitschrift* 47 (1954): 285–91.

Kaczynski, Bernice M. *Greek in the Carolingian Age: The St Gall Manuscripts.* Cambridge, MA: The Medieval Academy of America, 1988.

Kaczynski, Bernice M. "A Ninth-Century Latin Translation of Mark the Hermit's ΠΕΡΙ ΝΟΜΟΥ ΠΝΕΥΜΑΤΙΚΟΥ (Dresden, Säschsiche Landesbibliothek, Mscr. A 145b)." *Byzantinische Zeitschrift* 89 (1996): 379–88.

Khalifé, I. A. "Les traductions arabes de Marc l'Ermite." *Mélanges Université St Joseph* 28 (1949–1950): 117–224.

Kirchmeyer, Jean. "Hésychius le Sinaïte et ses Centuries." *Le millénaire du Mont Athos, 963–1963: études et mélanges* 1:319–29. Chevetogne: Éditions de Chevetogne, 1963.

Kirchmeyer, Jean. "Le moine Marcien (de Bethléem?)." *Studia Patristica* 5 [= *Texte und Untersuchungen* 80] (1962): 341–359.

Kohlbacher, Michael. "Unpublished Greek Fragments of Markianos of Bethlehem (†492)." *Studia Patristica* 29 (1997): 495–500.

Kohlbacher, Michael. "Unpublizierte Fragmente des Markianos von Bethlehem (nunc CPG 3898 a–d)." Pages 137–66 in *Horizonte der Christenheit* (FS Friedrich Heyer), 137–66. Michael Kohlbacher and Markus Lesinski, eds. Oikonomia 34. Erlangen: Lehrstuhl für Geschichte und Theologie des Christlichen Ostens, 1994.

Krüger, P. "Zum theologischen Menschenbild Babais des Großen nach seinem noch unveröffentlichten Kommentar zu den beiden Sermones des Mönches Markus über 'das geistige Gesetz.'" *Oriens Christianus* 44 (1960): 46–74.

Kunze, J. *Markus Eremita, ein neuer Zeuge für das altkirchliche Taufbekenntnis: Eine Monographie zur Geschichte des Apostolicums mit einer kürzlich entdeckten Schrift des Markus.* Leipzig: Dörfflig und Franke, 1895.

Lampe, G. W. H. *A Patristic Greek Lexicon.* Oxford: Clarendon Press, 1961.

Lavenant, René, SJ. "Le problème de Jean d'Apamée." *Orientalia Christiana Periodica* 46 (1980): 367–90.

McCarthy, M. F. "Notker Balbulus." *New Catholic Encyclopedia* 10: 525–26. New York: McGraw-Hill, 1967–.

Mingana, Alphonse. *Early Christian Mystics.* Woodbrooke Studies 7. Cambridge: Heffers, 1934.

Plested, Marcus. *The Macarian Legacy: The Place of Macarius-Symeon in the Eastern Christian Tradition.* Oxford Theological Monographs. Oxford University Press, 2004).

Sauget, Joseph-Marie. "Marco, Monaco in Egitto, santo." *Bibliotheca Sanctorum* 8:708–10. Rome: Pontificia Università Lateranense, Istituto Giovanni XXIII, 1961–1969.

Tillemont, L. S. Le Nain de. *Mémoires pour servir à l'histoire ecclésiastique des six premiers siècles justifies par les citations des auteurs originaux.* Brussels: E. H. Fricx, 1732.

Walraff, Martin. "Socrates Scholasticus on the History of Novatianism." *Studia Patristica* 29 (1997): 170–77.

(Ware), Metropolitan Kallistos. "Introduction." *Marc le Moine: Traités spirituels et théologiques*, ix–li C.-A. Zirnheld, trans. Spiritualité Orientale 41. Bégrolles-en-Mauges: Abbaye de Bellefontaine, 1985.

(Ware), Metropolitan Kallistos. "The Sacrament of Baptism and the Ascetic Life in the Teaching of Mark the Monk." *Studia Patristica* 10 [= *Texte und Untersuchungen* 107] (1970): 441–52.

Wright, William. *Catalogue of Syriac Manuscripts in the British Museum.* London: British Museum, 1871.

Volume Two

CHAPTER ONE

On Melchizedek

Introduction

On Melchizedek is the first of Mark's two controversial writings about Christology. Whereas the second (the *Doctrinal Treatise*) directly addresses a number of problems resulting from a refusal to accept the implications of Chalcedonian orthodoxy, this treatise is directed against a somewhat more exotic problem. A variety of sources indicate that several early Christian groups took up the biblical comparison of Jesus to the elusive and evocative figure of Melchizedek (see Heb 5–7) and developed this comparison in ways that did not meet with widespread acceptance. Epiphanius of Salamis, the relentless hammer of deviance, dedicates his *Panarion* 4.54–55 to describing the development in Rome of a community of Christians who affirmed that Christ was born a "mere man" (a claim that Mark rebuts in the treatise at hand) and that Melchizedek was a greater heavenly power than Christ. Epiphanius notes (*Pan.* 5.55.9.18) that this view is also held in Egypt—and it is not without interest that Melchizedek plays a prominent role in two documents of Egyptian provenance: *Pistis Sophia* and the Nag Hammadi tractate IX, 1 (*On Melchizedek*).[1] But more relevant for our purposes is the similar

---

[1]See *Pistis Sophia* 34–36, 194–95, 197, 291, 324–26, 333–34, 363 (C. Schmidt, ed., V. Macdermot, trans. & notes, NHS 9 [Leiden: Brill, 1978]). The discovery of these documents gives weight to Epiphanius' assertion, but it should not be assumed that he has accurately described the origin or thinking of the groups that produced and read *Pistis Sophia* and NHC IX, 1. The similarities between those texts and Epiphanius' description are superficial and trivial: cf. Epiphanius, *Pan.* 4.55.7.3 (K. Holl, ed., GCS [Leipzig: Hinrichs, 1980]) and NHC IX, 1.25.4–26.4 (B. Pearson and S. Giversen,

method used by both Epiphanius and Mark to refute the Christian speculation about Melchizedek. For their critiques, an attentive reading of Hebrews is the point of departure. They both show that such a reading does not lend support to identifying Melchizedek as an earlier incarnation of Christ, and they both attempt to relieve some of the mystery of Melchizedek by reconstructing an account of his identity that is less imaginative than what one reads, for example, in 2 Enoch 71–72.

Mark's explication of Scripture in *Melchizedek* can be considered a dress rehearsal for the lengthier scriptural arguments that we find in his *Doctrinal Treatise*. In both cases, Mark constantly asserts that Christ is no mere human. He also sets himself the rather more ambitious task of commenting upon the union of natures in Christ. In this chapter, he works under the constraint of relating what he says back to Hebrews, and probably for this reason, he tends to express himself somewhat elliptically. For example, he writes,

> Christ "has neither a beginning of days nor an end of life." If the Word, who is without beginning, set in motion the incarnation, it is clear that Christ is without beginning through union with his mother. So in this too Melchizedek resembles him, since by divine dispensation his birth and death are passed over in silence in order to reveal in advance the mysteries regarding Christ. (§4)

Mark moves breathlessly from the claim that we should think of Christ as being "without beginning" (Greek: *anarchos*) because the Word (who is without beginning) is Christ, to his comparison of

eds., *Nag Hammadi codices IX and X*, NHS 15 [Leiden: Brill, 1981], where Melchizedek seems to be assimilated to Christ. It seems more plausible that the Egyptian "Melchizedekians" were inspired by the enigmatic figure and worked him into their cosmological visions. Other comparable uses of the figure Melchizedek are found in a variety of ancient documents: see, e.g., 2 Enoch 71–72; the "Melchizedek" fragments from Qumran (11QMelch); the *Testament of the Twelve Patriarchs*, Levi 8.1–19; *Aboth d'Rabbi Nathan* A.34; Babylonian Talmud, *Sukka* 52b. Further references are given in note 17, below.

this dense theological assertion with Melchizedek. But because we have an expanded treatment of Christology from Mark's hand in the *Doctrinal Treatise*, we can with some confidence expand this claim and appreciate the thinking that underlies it. In the *Doctrinal Treatise*, there is abundant evidence that Mark considers it appropriate to describe Christ with certain words, even if those terms are, strictly speaking, appropriate only to one of his two natures. Because of the "union with his mother" and because the Word "set in motion the incarnation," Christ can accurately be described as both human and divine.

In addition to these strictly christological concerns, Mark seizes the opportunity raised by this discussion to enter into a lengthy treatment of typology in Scripture and how to interpret it. The first part of this discussion (§7) is technically interesting, even if it does not make for gripping reading. Here, Mark advances a detailed case for identifying Melchizedek's genealogy in general (if not in detail), and, on the basis of linguistic parallels, offers several explanations of how the king of Salem—or, as he argues, the king of Selgē—can be seen to be a type of Christ. He ends this rather dense segment with some playful cases drawn from conventional Greek names, to underscore that names do not necessarily reflect realities. The second part of his discussion applies these lessons to Christ, and includes the traditional claim that the 318 soldiers taken by Abraham to rout the troops of the four kings were types of the 318 bishops who assembled at Nicaea to defend and define the orthodox profession of faith against Arianism.

Along similar lines, he makes some general comments on the importance of tradition for theology (§10). Mark invokes "apostolic tradition" as early as the first page of the treatise, and it is clear from his extended discussion much later in the work that he regards the apostles as the font of tradition. He explains in general terms that preaching is the mechanism whereby this apostolic deposit is handed down. He also specifies that the community is self-regulating: "Even if someone at some point is suspected of being involuntarily deceived, either he will undoubtedly reform once he has been rebuked or, if he clings to falsehood, he will be considered outside the Church." The only topic mentioned by Mark in this connection is "the mystery of Christ and his divine economy." It is precisely because he attributes such importance to those themes that Mark dedicated two treatises to their defense.

On Melchizedek[2]

Heterodox interpretations of the name "Melchizedek"

1 The Lord, comparing the world to a field and the proclamation of the truth to sowing, says that the wheat is sown first and afterwards the weeds [Mt 13.24–25]. Because of this comparison, we can observe that after the apostolic tradition was handed down, there followed some kind of superfluous and devilish oversowing of concocted tenets. None of the Lord's holy disciples spoke less than the truth, nor was Saint Paul inferior to the "super-apostles" [2 Cor 11.5], but rather sowed the word throughout the world like one sowing grain. Although this is so, certain heterodox persons have popped up, sowing weeds on top of the grain; trying to transcend—so they think—what the apostles taught, they attempt to teach "more mystical" teachings of their own.

The disciples did not preach that Melchizedek was God by nature, as these people do. Yes indeed, these people introduce this and kindred notions; as a result, they disparage the Lord's divine dispensation on our behalf. If they divinize Melchizedek, whom Scripture in its reticence calls a human "without father and without mother" [Heb 7.3], they certainly disparage Christ, who has the Father in heaven and for our sake had a mother on earth. And if they should think that Melchizedek is great because he lacks a genealogy, they would consider Christ, who has a genealogy, as lesser. The promotion of such an idea as this is likely to carry off into a denial of their faith those who have even less sense than they, which brings with it even greater condemnation for the person who propagates such a notion [see Lk 17.1–2].

They suffer from these delusions, I believe, because they deliberately overlook the chapters of Holy Scripture that provide a

[2]Source: G. de Durand, ed., *Marc le Moine. Traités*, 2 vols., Sources chrétiennes 445, 455 (Paris: Cerf, 1999, 2000), 2:171–223.

context on this subject, and intentionally look for certain snippets that meet their purposes. Because of this, they take the divine name interpreted as belonging to Christ and assign it to a human being as to God, and this person, who, according to his priestly order [Heb 6.20], is assimilated to the Lord, they say is by nature Son of God. They say, in fact, "If this person were not Son of God, how could one say 'king of peace' and 'king of righteousness'?" Let them know, if they want, that the Apostle does not say that he is "king of peace" by nature, but that his name is interpreted that way. He says, "In the first place, [his name, Melchizedek,] is interpreted to mean 'king of righteousness'; next, he is also king of Salem—that is, 'king of peace'" [Heb 7.2].[3] They deliberately overlook this phrase "interpreted as" and, by doing so, think that the name given by interpretation belongs by nature to the person being so named.

How Melchizedek, as a priest, foreshadows Christ

2   Once again they say, "If he was not God, how was he 'without father, without mother'?"

By saying this, it seems to me, they are no longer saying that Melchizedek is the Son, but are probably saying he is the Father.

Then they say, "We are not saying he is the Father but rather is God the Word before he took flesh and was born of Mary."

And how was God the Word "without father," you empty-headed fools? Learn correctly what blessed Paul says: that all those things are said about Christ *who has taken flesh*. He says, "The one of whom these things are spoken belonged to another tribe . . . for it is evident that the Lord was descended from Judah" [Heb 7.13–14].

"But tell us," they say, "how Christ, who was descended from Judah, is without father and without mother, according to the order of Melchizedek" [Heb 6.20].

---

[3]In antiquity, Hebrews was commonly attributed to "the Apostle," Paul.

They do not know what they are talking about. When Paul speaks of "the order of Melchizedek," he is not talking about Christ being "without father" but is speaking solely about his priesthood. Thus he does not say, "You are without father and without mother according to the order of Melchizedek," but rather, "You are a priest for ever according to the order of Melchizedek" [Heb 5.6]. What does he mean by "according to the order of Melchizedek"? He means this: according to the symbolic representation, not according to the Law. The tribe of Levi was appointed to exercise the priesthood according to the Law [Num 3–4], while Melchizedek was appointed not according to the Law, but rather according to his role as a prophet who indicated certain things concerning Christ. Therefore Paul says, "You are a priest for ever," not according to the order of Levi, nor according to the order of Aaron—which are of the same tribe—but "according to the order of Melchizedek," who exercised the priesthood without being under the Law.

How Melchizedek resembles Christ; type versus reality

3 But what will they in turn say to us? "If Melchizedek is a human being, how can he remain a priest for ever [Heb 7.3]?"

And this they ask by making use of snippets and passing over the majority of longer passages from Scripture, for it says, "Resembling the Son of God, he remains a priest for ever" [Heb 7.3]. "Resemblance" and "substantive reality" are not the same thing, for one is the type while the other is the reality. Just as the prophet Jonah, because of his three-day entombment [Mt 12.39–40], resembles Christ and remains a prophet, and just as Moses resembles Christ because he rules the people and remains their leader for ever, Melchizedek, because of his priesthood of the nations, also resembles him and remains a priest for ever. Therefore Paul says, "You are a priest for ever according to the order of Melchizedek" [Heb 5.6].

And now they say, "Granted that Melchizedek is a human being who resembles Christ, show how he is without father and without mother, having neither a beginning of days nor an end of life (which is true of the Lord Jesus Christ), and how Melchizedek resembles him in these things; for the Apostle says, 'without father, without mother, without genealogy, having neither beginning of days nor end of life, but resembling the Son of God' [Heb 7.3]. Demonstrate resemblance in these areas so we may know that Melchizedek is a human being and not Christ himself."

By opposing us in this fashion, they draw themselves up in battle, not against us, but against Holy Scripture, for they have only to believe the Apostle when he says that Melchizedek *resembles* the Son of God, not that he *is* the Son of God [Heb 7.3]. When they say, "Demonstrate to us the resemblance by reason of the names that Scripture uses so we may believe," it seems they do not believe what Paul says. When we are at a loss how to offer any such demonstration, they give up on the faith because they have already given up on it. Since it is possible to find in the true Scriptures a multitude of names whose explication most people will find difficult to understand, is this a reason for the Church to turn away from the faith handed down to it and to put its faith in its own opinions? Heaven forbid! But we will not maintain an ill-considered silence just because of this, but will, to the best of our ability, demonstrate resemblance by using what we have already said.

Melchizedek's resemblances to Christ

4   The Apostle says that Melchizedek is "without father and without mother" because of the words that follow—"without genealogy" [Heb 7.3]—since in his genealogy no account is given of any father or any sort of mother, or when he was born or when he died. On account of this, he has "neither beginning of days nor end of life" [Heb 7.3]. Nor can a genealogy be given for him, since he descends from peoples who were taken away by force, as Scripture makes clear by showing his dwelling place.[4] In this he resembles the Son of God, since the Lord Jesus Christ did not have a father on earth and in heaven did not have a mother.

Since we have said that Holy Scripture, by divine dispensation, does not give an account of when Melchizedek was born or when he died, and because of this says that he has "neither beginning of days nor end of life," even in this phrase they look for resemblance, saying, "If you mean Melchizedek, tell us also about Christ: how 'he has neither beginning of days nor end of life,' so we may understand 'resemblance' in this too. We know that he was born of Mary and had a beginning and died and rose, in accordance with the Scriptures."

To this we say, "Do you believe what the Gospel says: 'The Word became flesh' [Jn 1.14], which means he did not turn into a human being, but rather assumed humanity to himself?"

"Yes," they say, "we believe this."

If you believe this, then, understand that Christ neither is a mere human being nor is perceived as one,[5] as someone who did not exist at one time as a single entity and was later united at some other time; rather, he was simultaneously united, begotten, and born. It is clear that God the Word achieved this beforehand in a manner worthy of God, in accordance with what is written: 'The Holy Spirit will come

[4] At §7, below, Mark will return to this theme. Although he does not explain himself fully even at that point, it is at least clear that he understands Melchizedek to have been the Jebusite king of Jerusalem, which was also called Jebus (see, e.g., Josh 18.28; 1 Chr 11.4) and is glossed as "the city of the Jebusites" (Judg 19.10–11), where "to this day the Jebusites live . . . with the Benjamites" (Judg 1.21; cf. Josh 15.63). Since the Jebusites were one of the seven tribes to be destroyed by the Israelites (see, e.g., Ex 23.23; Deut 20.17; Josh 3.10), Mark infers that Melchizedek lacks a genealogy because his people were among those "scattered" by the Israelites.

[5] The claim that Christ is a "mere human," which is sometimes called *psilan-thropism* from the Greek (*psilos anthropos*), was first propounded by Theodotus the Cobbler, a Greek who lived in Rome in the late second century and who was excommunicated by Pope Victor (see Eusebius, *Ecclesiastical History* 5.28; K. Lake, ed. & trans., Loeb Classical Library, 2 vols [Cambridge, MA: Harvard University Press, 1989]). As a result, adherents to this view are sometimes called "Theodotians." One of the earliest adherents to this view, Theodotus the Banker, appears to have brought Melchizedek into the discussion as well; see Epiphanius, *Panarion* 54–55.

upon you and the power of the Most High will overshadow you. Therefore the child to be born will be holy; he will be called 'Son of God'" [Lk 1.35].

Because of this we know that Christ "has neither a beginning of days nor an end of life." If the Word, who is without beginning, set in motion the incarnation, it is clear that Christ is without beginning through union with his mother. So in this too Melchizedek resembles him, since, by divine dispensation, his birth and death are passed over in silence in order to reveal in advance the mysteries regarding Christ.

The incarnation of Christ

5   He in turn says,[6] "Did the Lord assume the same body as we have, or not?"

"Yes," we reply, "the same body as we have. But he did not assume it separately, for the body was not brought into existence beforehand and then united with the Lord; rather, he effected the union from his mother without division,[7] as we have said."

They immediately say, "Why, then, do you add up his years?"

His years are not added up by taking into consideration only his nature, but by reckoning his birth when he came into existence as a human being. Scripture does not say that he was born a mere human being, as you say, or that God the Word was born, but rather that Christ was born: He is at one and the same time both God and human being, without separation and without division, Son of God.

[6]The text has *phēsi*, "he says," which should, it seems, be *phasi*, "they say," to match the plural "they say" immediately below, but Mark's pronouns are not consistent; see §9, for example, which alternates between second person singular, third person plural, and second person plural.

[7]Mark's use of the adjective "without division" (Greek: *adiaireton*) indicates that he was writing after the christological definition of the Council of Chalcedon made that term, and three others ("without confusion" *asynchytōs*, "without change" *atreptōs*, and "without separation" *anchoristōs*), the benchmarks of normative Greek Christology.

By divine dispensation his birth had a beginning, but by nature his union, effected through his mother, had no beginning. Tell me: To what do you attribute a beginning? To a mere body? But the Lord's body never existed independently as a "mere" body, in accordance with the Gospel voice that says to Joseph, "Do not be afraid to take Mary as your wife, for the child conceived in her is from the Holy Spirit" [Mt 1.20]. Despite this, will you still posit a beginning for the begotten Christ? Look! The Word himself took flesh, as is demonstrated in the Gospels. So you can posit neither division nor beginning for Christ, as has been demonstrated.

"Let us grant," he says, "that Christ does not have a beginning on account of the union. Does not the union also not have a beginning?"

Yes and no, for the reason that he who is without beginning became the beginning of the union. On account of this I said, "Yes and no." It is more orthodox to say "No."[8] Whenever elements are united in a substantive reality, even if one conceives of them as dual in origin, that which is united with the nature of the more powerful element takes both its conception and its name from the more powerful, just as a river that is maintained by rain and flows into the sea is no longer called a "river" but rather "sea": From the former it received its beginning, and in the latter it reaches its conclusion. If the bodily force, acting as the more powerful, influenced the Word and thus brought about the union, one would think that the union also had a beginning, in accordance with its bodily nature. But if God the Word, as befits God, influenced the body, in accordance with the Gospel, it is clear that, with reference to that nature, it ennobled the holy body, because in it "the whole fullness of Deity was pleased to dwell bodily" [Col 1.19, 2.9].

If it is "the whole fullness," it is clear that none of the Deity is lacking in any part of Christ's holy body, whether you call it "without beginning" or "Godhead" or "imperishable" or "almighty power" or

---

[8]G. W. H. Lampe notes this occurrence of the word *eusebesteron* and glosses it as "more reasonable," which also makes sense in this passage; see his *A Patristic Greek Lexicon* (Oxford: Clarendon Press, 1961), s.v., 576A(B).

"authority" or "might" or "incomprehensible wisdom." It has all of these because in it "the whole fullness of Deity was pleased to dwell" [Col 1.19, 2.9]. Therefore Paul says, "From now on we regard no one according to the flesh; even though we once knew Christ according to the flesh, we no longer know him that way" [2 Cor 5.16]. We know that in him "the whole fullness of Deity was pleased to dwell" and that we have come to fullness in him [Col 1.19, 2.9–10]. It does not say "in them," but "in him," for he is "the fullness who fills all in all" [Eph 1.23]. Thus one sees how Christ "has neither beginning of days nor end of life" [Heb 7.3].

What Scripture teaches about Melchizedek

6 They in turn say, "If Melchizedek is a human being, how does he remain a priest for ever [Heb 7.3]?"

This can be understood in two ways, not only with regard to Melchizedek but all the saints, too. First because "for ever" is adduced in Scripture, and second because they remain at God's side for ever. The prophet Isaiah remains a prophet for ever, and all the prophets remain prophets for ever, both in the presence of Scripture and in the presence of God. In like fashion, the apostles remain apostles for ever; otherwise, with what sort of hope did they die each day for Christ [1 Cor 15.31]? And all those who exercise the priesthood for Christ remain priests for ever. Likewise, holy Melchizedek, who exercised the priesthood for God, also remains a priest for ever, in accordance with what the Lord says: "To him, all of them are alive" [Lk 20.38].

This saying about Melchizedek also carries with it teaching about the Divinity, since God saw fit to regard him this way: "See how great he is! Even the patriarch Abraham apportioned him a tenth of the spoils" [Heb 7.4]. And why does this have the dignity of Divinity? Do you wish to see greater humility than Abraham's? When he accepted the cave for Sarah's burial, he prostrated himself before the people who sold it to him [Gen 23.7, 12]. Because the patriarch prostrated himself before them, do we also divinize these people? Heaven forbid! See how great their folly is? They put limits on the magnitude of God the Word and whittle him down to nothing!

Scripture does not say about Melchizedek, "See how great he is! He made heaven and the earth and the sea. He gave human beings the ability to think so they would have the initiative to act voluntarily. He apportions to everyone what they need, not as soon as they ask, but at the appropriate time, determining what is suitable as needs arise." Nor does Scripture say, "He weighed out with good measure rain and snowfall, the winter frosts and the fiery rays of summer so the world would not perish." Nor does it say, "With righteous compassion he preserves sinners and is able sincerely to have pity on them. He is everywhere indivisible and remains in the Father without confusion. He is the creator of everything good and knows and judges all things. In his weakness he bound the strong man, and in his folly he stole the cunning serpent's possessions [Mt 12.29; see 1 Cor 1.25]. He brought life out of death and made clear what was obscure." The Apostle said nothing like this about Melchizedek, but says, rather, "See how great he is! Abraham has apportioned to him a tenth" [Heb 7.4]. If Melchizedek were God, would Paul circumscribe his immeasurable power within what is measurable, and this with nothing remarkable but the ten percent given by Abraham, which, according to the Law, priests also receive?

When you read and find something written concerning Melchizedek, therefore, remember what the Apostle said, "The one about whom these things are said belonged to another tribe" [Heb 7.13], and do not err any longer, "for it is evident that the Lord Jesus Christ was descended from Judah" [Heb 7.14]. Follow with Paul's faith and do not attach divine messages prophetically received to the person himself who receives such messages, nor, again, assign things that happen typologically to the types themselves. To which tribe did Melchizedek belong that you suppose that what he said and did were done on his own? When you err in this manner, you will undoubtedly hold the lamb typologically slain to be God, saying,

"If it were not God, how did his blood drive away the destroying angel?" [Ex 12.5–13]. Perhaps you will also deify the bronze serpent, saying in response, "If it were not God, how did it heal those bitten by serpents?" [Num 21.8–9]. We, however, will repeat what the Apostle said: "The one about whom these things are said belonged to another tribe" [Heb 7.13]. Each person achieved what he did, not through his own powers, but through Christ, who is expounded in them. So too Melchizedek. Even if he was called "king of righteousness" [Heb 7.2], he was not king of righteousness by nature but, rather, his name was interpreted by Scripture to mean that: "The one about whom these things are said belonged to another tribe."

Explication of typological names

7   I also wanted to inquire about things that deceive those who deceive the soul [see Titus 1.10].

Why did the prophets or the apostles not proclaim him to be God? If they had been swept away by jealousy or fear, they would not have revealed to everyone, without fear and jealousy, the one whom Mary bore. If they had been ignorant, they would be infants compared with you people, and you would be more perfect compared with them, since what has been revealed to you was kept hidden from them.

But what do the pests say?

"Do not be amazed if the apostles were ignorant of this mystery, which appeared difficult even for Paul, who says, 'About this we have much to say which is hard to explain'" [Heb 5.11].

What pretentiousness! They think they are wiser than the Apostle! [But] "they understand neither what they are saying nor the things about which they make assertions" [1 Tim 1.7]. If they really believe that the subject of Melchizedek requires a long discourse and is hard to explain, let them clarify for whom it is difficult. Us or them? We say that Melchizedek is interpreted with reference to our

Lord Jesus Christ. If the discourse is long and the subject difficult to explain, that is also in accordance with what the Apostle has to say. They say that Melchizedek is God by nature, but if he is God by nature, how is he difficult to explain? God is universally believed in, but types have to be interpreted. On account of this, we see whom Saint Paul is bearing witness to when he says, "About this we have much to say which is hard to explain" [Heb 5.11]. If they believe the Apostle was speaking about Melchizedek as though he were God, let them expound their God, since they think that Melchizedek is God by nature. Otherwise, in the Lord and to the best of our ability, we will interpret the things having to do with Melchizedek as types, in accordance with the foundation laid down by Saint Paul, and let them stop their blaspheming.

What is now called "Jerusalem" was first called "Jebus."[9] Because of this, we know that Melchizedek comes from the seven nations that were destroyed [Deut 7.1], for he was Jebusite. Later, after the nations had been driven out and the people [of Israel] had settled there, God chose Jerusalem as the place to which the priests would bring their sacrifices from all over Judea. Because of this, and after the wars had ceased, they changed the name of the city to Salem, which means "peace." Jerusalem is interpreted to mean "vision of peace." For this reason Melchizedek is interpreted by Paul and by Scripture to mean "king of peace" [Heb 7.2]. He first ruled in Jerusalem, although some speak of him as king of Selgē and interpret "Selgē" to mean "chastity."[10] Therefore the person who rules Selgē is not unreason-

---

[9]On this section, see the references listed at n. 4, above.

[10]The interpretation that Mark offers here is striking, as G. de Durand has observed (for further details, see SC 455:206–7 n. 1). First, "Selgē" is nowhere mentioned in biblical literature, nor indeed does it occur in earlier etymologies of biblical proper names. Second, other sources such as the Souda and Zonaras's lexica offer an interpretation of the name's meaning that is completely opposite of Mark's; Eustathius, the twelfth-century archbishop of Thessalonica, knew both interpretations, but Mark's is the rarer of the two. It is not clear where Mark got his information, or who the authors to whom he alludes may have been. But he probably went to some trouble to find this interpretation. On this basis, de Durand concludes that this passage shows Mark to have been "rather erudite."

ably interpreted to mean "ruler of chastity," in accordance with the name of the city.

Nevertheless, Melchizedek is certainly not "ruler of chastity" by nature, but by designation, in accordance with the interpretation of the name "Selgē." Christ is the ruler of chastity by nature. Surely they do not believe that because of the interpretation of the name "Jerusalem," Melchizedek too is called "king of peace"! If this Jerusalem where he reigns as king is the heavenly Jerusalem, let him who rules over her also be "king of peace" by nature. But if this Jerusalem is a type of the Jerusalem above, it is clear that this person is also designated "king of peace" typologically because of his semantic identification with the city.

"King of righteousness" [Heb 7.2] is the proper interpretation of his name—that is, "Melchizedek" in the Canaanite language—as we have learned from those who are educated, just as some interpret the name "Ambrosios" to mean "immortal." So what does this mean? Since many people are named Ambrosios, are they because of this immortal by nature, in accordance with their name? Absolutely not! How many people are called Eugenios, and yet are slaves![11] How many are called Athanasios, and yet die![12] How many are called Polychronios, and yet live short lives![13] How many are called Dēmokratēs, and yet rule no one![14] How many names are found to have no correspondence with reality!

More explication of typology

8   Now that we have interpreted the names and designations to the best of our ability, come, let us turn our attention once again to

---

[11]The root of "Eugenios" is *eugenēs*, "well-born, of high descent," hence "noble," a member of the nobility.

[12]"Athanasios" literally means "deathless," hence "immortal."

[13]"Polychronios" literally means "many years," hence "long-lived."

[14]Mark is playing on the etymology of "democracy," which literally means "rule of (the) people."

actions. Just as Abraham armed 318 men along with his kinsmen and routed the foreign tribes in the time of Melchizedek [Gen 14.14–18], so too in the time of Christ, Christ's true kinsmen, the 318 patriarchs assembled in the city of Nicaea, apostolically armed, routed heresies.[15] See how the interpretation naturally follows: At that time, Melchizedek brought out bread and wine [Gen 14.18] as refreshment for those returning from battle. In the same way, Christ, the great high priest [Heb 2.17, 3.1, 10.21 etc.],[16] gives sanctified bread and wine to those returning to him from spiritual warfare and says, "Take, eat of it, all of you" [Mt 26.26–27]. Again, Abraham gives ten percent of the firstfruits to God's priest [Heb 7.4], and those who follow his faith offer Christ their firstfruits. The five senses offer him a double meaning—I mean in their own right and also spiritually. There are ten parts to our nature; it was held prisoner at one time by the foreign tribes, as the aforementioned narrative indicates. So, from what has been said, do you understand how "much of what we say is hard to explain," as Saint Paul says [Heb 5.11]?

Do not say, therefore, that the types are what is real, nor, when you hear that Melchizedek is without father and mother because he lacks a genealogy [Heb 7.3], think because of that that he is Son of God by nature. Have you not read what Holy Scripture, by making use of types, has to say about him in the narrative? It uses Lot, Abraham's nephew, with regard to those who were kings at that time; it gives the names of the places together with peoples' names, and clearly indicates Melchizedek and the city of Salem. None of this is interpreted independently of the incarnation of the Lord. If these names represent the true nature of things, there is nothing left to interpret; if they can be interpreted, they no longer represent the true nature of things. How, then, is the discourse long and difficult to

---

[15]Mark is alluding to the Council of Nicaea, convened by Emperor Constantine in 325. Different authors report different numbers in attendance; Hilary of Poitiers gives the number 318, which subsequently became traditional. It is possible that Hilary himself had Gen 14 in mind when he reported that number.

[16]Gen 14.18 adds that Melchizedek "was priest of God Most High."

explain [Heb 5.11]? Read what has been written! These types eventuate in those realities. What is written is written as a warning for us, upon whom the end of the ages has come [1 Cor 10.11].

What Scripture says about the priesthood

9   They must also inquire about this: How did God the Word, who had not taken flesh at that time, exercise the priesthood? And also, on behalf of whom did he exercise the priesthood? If you say, "On behalf of the world," then where is the sacrifice? "For without the shedding of blood, you have heard that there is no forgiveness of sins" [Heb 9.22]. Also, who are the heralds and witnesses of the priesthood? If they say that it is he himself, was he a type of those who were to come? Was the one without flesh, then, the type of him who took flesh and became incarnate? Is it better to say that he became a type of himself? But where is he who is not called a type but is rather the reality? If he was the reality at that time, what will we say about the incarnation? How does Scripture say that "this mystery was not made known to other generations as it has now been revealed to the holy apostles and prophets" [Eph 3.5]? At that time prophets did not cry out about this, nor apostles.

But what do they say? "If he was not God, how was he priest before the Law came into effect?"

Here is our response to them: "One speaks of the priesthood because an enfleshed human being offers sacrifice to God. Without flesh, he is not called 'priest.' So, just as Abel sacrificed to God before the Law took effect and because of this was designated a priest, and just as Noah sacrificed to him and was designated a priest, and just as Jacob sacrificed to him and was designated a priest, as were all of those who sacrificed before the Law took effect, so too was Melchizedek a priest before the Law existed."

"But," they say, "Scripture does not say that these people were priests."

Holy Scripture does not waste words, as you people do in making your irrelevant assertions. If you take any kind of look at the different situations, you will see that Melchizedek did not sacrifice; he was only *called* a priest. You are on more secure ground with those who sacrificed than with him who was called a priest only in name, since the act of sacrifice, rather than the name, is what defines the priesthood. We make this distinction in response to their unreasonable assertion. We have priests in the Lord; likewise we have Melchizedek and these others as priests of God, too.

The authority of tradition, and those who subvert it

10   I am amazed at how they have not listened attentively to blessed Peter on these matters, who cries out and says, "There will be false teachers who will secretly introduce destructive heresies" [2 Pet 2.1]. Quite rightly he says "they will secretly introduce." There is no doubt that they are looking for an opportunity and, as soon as they find those who happen to be present, they fashion their responses accordingly. Sometimes they clearly say that Melchizedek is God, while at other times they deceptively confess, "We give him the name 'priest of God'" [Gen 14.18; Heb 7.1], just as Holy Scripture says. If they believed at all in Holy Scripture, they would say everything in accordance with Scripture. First of all, Scripture does not say Melchizedek is God, so these people should not say he is. Let them confess, in accordance with Scripture, that "he resembles the Son of God" [Heb 7.3], for he is not the Son by nature, and that "[his name] is interpreted to mean 'king of righteousness'" [Heb 7.2], not by nature, and that "the one of whom these things are spoken belonged to another tribe" [Heb 7.13]. Let them not pick and choose ambiguous snippets so as to persuade the many through deceit and ensnare the more innocent and simple.

Because we have received such an important commandment and office from the Lord, we are compelled to persuade those who are led astray by ignorance. On the other hand, when they see that those who have been deceived by them want to repent, they prevail over them with persuasive-sounding arguments tailored to their audience. Thus they are always saying, "If even Melchizedek is not God by nature, we have not sinned in divinizing a human being, for it is written, 'I say, "You are gods, sons of the Most High, all of you"'" [Ps 82.6].

They do not understand that such a difference of opinion clearly demonstrates the shaky grounds on which their faith in Christ rests. Thus they opine that the Lord is the equal of all human beings and is no longer what he is—Savior and God and Master—and they are prepared to worship what is created more than the Creator [see Rom 1.25]. Like snakes, therefore, they coil themselves around and bind fast those who want to escape them. This in turn forces us to keep the commandment, "Be wise as serpents" [Mt 10.16], in order to imitate their deceitful ways and with even more rapid contortion of thought to release those around whom they have wrapped themselves. We say that even if Melchizedek is God, we would not sin in holding him as a human being and naming him as one, for it is written that "there is no other name under heaven by which we must be saved" [Acts 4.12] but that of our Lord Jesus Christ, "the fullness of him who fills all in all" [Eph 1.23]. Let them listen to the Apostle, who commands us not to accept the Gospel from a later preacher: "If someone comes and preaches another Jesus whom we did not preach, or if you receive a different Spirit which you did not receive from us, or a different Gospel that you did not receive from us, you submit to it readily enough" [2 Cor 11.4]. If Paul sets his seal in such a way on matters concerning the Gospel, why will those who introduce divisions[17] be believed or those who put their faith in such people?

But what do they say to us? "How then does everyone teach in the churches? As you teach here today?"

---

[17]Or "heresies": *haireseis*.

Let them understand that all the teachers confirm as perfect what the apostles taught, and no one has yet made innovations in what has been preached, as those people are doing. Even if someone at some point is suspected of being involuntarily deceived, either he will undoubtedly reform once he has been rebuked or, if he clings to falsehood, he will be considered outside the Church, where it is reasonable that such people should suffer. In this situation it is possible to ascertain their foolishness, since they are more evil than every heresy. Excommunicated from the holy bishops and anathematized, they are in unfamiliar territory and come together secretly and have fellowship—that is, as we said earlier, they disparage both the mystery of Christ and his divine economy. Not only this, but if at some time, on account of false piety, they have been able to convince bishops or supervising priests who act with the bishop's authority to put their faith in them, immediately they secretly calumniate the orthodox and those who possess true faith, accusing them of malignant thoughts, and they prepare them to be hated and persecuted. But the person who understands the way people think thwarts their deceptive practices; he reveals these people for what they are and steps aside for them to fall "into the pit they have prepared," as it is written [Ps 7.15].

Concluding distinctions between Melchizedek and Christ

11   Nevertheless, leaving behind their secret associations to do evil, let us return to the subject at hand and conclude by refuting their erroneous belief. That name the prophets did not preach, the apostles did not teach, the martyrs did not confess; none of the patriarchs declared him to be God, none of the holy Fathers wrote down his name. Come to your senses, therefore, you poor person, and realize that the Devil has filled you with superfluous knowledge in order to afflict your will with his own arrogance, so that from here on out you will fall into error along with him. How is this not done willingly? The person who has such a great cloud of witnesses [Heb 12.1], which establishes him in the true faith, has chosen and confessed what none of them has confessed. If all of them have been saved apart from that knowledge and confession, save yourself also by imitating them and say, as Saint Paul says, "I decided to know nothing except Jesus Christ, and him crucified" [1 Cor 2.2].

If outside of such a confession you think that you yourself cannot be saved, it is clear that you think all the aforementioned saints are not saved—except you, of course. Even if you do not say so with your own mouth so as to deceive people, the logic of the matter nevertheless demands a voice greater than your own. Do you see how you have come to grief over so many blasphemies and so many evils on account of your erroneous belief—or, rather, on account of your complete *lack* of belief?

Learn how this works: Melchizedek did not perform any miracles, did not set down commandments, did not determine any threats of punishment, did not die for us, did not bestow participation in the Holy Spirit. I do not know how, from now on, you can place such confidence in him! If you say, "He provided us with all these things by taking flesh," you only make yourself more liable for erroneous belief. The Lord revealed himself in words and deeds; he also commanded us to believe in these words and deeds, for Scripture says that he appeared to Abraham, but [only] in voice, giving him commandments, and prophesying what was to come, and promising benefits in the land of the Chaldeans, and near the oak of Mamre, and in many other places and with many other words and deeds [Gen 12–18]. Nowhere does Scripture secretly indicate that Melchizedek did such things or that such things took place through Melchizedek. Because of this, your faith in him is unfounded, your thinking is uncertain, and such knowledge of God as you possess is in vain.

Therefore, given the manifestation of the orthodox faith through many martyrs, whoever looks elsewhere and either with good reason or without reason calls Melchizedek God or Son of God by nature clearly acts as a Judaizer.[18] It is clear that Jesus Christ, who was born of Mary, is Son of the living God. He lacks nothing that we have to look for his fullness elsewhere, for in him the fullness of the Godhead was pleased to dwell bodily, and all of us have come to fullness in him [Col 1.19, 2.9–10], all who believe in his words as words spoken by the Son of God, through the favor and power and grace of God the Father and of the Son and of the Holy Spirit. To him be the glory and the majesty and the kingdom, now and for ever and ever. Amen.

[18]A claim like this unavoidably sounds jarring and anti-Semitic to us, but even so it may be that Mark is making a legitimate point here by drawing attention to an aspect of late ancient Jewish thought. Melchizedek is found in Jewish literature as a figure of some significance: e.g., in the *Testament of the Twelve Patriarchs*, Levi 8.1–19, Levi is assimilated to Melchizedek; at *Aboth d'Rabbi Nathan* A.34, it is concluded that Melchizedek is more beloved of God than Aaron. Sometimes, he is placed in a messianic role; e.g., Babylonian Talmud, *Sukka* 52b. Melchizedek's role as a messianic figure is also seen in the literature found in Cave 11 at Qumran (see M. de Jonge and A.S. Van der Woude, "11Q Melchizedek and the New Testament," *New Testament Studies* 12 [1966]: 301–26), which in turn can be connected to a Gnostic text discovered at Nag Hammadi, in which Melchizedek plays a similar role (see B. Pearson, "Melchizedek (NHC IX, 1)," in *The Anchor Bible Dictionary* [New York: Doubleday, 1992], 4:688–89). Against such a background, one can see why Mark might claim that Christians who stress the messianic character of Melchizedek are acting like Jews.

CHAPTER TWO

A Monastic Superior's Disputation with an Attorney and Discussion with His Fellow Monks

INTRODUCTION

All of Mark's writings that are translated in this volume are controversial in spirit. But his *Disputation with an Attorney* stands apart from the others because, in it, the Attorney is a realistic figure who interacts with the Elder. (This realism can be contrasted to the arguments found in *Melchizedek*, which by Mark's own admission are hypothetical.) Although it is not possible to determine whether this disputation is a record of an actual dialogue to which Mark was party, his descriptions are at some points so vibrant that they tempt the reader to take the text as an account of a real event. For example, when the Elder upbraids the Attorney for a cutting remark, we read this exchange (§11):

> The monk said, "Just as you wish—but to what do I attribute the unjust reproaches that you have heaped on me?"
> The lawyer said, "To the law of patient endurance, which you lectured me about previously."

The Elder gives as good as he receives, though, and there is biting wit in some of his words. For example, in the same section of the text, he compliments the Attorney backhandedly for his "wisdom, not to say cunning"; shortly thereafter, he elaborates on the word "cunning" and, in doing so, accuses the Attorney of hypocrisy (§13). The Attorney, stung by the remark, leaves the discussion. This ends the first part of the treatise. At the beginning of the second part, the Elder sighs deeply. He explains to his novices that his consternation was prompted by realizing that monks do not live up to the standards that they promote when talking with secular Christians. Perhaps we can take this to mean that the Elder is somewhat disappointed at himself, because he has responded to the Attorney's acid remarks with equally caustic rejoinders.

But even if there are echoes of an actual encounter in *Disputation*, it is clear that Mark has incorporated stylized elements into the work. At a few points, for example, the dialogue runs parallel to discussions in Athanasius' *Life of St Antony*. And in some other connections, Mark seems to draw on conventions that are best known to us through the writings of Evagrius Ponticus. These similarities are not strong enough to suggest that Mark wrote *Disputation* as a result of being inspired by earlier works, though they do indicate that he may have had some of those works in mind. It therefore seems prudent to suppose that Mark is retelling a conversation that actually took place, even though his retelling is enriched with allusions to other ascetic literature.

As for the discussion itself, the point of departure is the Attorney's two-pronged assertion that monks do wrong by refusing to judge wrongdoers and by claiming that their "spiritual works" exempt them from undertaking physical labor. After "praying interiorly," the Elder undertakes his answer, which he begins by underlining the importance of humility. The Elder's response treats refusal to judge wrongdoers and commitment to spiritual works, not as two separate subjects, but as two themes inextricably bound together.

This seeming lack of clarity, which can be very frustrating at first, is in fact the result of the Elder's consistent application of the insight that, in life, the mundane cannot be allowed to eclipse the spiritual. (The theme of how the perceptible—or "sensible"—realm (*ta aisthētata*) and the intelligible realm (*ta noēta*) are related recurs in one form or another throughout this writing.) He returns to the importance of humility when he addresses the problem of judgement. Aware that his interlocutor is a renowned lawyer, the Elder takes judgement to refer specifically to legal adjudication. And then he points out that it is better to suffer wrongdoing humbly than to seek retribution. Or, to use his own words, the Elder says (§2),

> For this reason, my wisest of friends, after being instructed in secular statutes and laws, a person should afterwards be taught the spiritual law, and take on sufferings for the sake of godliness, and patiently endure as his own whatever afflictions befall him. Without such sufferings and afflictions no one can become truly wise.

Thus the Elder encourages the Attorney to recognize the opportunities for growth in wisdom and godly love in situations where one's first instinct is to be avenged. He outlines some practical measures that facilitate this Christian response to being wronged; prayer he especially recommends.

What is particularly interesting in the Elder's teaching is that he sketches a way for Christians in the world (who are his special focus in the first part of the *Disputation*) to live according to the principles that are observed in a much more obvious way by Christian monks. It is only in the second part of the *Disputation* that the Elder directs his attention to the contemporary state of monks. So what he says in the first part should be taken as advice for everyday Christian life, as distilled from his experience in the monastery.

This advice—particularly as regards the acquisition of Christian humility—is restated in an even more profound way in the second part, when the Elder responds to questions from fellow monks. Here, the Elder returns to his earlier themes while bringing into the discussion topics that are often found in monastic literature. A good example is his extended discussion of thoughts (see Part 2, §§5, 8).

The expectation of many ancient monastic authors is that such intro-spection and scrutiny are characteristic of monks; secular Christians may or may not have the time for these undertakings. Be that as it may, it is important to note that the instructions offered by Mark (the authorial voice behind the treatise as a whole) are based on the same principles, irrespective of whether his readers are monks or not. There is no sense that the two groups are discontinuous. Rather, they make up a single body. And it is the privilege of an elder—such as Mark himself—to serve his fellow Christians in the world by offering them godly counsel (albeit sometimes godly counsel of an astringent sort). Mark's great expectation on the part of his readers is that they will not be upset by this counsel, and get up and leave.

A Monastic Superior's Disputation with an Attorney and Discussion with His Fellow Monks[1]

Part One
Disputation with the Attorney

The biblical basis of monastic belief and practice

1   A certain renowned lawyer asked a monastic elder the following question: "Please explain this to me; I want to know what you monks think. You say that wrongdoers should not be judged [Mt 7.1]. Furthermore, what sort of practices do you have in mind when you avoid sensible works?[2] I find great fault with you for these beliefs. By not passing judgement, you go against the law, and by practicing idleness, you go against nature. But if I discover that you do these things for the sake of philosophy, then even I will be forced to lay aside my complaint and will eagerly seek out the virtuousness you profess."

The monk first prayed interiorly and then replied, "If you are looking for answers to these questions, my learned friend, you need to get them from those who fully understand them. I am still a pupil, someone being taught. But since you, as someone wise,[3] have of your

---

[1]Source: de Durand, *Marc le Moine*, 2:11–93.

[2]In Platonic thinking, adopted by Christian intellectuals, the sensible or material realm (*ta aisthēta*) was inferior and opposed to the intelligible realm (*ta noēta*), the realm of Plato's Ideas, which for Christians corresponds to the divine. The lawyer's question implies that he expects monastic practices to be defended as "intelligible works." For other cases where monks are criticized for failing to undertake "sensible work," see also Augustine's *On the Work of Monks* and, in the Alphabetical Collection of the *Apophthegmata Patrum* (PG 65.71–440), John Kolobos 2 and Silvanus 5.

[3]*Sophos*. The lawyer has just appealed to philosophy (*philosophia*), the love of wisdom (*sophia*). The monk's response echoes one that Antony the Great gives to some philosophers; see *Life of Antony* 72, 75. The earlier "I am still a pupil, someone being taught" is a common early monastic teaching and trope; it does not mean that Mark was a novice at this time.

own accord come to those who are uneducated in order to find out what they think, listen. Monks adhere to no doctrines[4] estranged from the Church, but eagerly cling to that which belongs to Christ, in accordance with what the Apostle says: 'Let the same mind be in you that was in Christ Jesus, who, though he was in the form of God, did not regard equality with God as something to be exploited, but emptied himself, taking the form of a slave' [Phil 2.5–7]. You need to understand, then, that it is God-given and is the agent of great virtue—I am talking about humility—and this is something that the Lord commanded the Church to do when he said, 'Do not work for the food that perishes but for the food that endures for eternal life'" [Jn 6.27].

The lawyer then said, "Please, I too would like to know what sort of work this is."[5]

The monk replied, "To seek through prayer God's righteousness and the kingdom of God [Mt 6.33], which the Lord said was within us [Lk 17.21]. And he has revealed to those who seek his kingdom that they are to do so by all corporal means. Since we have heard these things from the Lord and have believed them and carried them out to the best of our ability, how can you say that we are acting outside of nature? If what we are doing seems to you to be contrary to nature, you should realize whom you are faulting. It is God who has commanded us. Similarly, not doing wrong to wrong-doers is God's commandment also. So how are those who keep this commandment breaking the law, since God has said through the Prophet,[6] '"Vengeance is mine; I will repay," says the Lord' [Rom 12.19],[7] and in the Gospels it says, 'Do not judge, and you will not

---

[4]The word translated here as "doctrine" is *phronēma*, and the verbal form of that word appears in Phil 2.5 (*phroneisthō*).

[5]Mark changes the tenses frequently in this work, but we have opted to translate it in the past tense.

[6]Mark strikingly refers to the Apostle Paul as "the Prophet."

[7]In Greek, "vengeance" (*ekdikēsis*), "wronging" (*adikein*), and "wrongdoers" (*adikountes*) all share the root word *dikē*, "justice," as indeed does "lawyer" (*dikanikos*).

be judged at all' [Lk 6.37], and the Apostle says, 'Do not pronounce judgement beforehand' [1 Cor 4.5], and again, 'Do not avenge your-selves' [Rom 12.19], and again, 'Who are you to pass judgement on another person's servant?' [Rom 14.4]? Who, then, has decreed laws more just than these? Who wants to judge wrongdoers before God as though he himself were sinless [cf. Jn 8.7]? Who brings charges against those trying to keep God's law? And who calls it evil to for-bear from evil?"

The primacy of spiritual law over secular law

2　When he heard these things, the attorney said, "So, do rulers sin when they punish wrongdoers and maintain justice for those who are wronged?"[8]

The elder replied: "It is not judges who sin, but rather those who hand wrongdoers over to the law instead of delivering them to God (see 1 Cor 1.8). First, because everything that happens to them increases their own sense of wrongdoing, and thus brings them to repentance and not to revenge. Second, even if they have suffered unjustly, they should forgive the wrongdoer whatever offense he has committed, listening to the Lord when he says, 'Forgive, and you will be forgiven' [Lk 6.37], and not, by exacting merely human retribu-tion, make their own wrongs unforgivable. 'Rulers,' according to the Apostle, 'are not a terror to good conduct but to bad' [Rom 13.3]. They do not force the faithful and godly to accuse wrongdoers, nor do they bring charges against those who show forbearance because the latter do not make use of the courts when they are wronged. Rather, they provide retribution for those who desire it. Those who

---

[8]Words built on *dikē*, "justice," continue in this section: "wrongdoers" (*adik-ountas*), "those who are wronged" (*adikoumenois*), "judges" (*dikastai*), "unjustly" (*adikōs*), "retribution" (*ekdikēsin*), and "vindicate" (*ekdikountes*). Later, *dikaiosunē*, which means both "justice" and "righteousness," will figure prominently in the discussion.

show forbearance for God's sake they honor and approve for pursuing the better course. So, just as they do not bring forward those who do not want to press charges, so too they do not sin when they vindicate those who do press charges. For this reason, my wisest of friends, after being instructed in secular statutes and laws, a person should afterwards be taught the spiritual law, and take on sufferings for the sake of godliness, and patiently endure as his own whatever afflictions befall him. Without such sufferings and afflictions no one can become truly wise."

The spiritual law concerning sufferings and afflictions

3   When the attorney sought to learn what the sufferings undertaken for godliness are, the elder said, "They are the commandments of Christ, of which the first and greatest is love, for 'love is not resentful but bears all things, hopes all things, endures all things' [1 Cor 13.5, 7], as Scripture says. If love practices these things, she cannot judge the person who seems to have wronged her. With such love we distinguish one person from another but leave each person with his dignity intact, awaiting, by the grace of Christ, the filling up of deficiencies, provided that we do not neglect to work to the best of our ability. God knows what we cannot do because of our weakness and knows that it is because of our neglectfulness that we do not do the work of love. Since a person is strengthened not only by sufferings voluntarily undertaken, but also by chance afflictions, we need great patience and humility from God. Therefore the Apostle says, 'The person who wants to become wise in this age should become foolish in order to become wise' [1 Cor 3.18].

"Such a person does not condemn his superiors for falling short of perfect love and makes an even greater effort with regard to his inferiors. When he reaches them, once again he searches out others greater than himself and, when he finds them, matches himself against them also, and does not stop running his race until he finds some who surpass him in love [2 Tim 4.7; Heb 12.1]. If someone does not compare himself to his superiors but instead condemns them for not being perfect, he passes judgement against himself without knowing it, for, it says, 'Do not judge others and you will not be judged at all' [Lk 6.37]. Because of this, those who are rhetorically wise think that only wrongdoers sin, while those who are spiritually wise find fault with themselves, even when they are wronged, when they do not freely endure injustices—and not only for that reason, but also because afflictions spring up from old causes and things they are responsible for, even if one sin is less than another. The person who justifies himself seems to be condemning God for not judging, while the person who endures as his own the affliction that comes his way confesses his own acceptance of it, on account of which he also endures the suffering of terrible things."

Prayer and humility: The essentials for keeping God's law

4   The secular, annoyed at the monk's reproaches, said, "If your spiritual law imposes these practices in accordance with God's decrees, as you say, why do some of the monks still fall, even though they keep the law?"

The elder said, "Those who keep the law do not fall. Rather, those who forsake it and neglect its essentials fall (by 'essentials' I mean prayer and humble behavior), beguiled by self-conceit and worldly concerns. Because of this fact, the Devil also does not deter us from thinking about and doing all sorts of worldly things; his only desire is to lead us astray from prayer and humble behavior. He knows that everything outside of these two virtues, even if it seems good, will later be taken away by him at some point. By 'prayer' I mean not only prayer demonstrated by means of the flesh, but also prayer offered to God by means of undistracted reflection. If one of these is diverted at an inopportune time, the other, on its own, does not serve God but rather its own will."

The attorney then asked, "Does the flesh have will apart from thought?"[9]

The monk answered, "It does, in accordance with what the Apostle says: 'We ourselves were once disobedient, doing the will of the flesh' [Titus 3.3; Eph 2.3], and again, 'What the flesh desires is opposed to the Spirit, and what the Spirit desires is opposed to the flesh' [Gal 5.17]. So, you see, the flesh has desire and will, and we are ignorant of this fact on account of the carelessness and assent of our thoughts. Because of this fact, not only those who neglect prayer, but also those who do not pay heed to their thoughts are injured. (I have said these things not as someone who condemns others, but rather as someone who confesses his own shortcomings.) The former is a mark of arrogance, the latter of humility. And 'the Lord opposes the arrogant, while he shows favor to the humble' [Prov 3.34]. His favor leads us not only to knowledge but also to the possession of holy virtue—I mean undistracted prayer, which blessed Paul in no way wishes us to neglect. He says, 'Pray without ceasing' [1 Thess 5.17]. At the same time, also indicating the lack of distraction in the mind,[10] he said, 'Do not be conformed to this age, but be transformed by the renewing of your minds, so that you may discern what is the will of God—what is good and acceptable and perfect'" [Rom 12.2].

"Since God has set down various commandments for our lack of faith and frailty, so that each person, in accordance with the fervor he demonstrates, may escape punishment and gain salvation, the Apostle guides us toward the perfect will of God, not at all wanting us to be condemned. Knowing that prayer assists in achieving all

[9]See Part Two, §8 below.

[10]"Mind" stands for one of the words that is assuredly among the most difficult to translate in the whole Greek ascetic vocabulary, *nous*. Some sense of what it does is given by Evagrius Ponticus in *On prayer* 35, where he writes, "Undistracted prayer is the highest function of the *nous*." In keeping with Evagrius' thinking (and indeed the Greek ascetic tradition as a whole), this function of the mind should be understood as an especially intimate form of human communication with God; the *nous* is thus the organ of communion with God. The reader should remember this when the word "mind" appears, and should not think in unduly restricted or narrowly intellectualist terms.

the commandments, at every opportunity and in every way possible he never stops giving orders about prayer: 'Pray in the Spirit at all times . . . and to that end keep alert and always persevere in making supplication'" [Eph 6.18].

Prayer leads to greater faith and the setting aside of daily worries

5 "From what I have said, we know that one kind of prayer differs from another. It is one thing to call on God with an undistracted mind, and another to present one's body to God when one's mind is distracted. Again, it is one thing to wait for an opportunity and to pray after setting aside one's worldly business, and another to prefer and seek out every opportunity to pray ahead of worldly concerns, in accordance with what the Apostle says, 'The Lord is near. Do not worry about anything, but in everything, by prayer and supplication, let your requests be made known to God' [Phil 4.5–6]. Blessed Peter agrees when he says, 'Be serious and discipline yourselves in prayer. Cast all your anxiety on him because he cares about you' [1 Pet 4.7; 5.7]. Most importantly, the Lord himself, knowing that all things are made secure through prayer, says, 'Do not worry about what you will eat or what you will drink or what you will wear, but seek only the kingdom of God and his righteousness, and all these things will be given to you' [Mt 6.25, 33].

"Perhaps the Lord is also inviting us to greater faith through this. Who, laying aside anxiety over transient things and being released from need, will not afterwards also believe in him concerning the good things of eternity? The Lord himself made this clear when he said, 'Whoever is faithful in a very little is faithful also in much, and whoever is unfaithful in very little is also unfaithful in much' [Lk 16.10]. By saying this he also showed his compassion for humanity: Knowing that concern for the daily needs of the body was inevitable, he did not exclude daily concerns but, yielding, ordered us not to worry today about tomorrow [Mt 6.34]. In doing so, he demonstrated that he was in complete accord with God while also demonstrating love for us. Indeed, it is not possible to be human and bear flesh and at the same time completely exclude physical, bodily life. It is possible, however, to curtail or put an end to many of these physical necessities through prayer and abstinence. If we neglect prayer and abstinence, however, it is absolutely impossible.

Prayer takes preference over service

6   "Because of this, the person who wants 'to come to maturity, to the measure of the full stature of perfection,' as Scripture says [Eph 4.13], ought not to prefer every kind of ministry over prayer or be drawn to them when the need arises, except out of necessity. Nor, when confronted with some necessity and the need to do God's work, should he avoid and reject them under the pretext of prayer; he should, rather, understand the difference between them and devote himself of his own accord to doing God's work. The person who does not think this way also does not believe that one commandment differs from another and is comprehensive, as Scripture says [Mt 22.36–40; Mark 12.28–32], nor, when confronted with doing God's work, does he want to carry out his obligations in accordance with all the commandments, as the prophet says [Ps 119.128]. When people are confronted with inevitable necessities and the need to do God's work, preferring prayer, they should excuse themselves from inopportune matters, especially those that draw us to great wealth and the coveting of possessions. To the extent that someone refrains from these things in the Lord and cuts himself off from superfluous material things, to that extent he keeps distracting thoughts away, and to the extent that he keeps distracting thoughts away, to that extent also he frees up space for pure prayer and demonstrates his faith in Christ.

"If someone, on account of lack of faith or some other kind of weakness, is unable to do this, however, let him at least acknowledge the truth, and, as far as he is able, let him advance by censuring himself for his immaturity. It is better to give an account of one's shortcomings rather than an account of one's falsehood and self-conceit. Let the Lord's parable about a Pharisee and a tax collector [Lk 18.9–14] convince you. In the same way, let us too, through hope and prayer, endeavor to ward off all worldly anxiety. Since we are unable to accomplish this perfectly, we offer to God the confession of our shortcomings without giving up our zeal for what is beneficial. It is better to be accused of a partial shortcoming than to be accused of total dereliction. With regard to what I have said about prayer and unavoidable service, we are in need of much discernment from God in order to know what kind of occupation we ought to choose over prayer, and when, since each person, when he occupies himself with some favorite employment, seems to carry out some required service, without realizing that he ought to judge matters with a view to pleasing God rather than himself.

"Something additional that makes this situation difficult to judge is that these mandatory and indispensable commandments are not always the same. One must be preferred over another at the appropriate time, since every service cannot be carried out at all times, but rather each at the appropriate time. Prayer without ceasing, on the other hand, is the service ordained for us [1 Thess 5.17]. Because of this, we must prefer it over occupations that are not indispensable. This distinction all the apostles teach when they instruct the multitude who want to turn their attention to service. They said, '" It is not right for us to neglect the word of God in order to serve tables. Therefore, select from among yourselves seven men of good standing whom we may appoint to this task. We for our part will devote ourselves to prayer and to serving the word." What they said pleased the whole multitude' [Acts 6.2–5]. What do we learn from these words? That it is good for those of us not yet able to devote ourselves to prayer to give ourselves to service, lest we fail in both; but for those who are able, it is better not to neglect what is superior."

The necessity of prayer

7   When the lawyer heard these words, he said this: "Those who are wise in the things of this world neglect prayer. Why then do they not fall? They manage to preserve themselves by means of philosophy."

The monk sighed and said this: "You're right. They do not fall; they fell once and for all when they suffered an extraordinary two-fold fall. I'm talking about self-conceit and negligence. Since they cannot stand up without prayer, they have no means of falling. Why should the Devil still occupy himself with wrestling with those who remain lying on the ground and who never stand again? There are some who are victorious at times and are defeated at other times: they fall and get up; they crush and get crushed; they wage war and have war waged against them. Others, on account of their great ignorance, are satisfied with remaining where they first fell and do not understand that they have come to grief because of their situation. The Prophet has pity on them and says, 'Does the person who falls not get up again? Does the person who goes astray not find his way again?' [Jer 8.4]. And again: 'Sleeper, awake! Rise from the dead and Christ will shine on you' [Eph 5.14].

"To those who refuse to take on the responsibility and difficulties of waking up and persevering in prayer in order to suffer affliction for godliness' sake on account of the coming kingdom, it says, 'I am your destruction, Israel. Who will help you?' [Hos 13.9]. Neither 'wound, or bruise, or inflamed sore' [Is 1.6], nor any of the evils that take place occur unless one wills them, for this wound is voluntary, this wound is 'sin that causes death' [1 Jn 5.16]; it cannot be healed through the prayers of others: 'We tried to heal Babylon,' it says, 'and she could not be healed' [Jer 51.9], because her illness was self-inflicted and there is no longer 'any emollient to put on it, neither oil nor bandages' [Is 1.6], remedies supplied by others. Holy Scripture clearly says these and similar things to those who disparage prayer and who restrict it, without reason of necessity or illness, to certain times and occasions, while the Lord says to pray 'always, night and day' [Lk 18.1, 7], and the Apostle ordains that we offer prayer to God Almighty 'without ceasing' [1 Thess 5.17].

The wisdom of godly work

8   "See too how the Old Testament restrains the person who puts his trust in himself and exalts his own wisdom. It says, 'Trust in the Lord with all your heart and do not exalt your own wisdom' [Prov 3.5]. These are not subtle words, as some seem to think. Because they think this way, they have acquired books and know the power of the words written therein without putting any of them into action. Puffed up with subtle concepts, they prop themselves up with propositions and questions and garner great praise from those who are ignorant of the love of wisdom—that is, philosophy. They do not bother themselves with being conscientious (that is, with a love of labor) and have forgotten all about hard work; by doing so, they bring much condemnation on themselves from God and from the godly and conscientious. Because they have made use of a superficial knowledge of the Scriptures, not for the purpose of work but for display, they have been deprived of that knowledge activated by the Holy Spirit. These persons are those who 'boast in outward appearance and not in the heart' [2 Cor 5.12].

"It follows that those inexperienced at working ought to apply themselves to it. What is said in Scripture is said not solely so that we will think about it but also so that we will do it. Let us start to work, then, so that, making steady progress, we find accruing to the faithful not only hope in God, but also firm faith, genuine love, a willingness to forgive, brotherly love, self-restraint, patient endurance, interior knowledge, deliverance from temptations, spiritual gifts, heartfelt confession of the faith, and fervent tears that come through prayer. And not only these, but also the patient endurance of afflictions that eventuate, sincere forgiveness of one's neighbor, knowledge of the spiritual law, the discovery of God's justice and righteousness, the visitation of the Holy Spirit, the bestowing of spiritual treasures, and all those things that God has promised to provide to people of faith, both now and in the age to come. To put matters simply and succinctly, it is impossible for the soul to shine forth in the image of God except through God's grace and through faith, if a person perseveres mentally with great humility and undistracted prayer.

"How then can those who are deprived of so many great and good things through ignorance and neglect of prayer say, 'We have not ever fallen'? They ascribe wisdom to themselves when they do not realize that they themselves have been overthrown, miserable because of their fall, even more miserable because of their ineptitude. The only profit from this is that they inspire in us even more faith in Scripture, which says, 'The wisdom of this world is foolishness with God' [1 Cor 3.19]. 'Wisdom comes down from above, from the Father of lights' [Jas 3.15, 1.17]. The sign of this wisdom is humility. Those who want to be people-pleasers have welcomed human wisdom instead of divine wisdom, and puffed up with this wisdom and reveling in it, have deceived many of the simpler sort, persuading them to practice philosophy, not by means of godly labors and prayer, but by 'plausible words of human wisdom' [1 Cor 2.4], which the Apostle repeatedly censures and blames for emptying the cross of its power.

"The Apostle says in the letter to the Corinthians, 'Christ did not send me to baptize but to proclaim the gospel, and not with words of wisdom, so that the cross of Christ might not be emptied of its power' [1 Cor 1.17], and again, 'God chose what is foolish in the world in order to shame the wise . . . and God chose what is low and despised and counted for nothing in order to reduce to nothing things that count for plenty, so that no one might boast in his presence' [1 Cor 1.27–29]. So if God is not pleased with Greek words of wisdom [1 Cor 1.17, 2.4][11] but with works of prayer and humility, as

---

[11]This seems to be an echo of 1 Cor 2.4, "with plausible words of wisdom." Paul, however, does not use the adjective "Greek." Athanasius does, however, in speech he ascribes to Antony in the *Life of Antony* 78.1 and 80.1 (ed. G. J. M. Bartelink, *Athanase*

has been demonstrated, why do they persist with their foolish ideas, abandoning the first method of godliness as being too difficult without wishing to be saved by the second or even the third?"[12]

Godliness versus the passion to please people

9   Since the attorney wanted to learn what the three methods of godliness are, the monk answered, "The first is not to sin. The second is for a sinner to patiently endure the afflictions that follow [see Jn 9]. The third is for the person who does not patiently endure afflictions to bewail his shortcomings and lack of endurance. This is so because the person who is not set right by attending circumstances here will by necessity be corrected by the judgement applied to all of us hereafter unless God sees us humbled and bewailing our sins. When God knows this, he blots out our sins by means of his all-powerful grace.

"If, however, through the above-mentioned neglect, we forsake humility and the bewailing of our sins and continue to justify ourselves with words of worldly wisdom, so that with these words we disparage those more godly than ourselves, how will we find mercy later, when we oppose ourselves to mercy now? How seductive the passion to please people is, and how difficult to discern! This passion even overwhelms common sense! The operations of the other passions are obvious to those who participate in them; as a result, these passions prepare those who are mastered by them to bewail their sins and humbly abase themselves. The desire to please people, however, disguises itself with the words and outward forms of godliness, so that those who are deceived by her cannot easily recognize her deceptions."[13]

d'Alexandre: Vie d'Antoine, Sources chrétiennes 400 [Paris: Cerf, 1994]). "Greek" also means "pagan." Immediately above Paul speaks of "human wisdom," a variant reading for 1 Cor 2.4.

[12]This section has strong affinities with Antony's debate with pagan (that is, Greek) philosophers in *Life of Antony* 72–80.

[13]"Deceptions" renders Greek *paratropas* and "methods" at the beginning of

The lawyer attacks the monk's understanding of what it means to please people

10   The secular inquired, "What sort of errors come from trying to please people? Rather than these, though, I want to know what pleasing people is. I can see that your responses do not follow any kind of natural logic, but make assumptions grounded in ignorance and censure what is beneficial with incoherent examples. So first explain to me what you mean by this term, 'pleasing people.' Only then will I, too, believe that it is as universally harmful as you make it out to be."

The monk said, "'Pleasing people,' it seems to me, is the *desire* to please people. That, I believe, is the proper sense of the term."

The lawyer, utterly amazed at this response,[14] said, "Now *that* is an entirely appropriate response! Why then, my devout friend, do you unjustly censure what is just? Does it not seem just to you to allow each person to test his own actions rather than turning it over to others to judge what is good? I myself insist that virtue consists neither of pleasing people nor of being praised by one's neighbor. I have heard Scripture say this very thing: 'Let your neighbor praise you and not your own mouth; strangers' lips and not your own' [Prov 27.2], and again, 'Let each of us please his neighbor for the good purpose of building up the neighbor' [Rom 15.2], and again, 'Give no offense to Jews and Greeks and to the Church of God' [1 Cor 10.32]. Who can give no offense without pleasing people? Why then do you go to such extremes in finding fault with pleasing people? If, according to you, we should accept those who do not please people over those who do, then you must think it entirely appropriate to praise brigands and murderers and thieves and conspirators, since they do not please anybody!

the paragraph *tropoi*. Mark is contrasting the deceptions of people-pleasing with the proper methods of godliness.

[14]Surprisingly, the attorney's amazement does not seem to be due to the fact that Mark's explanation is purely tautological (which is even more apparent in Greek than it is in English).

"If I have been silent up to now regarding what you have said, do not be surprised. It is not as though I had been opposing the Scriptures or ignoring what is more just; rather, I wanted to first hear what you had to say. We also know that we are to offer forgiveness to those who trip over their own words when they unintentionally stumble out of ignorance and ascribe evil to terms that are good. This has unintentionally befallen even you, my devout friend. You want, I think, to make self-centeredness manifest and to demonstrate its evils by calling it 'pleasing people.'[15] Since you have come to this conclusion not out of carelessness but out of ignorance, it would only be right that these terms that you use interchangeably be clarified and your charges passed over in silence as false. You have made them so injurious and hard to figure out that they have also overwhelmed common sense."

The monk agrees to lay out a scriptural argument against pleasing people

11   The monk, recognizing that the lawyer was clearly annoyed at his reproaches and rejected what the monk had said, was a little at a loss for something to say. As a result, it seemed to all those listening that, astonished at the lawyer's arguments, he was abandoning the debate. Opening his mouth, however, he said, "Since I wanted not to gain victory but rather to profit from proposing these words, and since you yourself have remained silent up to this point (not, as you say, because you were ignorant of what is more just, but because you first wanted to hear my explanation of matters), I beseech Your Excellency to keep your promise and teach me how Holy Scripture censures people-pleasing not in and of itself but under a different name. You clearly understand everything about Scripture, but, by keeping silent up to now, have not clearly demonstrated *your* under-

---

[15]In Greek, "self-centeredness" (*autareskeia*), literally, "self-pleasing," and "pleasing people" (*anthrōpareskeia*) share the root word *aresk-*, "please/pleasing." Concerning *anthrōpareskeia*, see Eph 6.6 and Col 3.22 and the discussion that follows.

standing. When you cite passages of Scripture as I have requested, not only will I be persuaded by what you have already said, but, on account of your many explanations, I will also trust that you have the better argument when you speak, even if, on account of my lack of education (as you say), I mixed up things and accused a virtue as if it were a passion."

When the layman heard these things, he replied, "I did not say I understand everything about Scripture, only partially, so do not urge me to speak. Since you began things, however, if you are at a loss at how to debate, be quiet and you will have my forgiveness. If, however, you are able to show that pleasing people is condemned by name, speak, and I will be forced, even against my will, to acknowledge the truth in what you are saying."

The monk said, "Just as you wish—but to what do I attribute the unjust reproaches that you have heaped on me?"

The lawyer said, "To the law of patient endurance, which you lectured me about previously."

The elder said to him, "My compliments on your wisdom, not to say your cunning: By promising to give compassion, you expect to receive it. Nevertheless, putting these things behind us, let me set forth what I have to say."

Scriptural testimony against pleasing people

12 "Listen, therefore, to the reproaches that Scripture pronounces against pleasing people. First, the prophet says, 'Because God has scattered the bones of the people-pleasers; they have been put to shame, for God has despised them' [Ps 53.5], and the Apostle says, 'not while attracting attention, in order to please people' [Eph 6.6], and again, 'Am I trying to please people? If I were still pleasing people, I would not be a slave of Christ' [Gal 1.10]. If you take the time to gather them together, you will find many other such passages in Holy Scripture."

The secular said, "Why should I? The responses I gave before are also written in Scripture.[16] Does Scripture contradict itself?"

The monk said, "Scripture does not contradict itself. We are near-sighted when it comes to comprehending the truth. Since not all people are impious and not all are godly, we ought not to please everyone, but only those who are good. Likewise, we ought not to displease everyone, but only the wicked. The Lord makes this clear in the Gospels when he says, 'Woe to you when all people speak well of you' [Lk 6.26]. He forbids us from pleasing people not only in these instances, but also in those instances that seem to be good: when we show our good side to people not for the sake of criticism or imitation, but for praise and some kind of reimbursement. And rightly so does he do this. If someone wants to please people for the sake of material reimbursement, he receives no spiritual gift from God, nor does he receive any reimbursement from what he is doing, since he has already received his wage, as the Lord also made clear in the Gospels, not once but on numerous occasions [Mt 6.2, 5]. When he gave commandments concerning prayer and fasting and charitable giving, he ordered us to hide these activities from people [Mt 6.2–6]."

A catalogue of evils caused by the people-pleaser

13   The attorney, while the monk was still speaking, said in a loud voice, "Enough's enough! I've had my fill on this subject. What you still need to do is to say clearly, without riddles and without conjectures, what these wicked and aberrant errors are, so I may know with certainty whether they are, as you have said, rather obscure and difficult to discover, since they are able imperceptibly to subjugate even common sense."

The monk said, "Pay attention, and I will spell it out for you. Consider whether you yourself have not discovered them to have

[16]See §10.

adapted to passion in every instance. The first of these wicked and aberrant errors, the mother of them all, is lack of faith. After her follow, like children, envy, hatred, jealousy, treachery, strife, hypocrisy, favoritism, servility, slander, lying, and feigned, not real, godliness, and many other such passions that are obscure and difficult to discover. Worst of all is that some of these, using the wisdom of words, represent themselves as good and conceal the harm inherent in themselves.

"If you want, I will clarify what 'cunning' means point by point.[17] The cunning people-pleaser gives one person advice while scheming with another, praises one person and finds fault with another, and upbraids his neighbor so as to commend himself. He advocates a case not in order to decide what is just, but to take revenge against his enemy. He makes his rebukes with flattery until he has overtaken his enemy with reproaches. He slanders anonymously in order to cover up his own backbiting. He calls upon the poor to acknowledge their neediness as though he wanted to provide for them, and, when they do so, he spreads it around that they are begging. He boasts in the presence of the inexperienced and acts humble in the presence of the experienced, pursuing praise from both. When the virtuous are praised, he acts as though he has a sour taste in his mouth and hurriedly talks about something else in order to deflect the praise. When those in charge are not about, he disparages them, and when they are present, he praises them to their face. He sneers at the humble and criticizes teachers. He casts aspersions on being uncultivated so he can pass himself off as wise. He belittles everyone's virtues and recites their vices by heart. In a word, he looks for the main chance and assumes slavish roles in order to satisfy his insatiable desire to please people. He tries to conceal his own vices by revealing the vices of others.

"Real monks do not behave this way, but do the opposite. With compassion they overlook the faults of others while they reveal their

---

[17]It should be remembered that, at §11, the Monk accused the Advocate of being "cunning."

own to God. On account of this, they are disparaged by those who do not know better. They do not desire to please mortal men so much as they desire to please God. Sometimes they do what is pleasing, sometimes too they diminish themselves; in both cases they receive recompense from the Lord, who says, 'The person who exalts himself will be humbled, while the person who humbles himself will be exalted' [Lk 18.14]."

The attorney, not persuaded, gets up and leaves

14   The attorney, upset at the monk's criticisms, said, "What amazes me, my dear monk, is not only the ideas you have propounded, but also what you have to say about 'cunning.' You accuse others of being cunning while you surreptitiously practice it yourself. Completely lacking in ordinary education, you make an appeal for foolishness sanctioned by God, saying that such foolishness is great wisdom and pleases God [see 1 Cor 1.25?]. Along with this foolishness, you have for my benefit ostentatiously made a show of prayer and godly sufferings in order to cover up your obvious lack of education with a dubious religiosity. Whether you are really the author of the propositions you have put forth or not, I will discover tomorrow when we continue our discussion."

With these words, he got up and left.

Part Two
A Discussion with His Fellow Monks[18]

A brother asks who is responsible for misfortunes that happen

1 (14) The elder escorted the lawyer to the door and, turning, groaned aloud. The brothers begged him to tell them the reason for his sighs, and he said, "I can see that some of you are troubled by what he said. For me this is proof that you consider the lawyer's words to be harmful, not helpful; you consider yourselves outraged, not benefited, by what he said. Here is the reason I am discouraged: We tell others about the spiritual law but do not keep it ourselves. If I have not properly adhered to the principles of those who are sullen and angry, but have followed rather those who themselves keep God's law and believe, in accordance with Scripture, that no afflictions come upon them unjustly, forgive an old man his narrow-mindedness. Only let us believe that we are responsible for the regrettable misfortunes that happen to us, even if they have not happened recently, even if they do not come about of our own doing but are the result of an ancient debt."

Then one of the brothers, who was confident of his ability to control his desires (thus ignorant of the truth) and ready to endure every sort of affliction, but thinking that he would suffer unjustly, as a martyr, audaciously responded, saying, "Where does Scripture say that the misfortunes that happen to people are their own fault and are the just judgement of God?"

The elder, very pleased with what the brother said, replied, "If you look for an answer to this question, beloved, you will find it in many passages of Scripture, both in the Old and the New Testament. If you want, I will elucidate a few passages for you, but as you learn you will have to set aside haughtiness—or rather folly—and acquire

---

[18]De Durand correctly separates the two parts of this treatise (a separation that the Greek text does not make) but follows the paragraph numbering of the text, which continues uninterrupted. We have renumbered the paragraphs in Part Two and have placed De Durand's paragraph numbers in parentheses for ease of reference.

the humility of Christ, who says, 'Take my yoke upon you and learn from me, for I am gentle and humble in heart, and you will find rest for your souls' [Mt 11.29]."[19]

With an analogy, the superior explains Christ's suffering

2 (15) His subordinate, eagerly latching onto the elder's words, said, "With regard to this matter, if each of us emulates Christ's humility and considers what happens to him to be his own responsibility, as you have said, it is clear that Christ too, in suffering, paid off his own indebtedness. Since this is so, I think that the person who says what you are saying blasphemes."

When the superior heard this, he said, "I tried to resolve first the question you asked earlier,[20] but since you have added this question too in order to bury my answers under a welter of confusing questions, with the Lord's help I will satisfy your demand also concerning this question by posing appropriate counter-questions. Tell me, are those who have borrowed money the only ones responsible for the debt they have incurred, or are those who co-sign for them also liable?"

The subordinate replied, saying, "It is clear that those who co-sign for them are also responsible for the debt."

The elder said to him, "You should clearly understand then that Christ also, when he took responsibility for us, made himself a debtor, as the Holy Scriptures say: 'The lamb of God, who takes away the sin of the world' [Jn 1.29]; 'He became a curse for us' [Gal 3.13]; 'He took responsibility for everyone's death and died for everyone' [2 Cor 5.14]. He did not take responsibility solely for you, did he? Acknowledge that he did, and I will admit defeat."

---

[19]In Greek "haughtiness" is *hypsēlophrosunē* and "folly" is *kakophrosunē*.

[20]That is, the brother's question in §1. (14): "Where does Scripture say that the misfortunes that happen to people are their own fault and are the just judgement of God?" and the superior's response.

The brother prostrated himself before the elder and said, "Even if I have erred like a child due to my ignorance, I do not deny the redeemer of the faithful who takes responsibility for all of us; for I know that no one else offers people hope of salvation, as the Apostle says, 'Since all have sinned and fall short of the glory of God, they are now justified by his grace as a gift'" [Rom 3.23–24].

Misfortunes are part of God's justice and righteousness

3 (16) With everyone profiting from the brother's acknowledgment and repentance, the elder said, "There remains for us only to demonstrate from Scripture that none of the painful things that happen to each person happens to him unjustly but rather that everything happens in accordance with God's just judgement. Some suffer on account of their own evil doings, while others suffer on account of their neighbor's misdeeds: 'We make our own decisions, but the Lord alone determines what happens' [Prov 16.33]. And again: 'Does any evil in a city happen that the Lord has not caused?' [Amos 3.6]. And again: 'All the Lord's works are done with justice and righteousness' [Prov 16.9]. And 'Each person reaps what he sows' [Gal 6.7], and 'If our injustice serves to confirm God's justice, what should we say? That God is unjust to inflict wrath on us? (I speak in human terms.) By no means!' [Rom 3.5–6].

"Look. The three children thrown into the furnace also instruct us on this very point: They acknowledge that it is their own fault and in accordance with God's command that they have been thrown into the furnace, even if they had to submit to the authority of others [Dan 3.8–30]. Saint David, too, afflicted by Shimei, confesses that he is being afflicted at God's command and because of his own faults [2 Sam 16.5–14]. Both Isaiah and Jeremiah, both Ezekiel and Daniel, and the rest of the prophets prophesied to the people and to the Gentiles that future afflictions would beset them on account of their own sin. These prophets clearly showed beforehand both the causes and the nature of the assaults, for, they say, in return for saying and doing such and such a thing, such and such a thing will happen to the people and to the Gentiles. Blessed David also makes this clear in one of the Psalms when he says, 'I know, Lord, that your judgements are just and that you have humbled me for the sake of the truth' [Ps 119.75]. And again: 'You have reproached me with the reproach due a fool. I am silent; I do not open my mouth, because it is you who have acted' [Ps 39.9].

"Therefore we, too, when we have heard such words appropriate to a jurist,[21] ought to say to God the words of Saint David: 'I am silent; I do not open my mouth, because it is you who have acted' [Ps 39.9], and we ought to give thanks that God sent him as a rebuke for the wicked thoughts hidden within us so that, carefully observing our thoughts, we may correct ourselves and have no doubts as to whether or not we are ignorant about most of our own evil doings. The perfect man is vigilant with regard to his own faults. If his conspicuous faults are hard to understand, how much more is this true of his ideas! So let us understand, as reasonable people, that the Lord brings assaults on us for our own good and through them works great good in us.

"First, these assaults bring out bad thoughts that secretly have a hold on us; after bringing these thoughts to the surface, these assaults bestow true and unaffected humility. Then follow deliverance from vain self-centeredness and, in general, the unveiling of every evil lurking within, as it is written, 'All those who work lawlessness are exposed in order that they may be exterminated for ever and ever' [Ps 92.9/91.8 (LXX)]. So, brothers, you ought to understand fully that if we do not patiently endure assaults with faith and thankfulness, we cannot discover the evil hidden within. If this evil is not plainly set forth, we can neither renounce bad thoughts that arise, nor seek to atone for evils done previously, nor gain assurance concerning those to come.'"

[21]"Jurist" translates Greek *dikanikos*, which contains the element *dika*, the root in Greek of *dikaiosunē*, which means both "justice" and "righteousness."

The nature of retributive justice

4   (17) Question: "If the attorney's words are a reproach to what we do, why do we not find ourselves responsible for what he said?"

Answer: "Assaults and reproaches do not in appearance resemble their causes; in accordance with what is spiritual, they preserve complete justice. We can know this because of what Holy Scripture says. Did those who were killed by the tower of Siloam [Lk 13.4] throw down the tower on others? No. And those who were led away to Babylon as prisoners for seventy years in order to repent [Jer 25.11–12], did they take other prisoners so they could repent? No. Misfortunes that happen for our instruction do not work this way. They are more like soldiers: when they miss the mark,[22] they are found out. Some are punished, but they do not suffer the same evils as they committed. In the same way, all of us are also instructed by the things that happen to us at appropriate times, and rightly so, so we may repent. But what happens to us bears no resemblance to what we have done, nor is the timing based on them. This is what leads many people into doubting God's justice: the postponement of retributive justice and the fact that the assaults bear no resemblance to what a person has done in the past."

Thoughts are the cause of misfortunes

5   (18) Question: "So, then, numerous afflictions beset us, and this happens because of what people do: They are envious, back-biting, slanderous, sycophantic, flattering, deceiving, cheating, undermining, defrauding, offending, enemy-making, disdainful, hateful, bellicose, violent, abusive, persecuting, and whatever other things people do to one another. Or afflictions come because of what we do with our bodies: We swell with anger or pride, we wage war, we desire ease and relaxation, we succumb to a variety of diseases and wounds,

---

[22]*Hamartēsantes* is the participial form of *hamartein* (*hamartia*, "sin"), which also means "to sin."

and become ill in any number of ways. Or, even aside from these internal occurrences, there are dog bites, venomous or man-eating beasts, and, in addition to these, occurrences of famine, pestilence, earthquake, frost, burning heat; there is old age, penury, loneliness, and similar things.

"All this happens on account of 'the spiritual forces of evil,' against which the Apostle made it clear we are to struggle [Eph 6.12] as we keep a close watch over our words and deeds, through which even our own thoughts contrive eventually to be our rivals. And rightly so, if our intellect, endowed with free will, does not, because of a lack of faith, befriend assaults that try us and, abandoning universal hope, stir up thoughts that neither produce speech nor follow through with actions. You said so yourself: All misfortunes have a cause; they befall a person in accordance with what he has done and bring us to an understanding of God's justice and righteousness. Clarify for us these causes so we may believe that we are responsible for what assaults us and that we ought to patiently endure the afflictions that befall us. I ask this lest, come judgement day, we incur more severe punishment, not only because we are sinners, but also because we would not accept treatment."

Answer: "The cause of everything that happens to a person is something that person has thought. I ought to have said that this includes both words and deeds, but since these do not precede thought, I attribute everything to thoughts. With thought leading the way, words and deeds follow, forming, for our benefit or to our detriment, a fellowship with each other. There are two types of fellowship: one comes from love, and one comes from wickedness. Because of this fellowship we assume responsibility for one another, even if we do not know it. Once we assume this responsibility, assaults necessarily follow, as Scripture says: 'The person who assumes responsibility for a friend offers his hand to an enemy' [Prov 6.1]. So each of us must bear whatever befalls him, not only on his own behalf, but also on behalf of his neighbors, those for whom he has taken responsibility."

How one assumes responsibility for others out of wickedness

6   (19) Question: "I would like to know what the first method of assuming responsibility is—I mean, the one that comes from wickedness."

Answer: "When a person assumes responsibility out of wickedness, he does so involuntarily. It happens this way: the person who defrauds another assumes responsibility for the other person's temptations, even though he does not want to. The same is true for the person who calumniates another and for the person who is calumniated, the person who mistreats another and the person who is mistreated, the person who slanders another and the person who is slandered, the person who denigrates another and the person who is denigrated, the person who defames another and the person who is defamed. And, so I do not mention each and every example of this, everyone who does wrong assumes responsibility proportionately for the temptations of the person wronged. Scripture testifies to this when it says, 'The righteous person extricates himself from being pursued; the impious person is handed over in his stead' [Prov 11.8]. And again: 'Whoever digs a pit will fall into it,' and 'Whoever starts a stone rolling will have it roll back on him' [Prov 26.27]. And again: 'We make our own decisions, but the Lord alone determines what happens' [Prov 16.33]. Therefore, if 'our injustice serves to confirm God's justice' in others, as the Apostle says, 'what shall we say? That God is unjust to inflict wrath' [Rom 3.5] on those who are being instructed by misfortunes, as well as on those who are ill-advisedly outraged at these misfortunes? No!"

How one assumes responsibility for another out of love

7   (20) Question: "After listening to you, I believe what you have said makes sense. Now tell me also how one assumes responsibility out of love."

Answer: "Assuming responsibility out of love is what the Lord Jesus imparted to us, first by healing our infirmities of soul, then by curing every disease and every sickness [Mt 10.1], taking away the sin of the world [Jn 1.29], restoring purity of nature for those who firmly believe in him, giving deliverance from death, imparting orthodox worship of God, teaching godliness, demonstrating that he would suffer hardship for love's sake even unto death, freely bestowing on us through participation in the Spirit the patience to endure such hardships for the good things to come, 'what no eye has seen, nor ear heard, nor the human heart conceived' [1 Cor 2.9].

"Because of this, he also accepted responsibility for our trials and temptations: was insulted, sneered at, betrayed, beaten, calumniated, persecuted, shackled, slapped, given wine vinegar and gall to drink [Jn 19.29].[23] What more can I say? Pierced with nails and stabbed with a lance. In this way, having entered into communion with us and having assumed responsibility for our sufferings by means of flesh and spirit, he in turn handed on this law to his apostles, prophets, fathers, and patriarchs, whom he taught in advance through the Holy Spirit and whom he instructed through the example of his body undefiled by sin. Making this pledge manifest, he said, 'Do not be afraid. I have conquered the world' [Jn 6.20; 16.33], and again, 'For their sakes I sanctify myself so that they also may be sanctified by the truth' [Jn 17.19], and again, 'No one has greater love than this: to lay down one's life for one's friends' [Jn 15.13]. Because of this, Saint Paul, emulating the Lord, also said, 'I am now rejoicing in my sufferings for the sake of you Gentiles, and in my flesh I am completing what is lacking in Christ's afflictions for the sake of his body, that is, the Church' [Col 1.24], he too intimating what pledging oneself out of love is.

"Do you wish to know more fully and clearly how all the apostles have entered into communion with us by means of thought, word,

---

[23] A variant reading of Jn 19.29, probably influenced by Mt 27.34, adds "gall" with the wine vinegar given to Jesus. Mark is either a witness to this variant reading or has himself conflated the passages from John and Matthew.

and deed and how, through this communion, they have taken responsibility for our trials and temptations?

"Using thought, they open up and explain the Scriptures for us, commending the prophetic utterances, persuading us to believe in Christ as the Redeemer, giving us the assurance to worship him as the Son of God by nature, praying for us, weeping, dying, and whatever other faithful actions come from thought.

"By means of words they exhort, admonish, reproach, rebuke our lack of faith, cast in our teeth our ignorance, interpret the Scriptures, clarify the times, confess Christ, preaching that he is the crucified one [1 Cor 1.23], the incarnate Word, saying that he is one and not two (even if he is thought to be united indivisibly from two),[24] restraining at all times and places and in every circumstance wrong or erroneous belief, refusing to give assent to falsehood, having no association with anyone who boasts in the flesh, spending no time with someone who is vain, in no way cowering before someone who boasts, despising the evildoer, preferring the humble, cultivating friendships with the godly, and teaching us to do the same.

"By means of deed, they are persecuted, sneered at, made indigent, afflicted, mistreated, imprisoned, killed, and whatever other things they suffered on our behalf. In this way, then, for the sake of community, they accepted responsibility for our trials and temptations: 'Whether we are being afflicted or whether we are being consoled,' he says, 'it is for your salvation and consolation' [1 Cor 1.6]. They received the law from the Lord when he said, 'No one has greater love than this: to lay down one's life for one's friends' [Jn 15.13]. They themselves have handed on this law to us, saying, 'If the Lord laid down his life for us, we too ought to lay down our lives for

---

[24]Mark's use of the phrase "indivisibly united from two" (Greek: *ek duo . . . hēnōmenon adiairetōs*) is a good example of how typically elusive he is in matters pertaining to christological formula. The most one can confidently say of this phrase is that its use of the adverb "indivisibly" is in line with Chalcedonian Christology. For further consideration of Mark's Christology, see the material in the general introduction to Vol. I, especially under the heading, "Dating Mark: The Internal Evidence."

our brothers' [1 Jn 3.16], and again, 'Bear one another's burdens, and in this way you will fulfill the law of Christ' [Gal 6.2].

"So, then, if we understand the two forms of communion with one another, both the pledge that necessarily and logically follows, and the corresponding trials that occur, we do not overly concern ourselves with why, or when, or on account of whom they happen. It is only for God to know what is appropriate for each person and urgent for his immediate situation, and how all of creation cooperates to this end. We need only to believe in God's justice and righteousness and know that everything that happens to us without our wanting it comes our way either on account of love or on account of evil. Because of this, we must patiently endure these things and not drive them away, 'lest we add sin after sin to our sins' [cf. Sir 5.5].

The superior concludes with some words on the will of the flesh

8 (21) "Above all, brothers" [the superior said], "I urge you to give serious attention to what has been said lest I fruitlessly undergo trials concerning words and lest you, because of your apathy, surrender to forgetfulness. Forgetfulness is the daughter of apathy, and both are granddaughters of a lack of faith."[25]

To these words the brothers replied, "Have more confidence in your discourse, father. We understand what we have heard and are assured that Holy Scripture affirms these things: It says that nothing happens to people against their will apart from God's justice and righteousness, even if we, as human beings, do not grasp the mysterious concurrence of events in what happens to us and their concordant necessity, as you yourself have correctly stated. Having no anxiety, therefore, about what you told us earlier, tell us finally what the will of the flesh is [Jn 1.13] and how it exists independently

---

[25]These genealogies of vice (or, in some cases, of virtue) are popular in Byzantine monastic literature. They present important observations in a memorable way and are used very effectively by spiritual masters like Evagrius; see, e.g., *On the eight spirits of evil* (PG 79.1145–64).

of the mind. The attorney asked you only if it exists; he did not inquire what it is or how it works."[26]

In response to these words, the monk said, "The will of the flesh is the natural movement of the body with the accompanying inflammation that takes place independent of thought; it gains strength through sleep and the relaxation of the bodily members. Saint Peter has this to say on the subject: 'Beloved, do not be surprised at the fiery ordeal that is taking place among you to test you, as though something strange were happening to you' [1 Pet 4.12]. And blessed Paul says this on this matter: 'What the flesh desires is opposed to the Spirit, and what the Spirit desires is opposed to the flesh' [Gal 5.17]. On account of this he also commands us, saying, 'Live by the Spirit, and do not gratify the desires of the flesh at all' [Gal 5.16]. They said these things because they wanted us not to get involved with movements such as these."[27]

In Christ Jesus our Lord, to whom be the glory for ever. Amen.

[26]See Part One, §4 above.

[27]The Syriac version has a variant ending: ". . . and not to be harmed by a speech that incites us to impassioned movements, but that, by inerrant prayer, protecting our thoughts and continual patience, we might find safety in Christ our Savior—to whom be glory and honor with the Father and the Holy Spirit for ever. Amen."

CHAPTER THREE

On the Incarnation
Mark's "Doctrinal Treatise"

INTRODUCTION

Mark's "doctrinal treatise" offers his longest sustained reflection on Christ and the Incarnation. But far from being a leisurely meditation in systematic form, the treatise is characteristically urgent and often confrontational. As the title in full states, his purpose is to correct the misapprehension of those who think that Christ "wore" his humanity like a garment. Counter to this view, Mark insists that the union of the human and the divine natures in Christ resulted in a single "substantive reality" (in Greek, *hypostasis*). As he puts it in a key passage, "My sole aim at this point is to demonstrate that none of the saints and Spirit-bearing men dared to divide as an entity him who had been united in a manner worthy of God in accordance with the Father's good pleasure" (§9). But even though Mark is concerned that some have attempted to divide Christ in that way, he addresses himself less to those who are in error than to those who might be squeamish about robustly affirming the hypostatic union. Thus, he signals in advance his intention to propose hypothetical arguments and respond to them (see §§10–11). In other words, Mark's aim is to preclude certain misunderstandings and sloppy thinking; to that end, it is convenient for him to present his treatise as a polemic.

But Mark's argument is not simply negative. He also constantly promotes his teaching about the hypostatic union by regularly encouraging the reader to think in terms of Christ's divine characteristics being attributed to his human nature, and *vice versa*. Because the two natures exist in a single substantive reality, it is considered legitimate to apply to one nature the language and terms that are appropriate to the other. This is called the *communicatio idiomatum*, and it is a christological insight that Mark employs with zest. An excellent example is found in Mark's explanation of why Christ's body and blood are considered holy (§42): "They are holy by nature, united in substantive reality with the Godhead from the time he was conceived in his mother's womb, and not after he was begotten, derivatively by participation." Because the body and blood are truly the body and blood of God the Son, they share in his attribute of holiness; or, to use Mark's language, they are holy by nature, not by participation.

We can also see how Mark applies the principle of the *communicatio idiomatum* in his insistence on the "double filiation" of Christ. That is, Mark insists that Christ must be understood as being at one and the same time both the son of God the Father (with respect to his divinity) and the son of Mary the virgin (with respect to his humanity). As regards his divinity, Christ is without mother; as regards his humanity, he is without father. (This thinking is implicit, e.g., in his argument at §52.) Surprisingly, Mark does not relate this analysis to the question of the status of Christ's mother. Nowhere in his corpus do we find the word *Theotokos*. But perhaps it is unreasonable to expect terms like that to appear ubiquitously. And in any event, Mark seems more concerned about addressing narrowly christological concerns: It is in precisely that context that he uses technical terms like *hypostasis* ("substantive reality") and *henōsis asynchytos* ("unconfused union").

Even so, Mark is conspicuously interested in these philosophical niceties first and foremost because they help explain how various scriptural claims about Christ can be understood in reference to a single person. Scattered throughout the *Doctrinal Treatise* are passages in Scripture that Mark marshals into a coherent account of Christ by means of a few key philosophical concepts. Similarly, his refutations of hypothetical objections do not demonstrate the philosophical incoherence of those objections; instead, he confronts them with further evidence drawn from the Bible. This technique is not bare proof-texting. Mark's use of technical descriptions (minimal though it may be) indicates his sense for how these biblical passages ought to be interpreted. It is this interpretive approach to the passage, rather than some supposedly self-evident meaning, that makes Mark's case.

Before turning to Mark's treatise itself, a final word about translation is in order. As we have already mentioned, Mark is addressing himself in this treatise against those who maintain that Christ's humanity "partially clothed" him, "like a cloak." The metaphor of humanity as clothing is found across the entire treatise, because Mark repeatedly uses the word *gymnos* ("naked") to characterize his opponents' view. Frequently, he uses the word without elaboration, though at one point he does helpfully gloss the expression (§28): "Yes, he is God—but not God stripped of his humanity [*gymnos anthrōpotētos*]." His regular use of the term culminates in one particularly striking instance, where he uses the term *gymnologia* to describe the view he is opposing (§27; in fact, it seems that Mark coins that term, which is not attested in the classical and patristic Greek lexica). We have translated that particular word somewhat expansively as "talk about a stripped-down God" because, here as elsewhere, it is very difficult in idiomatic English to convey Mark's meaning with a single term. For that reason, we have resorted to a small group of words to translate *gymnos*. They are "bare," "naked," "stripped" or "stripped down," and "unconcealed." It may help the reader to keep in mind Mark's specialized meaning when meeting any of those words.

On the Incarnation:
A Doctrinal Treatise Addressed to Those Who Say That the Holy Flesh Was Not United with the Word but Rather Partially Clothed It, like a Coat. Because of This, They Say, the Person Wearing the Garment Was Different from the Garment Being Worn[1]

Mark replies to a request; he distinguishes between truth and error

1   Since you [pl.] have often sought from me answers concerning the faith directed to those who oppose it, as well as responses to their arguments, and have also sought forthrightly to compare the disagreements between those on either side, I felt compelled to tell you what I have said before and, to the best of my ability, explain the cause of the disagreements that many people have.

Since the truth reveals itself to those who love her and are her friends because they do what she wishes, by their activities those who are her rivals demonstrate the error of their ways to those closest to her. Doing the truth means the patient endurance of suffering and disgrace, while participating in error means seeking approval and sensual pleasure. On account of this, because of suffering one accepts doing the truth with difficulty, while most people gladly

---

[1]Source: de Durand, *Marc le Moine*, 2:227–315.

participate in error because of the pleasure it brings them. Those who love suffering confess as teacher and master and lord the Son of God, who was crucified for our sake and looked with contempt on disgrace and dishonor, while those who love pleasure—or, rather, those who relish praise—are ashamed to make this confession.

We are called to do battle with the enemies of the cross

2   With the two parties fighting this way, certain people who cannot decide one way or the other see the aforementioned difference of opinion and, not knowing how to judge what is better from what is worse, decide that it is not possible to recognize which belief is true. This, then, is the way that disagreements arise about the two. All of Holy Scripture persuades those who love suffering that these people err in being unable to distinguish between these contrary opinions, while blessed Paul necessarily does so also. He is "the chosen instrument" [Acts 9.15] who rouses us to the truth even in our ignorance and forces us to do battle against the enemies of the cross [Phil 3.18], not only against Jews but also against heretics, who emulate them. Just as he called the former enemies, so too did he name the latter enemies, since one who really is an enemy ought to be called such. The former, in fact, are an enemy, and Paul, accordingly, calls them that [Rom 11.28]. If these people do not call the crucified Christ a mere man and do not share in the enmity that the Jews have for us, let them not be called enemies, but if they hold the same opinions as the Jews, how will they escape being so designated? On all occasions, someone who works closely with another will inevitably share the same name.

A refutation of those who attempt to divide Christ

3   How are they not enemies who divide the Lord of glory in two—I mean the crucified Lord [1 Cor 2.8]? No doubt they will attack the phrase "Lord of glory" and will say to us, "So, was the 'Lord of glory' crucified?" When they do, I will confess the source of my salvation and will not deny the truth.

4   I will say, "Yes, the Lord of glory *was* crucified." I have Paul as advocate and witness to these ineffable matters. He says, "We speak wisdom couched in mysteries, hidden throughout the ages and generations, which none of the rulers of this age understood. If they had, they would not have crucified the Lord of glory" [1 Cor 2.7; Col 1.26; 1 Cor 2.8].

So, now I want to question those who divide God: "Who is he who is both the crucified one *and* the Lord of glory?" I will be amazed if they surreptitiously introduce division into even this phrase. If, in running away from unity, they say that he is "a mere human being," I will say, "And how is it possible for a 'mere human being' to be Lord of glory?" If they say that God the Word is "bare," how was the "bare" Word crucified? So what do they say? "The Word is the Lord of glory, but the human being was crucified."

But Saint Paul did not say "two," nor did he introduce a division; he spoke, rather, of *one* Lord of glory, and him crucified [1 Cor 2.2]—"for if they had known," he says, "they would not have crucified the Lord of glory" [1 Cor 2.8]. And you, you heretic, must confirm the unity that Paul talks about. If they are bound by the truth, they will confess that the Word became flesh, who is Christ Jesus. Then we will say to them, "Now you have got it right."

Holy Scripture confesses God the Word as one and the same Christ

5   The Apostle, then, neither divided the Word from the flesh within the sovereignty of glory nor, in turn, the flesh from the Word in the crucifixion. Instead, he confessed unity without division both with regard to Christ's glory and with regard to the cross. So too ought we to believe, and we ought not to meddle with "division" concerning the Son of God, either by thinking or talking about it.

All of Holy Scripture, both the Old and the New Testament, confesses God the Word, with his own flesh, to be one and the same Christ and Son of God, in everything he did. Whether it be angels, or prophets, or apostles, or martyrs, in speaking and teaching about Christ, about—to be brief—not only the complete divine dispensation taking place for our sake but also Christ's coming advent and kingdom undefiled by sin [Heb 4.15], they made their confession affirming the one and undivided Son of God. They did so whether with regard to his revelation or his glory, his signs and wonders, his admonitions or healings, his sufferings and the violent assaults against him, or his cross and death.

6   See why Isaiah says, "Like a lamb led to the slaughter, and like a sheep that before its shearers is silent, so he did not open his mouth. His judgement was contained in his humility. Who will speak of his generation?" [Is 53.7–8 (LXX)]. Tell me, you heretic: Who is [the one who is like] a lamb led to the slaughter, and who has an indescribable generation? Do not say, "You are talking about two different persons"! The prophet was speaking about one and the same person in both cases. If you tell me Christ is a mere human being, how can his generation be at the same time ineffable? And yet Christ can trace his genealogy according to the flesh. If you say that he is God the Word, how can a bare God at the same time be led to the slaughter? All that remains, then, is to tell the truth about both cases: Christ, according to the prophet, is indivisible.

7   Listen, too, to what the prophet Jeremiah has to say: "This is our God; no other can be compared to him. He found the complete path to Knowledge and gave her to his servant Jacob, and to Israel, whom he loved. Afterward, she appeared on earth and lived among humankind" [Bar 3.35–37].[2] Once again, if you want to divide him,

---

[2]"She" and "her" in this passage refer to knowledge personified (*epistēmē*).

I will repeat to you: Who appeared and lived among humankind? If you say to me "a mere human being," listen: How, then, is he God, to whom no other can be compared? But if you say, "It is the bare Word"— how then was he seen on earth and how did he live among human beings? All that remains to do here too is to confess Christ without division in both situations.

8   What did both Daniel and Ezekiel and the twelve[3] say? To introduce such witnesses as these one by one in support of my position will only make it more difficult to grasp and will, perhaps, also be pointless. The throng of ideas will overshadow what we are seeking to accomplish[4] and will be above the heads of those reading this treatise, so that it may come to pass in terms of the intellect as it was written, "Jesus vanished since there was a throng in the place" [Jn 5.13]. There again, we might become the cause for a more severe condemnation of the faithless due to the surplus of our arguments, as it says: "If I had not come and spoken to them, they would not have sin, but now they have no excuse for their sin" [Jn 15.22].

The aim and task of this treatise

9   My sole aim at this point is to demonstrate that none of the saints and Spirit-bearing men dared to divide as an entity him who had been united in a manner worthy of God in accordance with the Father's good pleasure. There are, to be sure, certain heretics who, after being refuted, know the truth in their conscience, but neverthe-less neither acknowledge it nor cease being argumentative. The aim

---

[3]The so-called "minor" prophets, Hosea through Malachi.

[4]The term *zētoumenon* was frequently used, e.g., by Clement of Alexandria and Origen, to designate subjects for exegetical or theological research. See Clement, *Stromateis* 8.2, 8,6, *Fragment 67* (O. Stählin, ed., *Clement Alexandrinus: Werke* 3, 3rd rev. ed., GCS 17 [Berlin: Akademie, 1970]). But already from the time of the Apostolic Fathers, this language had acquired overtones of seeking specifically after Christ. See Ignatius, *Romans* 6.1; *Epistle to Barnabas* 2.9, 21.6. B. Ehrman, ed. & trans., *The Apostolic Fathers*, Loeb Classical Library, 2 vols. (Cambridge MA: Harvard University Press, 2003)

of these people is not to establish right belief, but to self-importantly draw attention to themselves by being victorious over their opponent. What is obvious from this? They want to hang on to a careless way of life and seek after self-conceit rather than seeking the will of Christ. If they were to seek him properly, they would successfully keep his commandments to the best of their ability.

10   Our task, by contrast, is not to be puffed up with self-conceit, but rather to help these people in the Lord. Thus, with confidence in the truth of Christ, we thought it necessary to proclaim not only what they are saying now, but also whatever deleterious notions they are likely to come up with later, and to propose solutions for them. In this way both parties will benefit. When those among them who are wise see us foretell all the machinations involved with these people's notions and see the rightful solutions, if they are lovers of the truth they will, without a doubt, be directed to the truth. If, however, because of long-held prejudices, they do not change their minds,[5] they will at any rate be put to shame by what they so confidently teach. Those who, due to their ignorance, have been carried away by the wise, but who now recognize the truth, will undoubtedly no longer allow themselves to remain in their error.

11   If one of them should be so foolish, however, as to conceal the solutions offered by us and propose instead mere words in order to deceive the simpler sort, and does this not by using whole chapters but rather snippets from the Scriptures, we are not responsible. We have laid out both the chapters and the solutions to the problems, but they, clearly, are word thieves who will also have to give an accounting for this wickedness: "They will be put to death for the harm they inflicted on the innocent" [Prov 1.32], says Holy Scripture. Likewise, they will not harm those well-grounded in the faith, for, it says, "Even if they drink something deadly, it will do them no harm" [Mk 16.18].

---

[5]Or: repent (*metanoēsōsin*).

Christ: The indivisible Lord of glory

12   What, then, are the notions that accord with these erroneous beliefs that they have not discovered the means to express to us? First, this: "Even if," they say, "the Apostle said that the crucified one and the Lord of glory are one and the same person, he said this because the crucified human being was worthy of glory *after* the resurrection." Thus they pilfer away the indivisible unity that existed before the crucifixion!

Nevertheless, their refusal to think that Saint Paul called Christ the Lord of glory *before* the crucifixion smacks of blindness and not of the truth—for, he says, "if they had known, they would not have crucified the Lord of glory" [1 Cor 2.8]. Besides, he did not say that Christ "participated" in glory but rather that he *is* the Lord of glory. The Lord has power over all glory, just as he is also able to give power to whomever he wishes, for, it says, "all of us have received from his fullness" [Jn 1.16], and "we have seen his glory, glory as of a Father's only Son" [Jn 1.14].

Since you have heard Scripture affirm the same thing on numerous occasions, my friend, you should know that the Lord Jesus Christ is one and the same Lord of life and death in every time and place and in every mighty work and circumstance. To say "Lord of glory" is to say "Lord of eternal life," and to say "they crucified him" [Mk 15.24; Jn 19.18] is to make clear that he died on our behalf. If life and death, therefore, the most powerful elements in all of nature, have been unable to divide Christ, as Paul demonstrates [Rom 8.38], neither can every sort of ruler and power, or height or depth, or things present or things to come [Rom 8.38–39].

Word and flesh united save us

13   Why, then, do you stumble over the stumbling stone [Rom 9.32] and say that the Lord's body is mere flesh? If it is mere flesh, how is it the life of the world and bread come down from heaven [Jn 6.32–33]? If, on the other hand, you believe the Lord's body to be God the Word alone, understand what the Lord says: "The bread that I will give is my flesh, which I will give for the life of the world" [Jn 6.51]. The world died on account of Adam's transgression. If the Lord's flesh were merely human flesh, therefore, not sharing in the substantive reality[6] of God the Word, it would clearly derive only from Adam and would fall under sin. How, then, was the flesh given for the life of the world when, in your opinion, it itself needed the same redemption as the world itself?

14 The Word did not suffer divested of the humanity. If the Word were mere flesh—I am speaking as you do—in need of purification, where, as a consequence, would salvation come from for us? If he who suffered were exclusively and merely human, he would scarcely have suffered even on his own behalf! Thus those who believe this are still in their sins [1 Cor 15.17]: They live for themselves, and not for him who died and was raised for them [2 Cor 5.15].

Our concern should be with keeping the commandments

If, on the other hand, they believe absolutely that Christ died not for himself, but for us, in accordance with the Scriptures [1 Cor 15.3], they should not say that the one who suffered was a mere human being, nor should they meddle in how the union came about. Instead, they should believe and concern themselves[7] with keeping his commandments, in accordance with what Saint Paul says: "For we hear," he says, "that some of you are living in idleness, not doing

---

[6]The substantive reality of God the Word is his *hypostasis*.

[7]The contrast between responsible concern and meddling is stronger in Greek: "concern themselves" is *ergazesthai,* whereas "meddle" is *periergazesthai.* The word play continues with Paul's words in the next sentence: "work" translates *ergazomenous* (the noun *ergon,* "work," will also figure below), and "busybodies," that is, those with time on their hands to meddle, *periergazomenous.*

any work, acting as busybodies. Such persons we command to do their work quietly and to earn the bread they eat" [2 Thess 3.11–12].

15   It is clear that the work the Apostle is talking about is the work of keeping the commandments, that is to say, such work is what we really ought to be doing, just as "bread" is really the Lord's flesh, as he said earlier. But what do they say? "One must first believe, and then work." These are words that cause internecine strife! As a consequence, they deny both the faith and their Baptism. If they were not initiated in the mysteries of the Church, they would have every right to say these things and to meddle in such matters. But if they have received the seal [of Baptism] as believers and have confessed not a mere human being, not a stripped-down God, but the Word incarnate, and have been baptized into Christ [Rom 6.3; Gal 3.27], having confessed him to be the Word incarnate, as I said earlier, they as a consequence have an obligation to keep the commandments and will have renounced making such meddlesome statements.

The truth of the incarnation

16   When we say these things, we are not presenting the orthodox faith as unknowable and devoid of witnesses—Holy Scripture is full of supporting statements concerning the faith—but, rather, are confessing in our Baptism that God the Word took flesh and became human and in the flesh was crucified, died, and was buried, and for us rose from the dead on the third day and ascended into heaven and will come to judge the living and the dead.[8] They, by contrast, are even now dividing Christ and splitting him asunder, on the one hand dividing the flesh from the Word and on the other the Word from the flesh, and, using human logic, are meddling with his ineffable union, inquiring into what is indescribable and asking "How?" And if they do not get an answer, they refuse to believe any longer. So those who

---

[8]This concise summary by Mark corresponds to the kind of creed that a candidate for Baptism would affirm.

were once united to the Lord through the spiritual mysteries are called adulteresses so long as their husband is still alive—and indeed he is alive—[Rom 7.2–3] for he himself lives and abides indivisible and incarnate, seated at the right hand of the Father [Rom 8.34; Col 3.1]. Incarnate, he will come to judge the living and the dead; incarnate, he is worshipped by the angels; incarnate, he is escorted by the powers; incarnate, he is glorified by the archangels; incarnate, he is praised in song by the whole creation; incarnate, he is prophesied by the prophets; incarnate, he is preached by the apostles; incarnate, he is confessed by the martyrs; incarnate, he is witnessed to by John [the Baptist]; incarnate, he pleases the Father; incarnate, he is witnessed to by the Spirit; incarnate, he is praised by the Church. Incarnate, he is the indivisible and immortal Son of God forever and remains incarnate forever.

One, not two: Jesus Christ indivisible, divine and human

17 Do you not shudder [James 2.19], you heretic, when you attempt to use his actions to divide him who is unified by hypostasis and indivisible by grace? If not, starting from "all the fullness of the Godhead was pleased to dwell bodily in him" [Col 1.19, 2.9], show me where in Holy Scripture he is divided at such and such a time or in such and such a place, or when doing some mighty work or performing some action, and I will put up with your perverse folly!

Even if you say "he was begotten," that does not mean that God is "bare" or that Christ is "a mere human being." Scripture does say that Christ was begotten, but it also says that the divine and the human were united in him. Thus does Holy Scripture everywhere confess him, not as God here and as a human being there, but one Christ Jesus, from both God and human being. Thus too you will find him everywhere in Holy Scripture: Jesus Christ, whom we profess and in whom we believe.

18   Now I want to ask you a question on this subject, you heretic, and, since you say you love the truth, give me a truthful answer, without resorting to clever circumlocutions. Give me an answer that responds to the question. Tell me, is Christ one or two? Undoubtedly you will say that he is one, in accordance with what Scripture says: "one Lord, Jesus Christ" [1 Cor 8.6]. If that is the case, that he is one, then tell me: In your opinion, what is he? A mere human being or unconcealed God? If you tell me, "He is one, from both," as you confessed at the time of holy Baptism, you have spoken well. But if you say that he is a mere human being, how can he also be God over all [Rom 9.5], begotten from the being of the Father? If you say, "The Word is unconcealed," you will hear [the question], "How was the Word begotten unconcealed from a woman?" [Gal 4.4][9] and will finally be forced to tell the truth: that Christ is both divine and human.

I am amazed at how they show no respect for Holy Scripture, which clearly says concerning these things that "they have left us, but they never really belonged to us; if they had belonged to us, they would have remained with us" [1 Jn 2.19]. Notwithstanding this, their spikes are mercilessly aimed at our hearts; they stab us with their sudden barbs, saying, "You are the ones who left us"! What a pitiable and perverse belief! Have we set ourselves up in opposition to Holy Scripture? No! Are we, after our Baptism, putting Christ to the test? No! Are we renouncing the confession of faith that we professed? No! Listen to Paul, who says, "From now on, we know no Christ according to the flesh,[10] even though," he says, "we once knew Christ according to the flesh. We no longer know him that way. If anyone is in Christ, he is a new creation. The old has passed away" [2 Cor 5.16–17].

---

[9]Paul does not use the word "unconcealed" (*gymnos*) in Gal 4.4.

[10]In 2 Cor 5.16, Paul does not use the word "Christ," but says, "we know no one according to the flesh." Mark has added "Christ."

Christ crucified, the power and wisdom of God

19   Once you have been baptized and have become a new creation [2 Cor 5.17], you impious wretch, do not become a new Tertullus, publicly declaiming against the truth [Acts 24.1–8], and do not employ sophistical arguments against Paul, the equal of Wisdom herself.[11] Learn what the gospel proclaims and show some shame in opposing it. Paul did not say, "We proclaim crucified flesh," as you say, nor the opposite, "the Word crucified," as you think we say. No, he gave a name to the union and said, "We proclaim Christ crucified, a stumbling block to Jews and foolishness to Gentiles" [1 Cor 1.23]. So, if you too stumble over this and say, "It is foolish to believe in someone crucified as Son of God," see how Saint Paul identifies you as a Jew and a Gentile, for he says Christ is "a stumbling block to Jews and foolishness to Gentiles."

It is clear, therefore, that those who stumble over this are Juda-izers, and it is obvious that those who think the proclamation about the crucified one is foolish are practicing paganism; for, he says, "a stumbling block to the Jews and foolishness to the Gentiles, but to those who themselves are called, both Jews and Greeks, Christ is the power of God and wisdom of God" [1 Cor 1.23–24].[12]

20   I will ask you a question, therefore, you apostate: Who is the crucified one, and how is he "the power and the wisdom of God" [1 Cor 1.24]? You have heard the Apostle say that Christ is the crucified one and that Christ is the power of God and wisdom of God. By no means does he say there are two Christs but that both descriptions describe one and the same person! So tell me: Who is he talking about? The bare Logos or a mere human being? Confess one, as the Apostle does—and say which one you mean. If you say, "The Word is bare," I will repeat the question, so listen: How was God the bare Word crucified? If you say, "He was mere flesh," tell me:

[11]In Greek, wisdom (*sophia*) forms the root of "employ sophistical arguments" (*sophizou*).

[12]"Gentiles" in Greek is *hellēnes* (which also means "Greeks") and "to practice paganism" is *hellēnizein*.

How could mere flesh be both the wisdom and power of God? If you admit that you are at a loss to explain this too and that you want to learn, do not divide Christ, and your difficulties on both accounts will disappear, for Christ is himself both the crucified one and the power and wisdom of God, being God the Word united with the humanity of the Savior.

21   So, having heard about Christ Jesus in Holy Scripture, you will understand that in every case it means God the Word, united with his own flesh: "Jesus Christ" defines the indivisible conjoining of divinity and humanity. It is clear, therefore, that the person who denies the union with regard to God's divine plans will also deny that Jesus Christ defines this union. So then, my friend, are you not afraid to call him a mere human being and dead body whom Paul confesses to be the power of God and wisdom of God and the Lord of glory? With these merely human conceptions of yours, are you not dividing that which has been indivisible for all time and has in actual fact by its very nature been united in a manner worthy of God?

We proclaim Christ crucified

22   If Christ was crucified for himself and not for us, we will allow also your assertion about him being merely a corpse. Listen how Saint Paul anathematizes those who do not believe that he was crucified for us—not once, but twice even: "Even if we or an angel from heaven should proclaim to you something contrary to what you received before, let him be accursed!" [Gal 1.8–9]. Why does he say this? "For I handed on to you," he says, "what I in turn first received: that Christ Jesus died for our sins in accordance with the Scriptures" [1 Cor 15.3]. And again: "He died for all," Paul says, "so that those who live might live no longer for themselves but for him who died and was raised for them" [2 Cor 5.15].

23   If he who died and was raised is a mere human being, we live for a mere human being and live no longer for the Son of God, for it is written that we live no longer for ourselves but for him who died and was raised for us [2 Cor 5.15]. Hearing these words from Scripture, then, will you finally acknowledge the lordship of him who died for us? If you still say he is a mere human being and a corpse, how can a mere human being be Lord of glory and the power and wisdom of God? For the Apostle says that the crucified Christ was these things. And if he was a mere human being, how did he die for all, since he himself would still have needed someone to die for him? If you tell me that he did not commit sin and, on account of this, did not need someone to die for him, you must realize that the righteous, as well as sinners, are ruled by death, for, the Apostle says, "Death exercised dominion even over those who did not sin" [Rom 5.14]. Everyone, from the time of Adam, has been ruled by death, not because of their own transgressions but because of Adam's.

24   Since even Christ himself and the holy apostles command us to believe in him as the crucified one, are they forcing us to believe in a mere human being? If, however, by once again making use of sophistries, you say that they are not talking about believing in him as the crucified but rather about believing in God who indwelled him, think about this: Either prove what you have said, so we too may understand, or we will demonstrate our faith in the Lord and, once you understand, you will no longer contradict what we say.

25   Pay attention! What does blessed Paul, the Lord's chosen instrument [Acts 9.15], say? He makes his confession not for himself alone but also on behalf of all the apostles. He says, "But we proclaim Christ crucified" [1 Cor 1.23], and confirms this when he again says, "Whether it was I or they, so we proclaim and so you have come to believe" [1 Cor 15.11]. And again: "I decided to know nothing among you except Jesus Christ, and him crucified" [1 Cor 2.2]. If, therefore, you do not accept the union even upon the cross, you will not be able to escape the fact that you are denying what the Scriptures proclaim, for the holy apostles say that neither a bare God nor a mere human being suffered, but rather he who is at one and the same time God and human: Christ Jesus, the Lord of glory. They do not divide the divine economy but confess one from both, Christ Jesus, the Son of God, who suffered in the flesh: "We preach Christ crucified" [1 Cor 1.23]. Thus the apostles proclaim, and thus we believe.

Our opponents immediately respond to this by saying, "And so God is crucified? Or does God die? Or have hunger? Or grow weary?"

You fool! Having heard numerous passages of Scripture concerning the Word incarnate, do you still unsatisfactorily call him God unconcealed, even given these workings of the divine economy that I have enumerated? It seems to me that you have forgotten not only what the apostles say but also the Holy Gospels!

Christ's suffering

26   Have you not heard that "the Word became flesh and dwelt among us" [Jn 1.14]? He who became flesh for us received wounds corporeally but did so without division. In addition, he who pre-existed embraced his passionless Passion.

"If he unites the divine and the human in substantive reality," one might say, "how was he able to embrace his passionless Passion?"

I believe that asking this question of God is blasphemy. All the same, I will point out to you things in creation that people can do that are not invisible but can be seen by the eyes or held by the hands. Now, you tell me how the following happens: How is the flame united with smelted gold, or melted together with it, or penetrated so as to flow together with it, or incised together with it, or carried together with it, without suffering a change? The fact that fire undergoes these things when it comes into contact with gold without suffering a change makes it clear that you do not know what you are talking about when you ask "How?" If it is possible among created things to see something that in its essence is ungoverned and unharmed by what it is governing, does not melt together with what it is melting and, when being united with what it is taking possession of, can affect that substance without being affected in its own substantive reality, why do you still refuse to believe in the all-powerful Divinity? Why do you go on asking how he does it?

27   So do not ask specious and malicious questions such as "Does God die?" or "Does God suffer?" You conceal the incarnation and indivisible union with all this talk about a stripped-down God. Say, rather, what is true—"Did *Christ* die, or suffer, or get hungry?"—and you will get an answer: Yes, he both suffered and died, and all the other things that Holy Scripture says he endured in the flesh. He was not forced to endure them by his nature but rather by grace endured them for us. If, having died, he lives, how much more easily could he have not died! In addition, if he walked on the sea [Mt 6.48], he was also able to walk on the earth without getting tired. And if he walked through closed doors, how much more easily could he have walked right through those attempting to seize him [Mt 26.53–56]! But since he suffered not for himself but for us, he willingly endured all things.

The danger of dividing the Lord's ineffable unity

28   What do they have to say to these things?

"Is he who suffered for us God, or not?"

Yes, he is God—but not God stripped of his humanity. I am telling you that he was a human being, but a human being united with the Godhead. When you hear about the great things that Christ did as God, do not talk about a stripped-down God as you observe these wonders; instead, speak of Divinity united with humanity. And again, when you hear about all of his sufferings, do not retort that because of his sufferings he is a mere human, but say instead that he is humanity united with Divinity. When the angels saw him incarnated on earth, they did not divide him in two, as you people have attempted to do; instead, recognizing the divine union, they wondrously offered their praises, saying, "Glory to God in the highest, and peace, goodwill among people" [Lk 2.14].[13] Do you see how they joined together praise in the highest places with goodwill among people and how they clearly proclaimed to the shepherds the good news of the birth of Christ the Savior [Lk 2.14], speaking of one—not two, as you do?

29   "We too," they say, "speak of one Christ and appropriately divide the natures depending on what he did."

Who, when he hears what we have said, will not shudder at the way they war against God? These people! Rectifying the Lord's ineffable make-up! They divide the things that he himself did not divide. He did not hobble our faith! These people, acting as though they were preachers second only to the apostles and prophets, claim they are making perfectly clear whatever Holy Scripture—both the prophets and the apostles—is silent about. They do not realize that this is leading them into committing great blasphemy. Sometimes they divide him who is indivisible and sometimes they join him together, dressing and undressing the Word like a coat that one puts on and takes off. In doing so they are destroying nothing but their own lives.

The soteriology of the incarnation

30   If Christ has not assumed our flesh in substantive reality, how will he give us the gift of the Spirit? We believe Holy Scripture: When God the Word was pleased to become human, he did not turn himself into flesh but rather united human flesh to himself. By doing this, he made every human being capable of receiving the Holy Spirit. He himself, by virtue of this union, assumed flesh as God, while we, by participation, receive the Spirit as human beings.[14]

---

[13]The reading of Lk 2.14 that Mark employs is probably secondary; the better reading is "peace among people of goodwill." The difference in Greek is one letter.

[14]See St. Athanasius, "He became human so that we might be made divine" (Greek: *theopoiēthōmen*). See *On the Incarnation* 54.3; C. Kannengiesser, ed., Sources chrétiennes, 199 (Paris: Cerf, 1973).

He became incarnate for us and died for all human beings "so that through death he might destroy the one who has power over death, that is, the Devil" [Heb 2.14], and save all people who believe in him, and graciously bestow the kingdom of heaven on the faithful through his incarnation. Did a dead man do all these things, as you say, or were they, rather, extraordinary events exceeding all power and wisdom, as the Apostle says [see Eph 1.3–14], which demonstrates that these works are even more wondrous than the wonderful things God did in the beginning? For Scripture says that "all things are summed up in Christ, things in heaven and things on earth" [Eph 1.10]. In the beginning God made heaven and earth [Gen 1.1], the sea, and everything in them, for our sakes, as it is written: "all things are ours, and we belong to Christ, and Christ belongs to God" [1 Cor 3.22–23].[15]

31　As marvelous as these benefactions and extraordinary doings are, his incarnated presence is even more marvelous and defies comparison, because it has illuminated the previous marvels God did for us in creation, and bestowed even greater gifts on us. The first human, after enjoying the aforementioned bounties through created things, was tricked by the Devil's sophistries and disobeyed God. Because of this disobedience, he fell under sin and, because of sin, was handed over to death [Rom 4.25, 5.12]. Because of him, we all have fallen from eternal life, whether sinners or righteous. No human being has escaped accusation, because the root of our nature, I mean the first human being, is mortgaged to him. Afterwards, danger was inevitable; death, likewise, became inescapable.

If the commandment was prescribed, then the condemnation for transgressing it was determined, the judge infallible, his verdict trustworthy, his law truthful, his justice unvarying, repentance impossible because it does not have an undefiled priest.[16] Everyone is liable to condemnation. If only the effects of sin had stopped there!

---

[15]1 Cor 3.22–23 reads "all things are yours, and you belong to Christ," but in late antiquity "ours" (*hēmōn*) and "we" (*hēmeis*) sounded the same as "yours" (*humōn*) and "you" (*humeis*) and are often interchanged in the manuscripts.

[16]That is, before Christ, the great high priest.

Sin has in addition introduced a plethora of impious acts. Once human beings were cut off from the light of paradise, they forgot about the light and became enamored of its opposite. Error became more characteristic of them than the truth; wickedness became second nature; idolatry acceptable, pleasure-seeking legitimate, covetousness something to be deliberately sought, sin something to be multiplied, rage more fearful, the serpent more audacious; human beings are at times befuddled and at other times distracted, ignorant of the future while being wrapped up in the present, while still "the creation was subjected to futility," as it is written, "not of its own will but by the will of the one who had subjected it, in the hope" [Rom 8.20] of his own coming.

The Devil, and Christ's defeat of the Evil One

32   The person who lets loose a swarm of such evils in the end becomes captive to them, unable to get free. It necessarily follows that all these evils turn out to be a just sentence for an initial transgression. If death was decreed for a single act of eating [Gen 3], what further penalty can be levied commensurate with such additional wrongdoing except for a person to live under eternal punishment?

The Devil sentenced human beings to just such a punishment. In all likelihood he endeavored to make his situation our own, saying, "Just as they have become my partners in evil, so too shall they be my companions in punishment. God is just and truthful and does not weaken his own law: Just as he cast human beings out of paradise because of their one transgression and handed them over to death, so too shall he condemn them to be punished eternally with me for the additional evils they do."

33   The Evil One understood God's righteousness; nevertheless, he did not realize that God is all-powerful, just as the Devil's followers fail to understand now, those who ask God, "How?" and who attempt to pry into the nature of Christ, the power and wisdom of God [1 Cor 1.24]. Therefore, the Power of God came to battle the power of the Enemy. Taking flesh, the Power of God redeemed human beings, not by arrogating power to himself, lest he abrogate justice, but by exchanging himself for us and acting with justice. He was begotten in human fashion,[17] taking upon himself a perfect human—or, rather, through this unique human being he took upon himself all human beings. He also suffered for us in order to release us from judgement, establish justice, fulfill his own purpose, and free human beings from death. To do so, he himself died for all and nullified the power of the Devil, without giving him the opportunity to arrogate power to himself and do what he wanted, just as he rescued us without arrogating power to himself, but by acting lawfully and using his almighty power.

The incomprehensibility of the incarnation

34   So, you blaspheming and unbelieving wretch, all these wondrous things take place on your behalf and on behalf of us all. Do you still say he is a "dead" power and not the power of God and wisdom of God [1 Cor 1.24], as Saint Paul affirms?

In an abbreviated fashion we have reminded the unbelieving of these things so we may persuade them that the Word became flesh [Jn 1.14] for us, as Holy Scripture says. He did not turn into a human being, but in substantive reality united himself with humanity.

But you say, "How?"

And I tell you, "Incomprehensibly. With regard to God, one does not ask, 'How?' He suffered as a human being and yet did so impassibly."

Once again you say, "How?"

And I tell you, "In the manner of the Lord. He was crucified in the flesh but was not altered in spirit, for flesh and spirit were united in his mother's womb."

[17]Mark uses the same verb to describe divine generation and human birth.

You say, "How?"

And I tell you, "Incomprehensibly. He died physically but in his actions was immortal."

Once again you say, "How?"

And I tell you, "All-powerfully. He was buried as a mortal and rose from the dead as God."

Once again you say, "How?"

And I tell you, "Unfathomably."

The Son of God is all-powerful

35 Once again I will ask you a question, and I want you to give me an answer. Do not talk all around the matter, but give me a straight answer.

Is the Son of God all-powerful? Yes or no?

If you say, "I do not know because I do not comprehend what 'the power of God' is," I will say to you, "If you do not comprehend what 'the power of God' is, how is it that you divide the union in two without understanding by what sort of power the union is effected?" If you say the opposite, that he is not all-powerful, look here: Holy Scripture refutes you when it says, "I know you can do all things and nothing is impossible for you" [Job 42.2].[18] If you confess the truth, however, and say, "Yes, God is all-powerful," do not seek any longer to find out "How?" with regard to what has taken place and what is written concerning the divine economy. By doing so you seem not to believe that he is all-powerful. If he is, do not seek how. If you find it necessary to know how, he is no longer all-powerful as far as you are concerned.

36 Tell me, then, a minor point—for it is minor—as I said earlier: How did he *ex nihilo* make heaven and the earth and the sea and everything in them [2 Mac 7.28]?

[18]In Greek, "power" (*dunamis*), "can" (*dunasai*), and "impossible" (*adunatai*) are all related etymologically.

If you have nothing to say on these matters, do not meddle with what is even more marvelous—how he became human or how, by means of the flesh, he suffered impassibly—nor seek to explain in terms of the natures how these things took place. Instead, believe that God, being all-powerful, does exactly as he pleases. Or have you not heard the Scripture that says, "The Lord does whatever he pleases" [Ps 135.6]?

Holy Scripture affirms the unity of Christ incarnate

37   So, then, we ought to believe only those things that Holy Scripture says about him and not meddle with "How?" Scripture says that Jesus Christ is Son of God, and that for us he became incarnate, and for us suffered, and for us was crucified, and for us died, and for us was buried and rose again, and was taken up into heaven, and is seated at the right hand of the Father, and will come to judge the living and the dead, and remains for ever.[19]

Let us therefore believe whatever Holy Scripture says the incarnate Word suffered impassibly or did. Since Scripture does not say *how* these things happened, let us not meddle there. It is written: "All the fullness of the Godhead was pleased to dwell in him bodily" [Col 1.19; 2.9]. If God himself was pleased to act in this manner, why do we inquire "How?" or attempt to divide him with regard to his activities? Why do we attempt to discern by our own powers of discernment in what way he bodily existed or how he dwelt, as though sometimes he dwelt and at other times did not? Again it is written: "From them, according to the flesh, comes Christ, who is God over all" [Rom 9.5]. Do you see how Holy Scripture everywhere confesses the Son of God incarnate and inseparable?

38   Let us imitate Peter, who, when he heard the Son of Man, confessed him to be Son of God and, on account of this, heard, "Blessed are you" [Mt 16.13–17]. Let us imitate Mary, who, when she

[19]For another creedal formulation, see §§18 and 40.

was looking for his holy body, said, "They have taken my Lord, and I do not know where they have put him" [Jn 20.13]. Let us imitate the blind man, who, when he heard the Son of God speaking to him and saw him, believed, and worshipped him by taking hold of his feet [Jn 9.35–38]. Does Scripture say that Christ answered the woman with the hemorrhage, "Who touched 'the human being'?" [Mk 5.30]? No. Does it say, "The soldier struck 'the human being'" [Jn 18.22]? No. Did Christ say to Pilate, "The one who handed 'my body' over to you is guilty of the greater sin" [Jn 19.11]? No. Does Scripture say, "They crucified 'the human person'—or 'the body' of Christ" [Jn 19.18]? No. Does it say, "They clothed 'the human person'—or 'the body'—with a scarlet robe" [Mt 27.28]? No. Does it say, "'A person' placed his hands upon the eyes of the blind man" [Mk 8.25]? No. Does it say, "'The human person' is going to my Father" [Jn 16.28]? No. Does it say, "Place your hand into the side of my 'person'" [Jn 20.27]? No.

No, everywhere Holy Scripture says there is one Christ and Son of God, God the Word, with his own flesh. If Scripture says, "Son of God," it is speaking about Christ in unity. If Scripture says, "Son of Man," it is likewise speaking about one and the same person. If he is slapped, if he is betrayed, if he is persecuted, if he is disbelieved or believed, or hungers or grows weary or, in general, whatever Scripture says about him, it is speaking about one and the same person, God the Word, with his own flesh, united, without division or separation: Jesus Christ, the Son of the living God.

39   Believe, therefore, in accordance with what Scripture says, that he came in the flesh, not that flesh came; that he grew weary in the flesh, not that flesh grew weary; that he suffered in the flesh, not that flesh suffered; that he died in the flesh, not that flesh died; that he was crucified in the flesh, not that flesh was crucified; that he rose in the flesh, not that flesh arose; that he was taken into heaven in the flesh, not that flesh was taken into heaven; that he healed in the flesh, not that flesh healed; that he was seated at the right hand of God in the flesh, not that flesh was seated. And, in general, whenever Holy Scripture speaks about him bodily, you cannot show that it is speaking about the flesh as one part of the whole, but rather united: he made the deeds of the flesh his own. For Scripture says: Christ was begotten, Christ healed, Christ ate, Christ slept; Christ's body, Christ's blood, Christ's feet, Christ's wounds. The soldier slapped Christ on the face, Christ grew weary, Christ suffered, Christ died for us, Christ was crucified, Christ arose, Christ was taken into heaven, Christ was seated at the right hand of God, Christ will come to judge the living and the dead, Christ is the Son of God, Christ is God over all things. Nowhere does it say, "his humanity suffered something," or "God the Word did something." It says everywhere in Scripture, rather, that he claimed the deeds of the flesh as his own, not only on earth in the here and now, but also in heaven for ever.

Our baptismal profession of belief

40   If these words you have heard from Holy Scripture are true, you ought to believe and not ask meddlesome questions.

What does somebody say now? "How am I supposed to believe what I do not understand?" or "What is belief?"

Belief is confessing what you professed at your Baptism, when you said, "I believe in God, the Father almighty, and in the Lord Jesus Christ, God the Word, God from God, light from light, power from power, who, in the last days, for us took flesh, was begotten, became a human being, was crucified, died, rose from the dead, ascended into heaven, and will come to judge the living and the dead." Did you not confess these things, either for yourself or through someone else? Were you not "buried with him through Baptism" [Col 2.12] and raised with him by means of the resplendent robe and the Holy Mysteries?[20]

---

[20]This seems to be referring to Baptism and Chrismation and Eucharist.

The sanctifying and forgiving nature of the union in the sacraments

41   Seeking what is godly, therefore, describe to me first what your concerns are and reflect on them with discernment, so that through what you say and think I may believe that you too are capable of understanding Christ's nature. How, being alive in the flesh, did you die with Christ and become buried with him? How did you also eat his body if it is merely flesh? How did you also drink his blood if it itself is merely blood? You receive neither God the Word nor Christ himself, but instead hear "the body of Christ" and "the blood of Christ." So, if they are not united—I am talking as you do—how will the body and blood give you life? If these things are not made holy by means of the union, how will they make you holy or grant you forgiveness of your sins?

42   If I were to speak to you about Christ, once again you would quibble and divide Christ. But now I am talking to you about the body and the blood. Tell me how they bestow life on you in and of themselves. Do you hear what the holy priest says? "The holy body of Jesus Christ, for eternal life." If he were to say, "The holy Christ, for eternal life," you would once again say, "He is holy because of the indwelling God." But now you hear the body and blood each on its own called holy. You should understand, you poor man, that they are holy by nature, united in substantive reality with the Godhead from the time he was conceived in his mother's womb, and not after he was begotten, derivatively by participation.

The person who believes this keeps the commandments of Christ afterwards and does not ask meddlesome questions about his nature. We learn this from Saint Paul, knowing for a fact that no one who asks meddlesome questions about Christ's nature keeps his commandment[21] [2 Thess 3.11], but that the person who believes and keeps Christ's commandment receives the Holy Spirit and becomes

---

[21]In Greek, the person who keeps Christ's commandment is described with the participle *ergazomenos,* whereas "meddling" is the verb *periergazetai*, both derived from the word *ergon*, "work."

someone taught by God [1 Thess 4.8–9]. Like a river, he pours out the truth for others too, in accordance with the word that the Lord spoke when he said, "'As Scripture has said, "out of the belly" of the person who believes in me "shall flow rivers of living water."' Now when he said this, he was speaking about the Spirit, which those who believed in him were about to receive" [Jn 7.38–39].²²

Who is the Son of Man?

43   Again listen to what Paul says about him whom you so confidently divide. "Every knee shall bow to him," he says, of those "in heaven and on earth and under the earth, and every tongue shall confess that Jesus Christ is Lord, to the glory of God the Father" [Phil 2.10–11]. Will you not tremble on that day when the above-mentioned holy powers simply worship him, without asking meddlesome questions, and give glory to God for the ineffable mystery of the union? Are you going to divide him even then and ask, "How?" There, it seems to me, wasted with fear,²³ you will undoubtedly neither say these things nor think them. No, consider that what you think here will be reckoned against you there. Therefore, you poor man, repent your wrongheaded belief and believe as Christ wants you to believe.

44   Listen to what the Lord says to his disciples: "Who do people say that I am? The Son of Man?" [Mt 16.13].²⁴ Carefully observe how he did not say, "Son of God," but rather "Son of Man." After hearing the disciples say, "Some say John [the Baptist], others Elijah," he said to them, "But who do you say that I am?" The foundation of the apostles (see Mt 16.18), Peter, answered by saying,

²²The Greek on Jn 7.38 uses "belly" (*koilias*); the NRSV uses "heart"; the NIV "streams of living water will flow from within him."

²³Reading *kekakōmenos* instead of the text's *kekarōmenos*, which is a misprint.

²⁴The best reading of Mt 16.13 has, "Who do people say that the Son of Man is?" Mark bears witness to a textual tradition that probably conflated Mt 16.13 with Mk 8.27 and Lk 9.18, "Who do people say that I am?"

"You are the Christ, the Son of the living God," and to these words the Lord responded, "Blessed are you, Simon Peter, son of Jonah, because flesh and blood"—that is, human ways of thinking—"has not revealed this to you, but my Father in heaven" [Mt 16.14–17].

The Lord praised Peter because when the latter heard "Son of Man," he confessed the Lord to be Son of God. And what did the Lord say to him? "You are Peter, and on this rock I will build my Church, and the gates of hell will not prevail over it" [Mt 16.18]. So, if you too transcend human ways of thinking, you will confess the Son of Man, whom Mary bore, to be Son of God. He will surely call you blessed, just as he did Saint Peter, and he will build on this rock of faith the whole church of your thoughts, and the gates of hell will not prevail over it because, in coming down from heaven, he loosened the bonds of Hades by means of his holy body in order to save those who believe in him without making divisions.

45 If you oppose even these arguments, however, and still attempt to divide the Lord, tell me, who is the Son of Man?

If you tell me, "God the Word," then how is he also Son of Man? If you say, "He is a mere human being," how did Peter call him Son of God? If, unable to slip out of this bind, you say, "He is both a mere human being and is called Son of God," you are introducing two Christs—one God the Word, and one a human being, for Saint Peter says, "You are the Christ, the Son of the living God" [Mt 16.17].

Jesus Christ, Lord and God

46 Will you accept how blessed Thomas bears witness to the truth? He touched the Savior's side and hands and confessed him to be Lord and God [Jn 20.24–29]. He did not pronounce him Lord and God either because of the Lord's wondrous works or because of his divine words, lest you should say that he was talking about God "indwelling" a human being. No, having touched the Lord's holy body with his hands, he explicitly confessed him also to be

God. What do you have to say to that? Who is the person who was touched? A mere human being? So how did Thomas confess him to be both Lord and God? But was he the Word "stripped down"? How was even a "stripped-down" God touched? You need to confess the truth here too: Jesus Christ is Lord. Or have you not heard in the Gospels how he accused the apostles on this point, saying, "Come and see that it is I myself, for a ghost does not have flesh and bones as you see that I have" [Lk 24.39]. Why did he not say, "Come and see that it is my humanity"? Instead, showing them flesh and bone, he said, "See that it is I myself."

Why am I still seeking testimony concerning the orthodox faith? All of Holy Scripture clearly states that he was one and the same Son of God with regard to both kinds of actions—divine and human, I mean—that our Lord Jesus Christ both did and suffered.

The reality of the incarnation

47   If Holy Scripture particularly mentions the Lord's holy body after the crucifixion, it does not do so to divide it from his divine dignity or from the holiness that was his by nature, but rather wants to demonstrate that the Lord Jesus Christ came not as some sort of apparition—as some think—but truly came in the flesh and died for us. Therefore, Scripture also clearly says, "If someone does not confess that Jesus Christ came in the flesh, this person opposes Christ" [1 Jn 4.2–3]. Where did he come except, clearly, into the world? Why did he come except for us? Why? In order to teach perfect truth, which no one else had taught—to believe in Father, Son, and Holy Spirit, but through keeping the commandments, however, and not through mere knowledge—and in order to suffer on behalf of all the faithful, to be despised, spat upon, beaten, tied up, scourged, crucified, to drink gall and sour wine, to die, be pierced with a lance, and rise from the dead on the third day. He likewise came in order to do himself the things of God in the flesh so we might see the angels ascending and descending on him [Jn 1.51], to give the Holy Spirit to those who show their belief in him by keeping his commandments, to save them, and to be taken into heaven and sit at the right hand of Power [Mt 26.64], and come to judge the living and the dead, and abide with the Father for ever. Having heard these things from Holy Scripture, we believe in Father, Son, and Holy Spirit.

48   No doubt you will say to me, "I too believe in the Father, Son, and Holy Spirit," understanding by "the Son" the Word bare and not with his own holy flesh.

But hear what the Lord, too, says on this subject: "This is eternal life: that they may believe in you, the only true God, and in Jesus Christ, whom you have sent" [Jn 17.3].[25] You have heard that Jesus Christ came "in the flesh" [1 Jn 4.2; 2 Jn 1.7], not "without flesh"! If you do not believe what Holy Scripture has to say about this, explain to me how the Word came "stripped down," or how the Father sanctified the Son and sent him into the world [Jn 10.36]. According to you, did this happen by displacement or alteration or mutation, or by apparition and imaginary appearance?

Heaven forbid that we think this way about the advent and appearance of the Lord! No, the union with holy flesh came about through the Father's commissioning and sending him down and sanctifying and anointing him: God the Word, from the time he was conceived in his mother's womb, made the flesh his own, uniting in himself everything about the flesh, ineffably and without change. The Lord's advent and presence is nothing other than the marvelous incarnation, and whatever things he said or did or suffered—and does and will do—by means of that advent and presence.

The real and compassionate humanity of Christ

49   Just as he came and suffered for us, so too does he maintain his priesthood and intercede for us, as Saint Paul confirms [Rom 8.34;

[25]Jn 17.3 reads "know you" rather than "believe in you."

Heb 7.24–25], acting not as a subordinate but by divine dispensation. As a result, in accordance with the Father's good pleasure, by becoming human he took responsibility for us, so that he himself might do for us all those things we ought to do but are unable to do.

He himself, by doing for us what we ought to do ourselves, demonstrates to us what it means to be truly human. For this reason, he fasted forty days and afterwards was hungry, in order to show us how, for love's sake, not to lose heart, even if we are hungry, or listen to the Devil, who commanded the stones to become loaves of bread [Mt 4.2–3]. So too he thirsted and grew tired and slept and ate with sinners [Mt 9.11], and prayed and said that the Son did not know the hour or the day of the final consummation [Mt 24.36], and went to a wedding [Jn 2.2], and sorrowed at hardheartedness [Mk 3.5], and was deeply grieved, even to death [Mt 26.38], and ate with sinners [Mt 9.11], and prayed that, if possible, the cup of death might pass him by [Mt 26.39], and wept for the dead [Jn 11.35], and ordered [the disciples] to catch fish [Jn 21.6], and did not stop them from buying food [Jn 4.8], and, in general, took upon himself and demonstrated everything possible for human beings, except sin [Heb 4.15]. He not only assumed flesh for us, but also assumed all of its physical attributes, except for sin [Heb 4.15], in order that we might know that nothing physical compels us to sin.

When you hear, then, that Jesus did or said something corporeal or human, do not think that he was incapable of doing something better, but instead marvel at his love for humankind and his accommodating himself to our human condition. If he became human for us, it is clear that for us he spoke and acted and suffered as a human being. Do not judge all of Christ's power by the fact that he became human for us, so that as a result you divide him according to his different activities, ascribing some to "mere flesh" and others to the "bare Godhead."

The union of divine and human in Christ

50   Since we have learned not to put our faith in his command-
ments but rather to persevere in what is hidden, perhaps if you too
reflect on this, you will say to me, "Tell me, whom, according to
Scripture, did the Father beget before the morning star [Ps 109.3
(LXX)], God the Word, or humanity?" I will tell you, "By nature,
God the Word—but, by grace, he made the humanity his own, too.
This is so because God the Word, by means of the good pleasure of
God the Father, also united humanity with himself, in accordance
with Scripture, which says, "This is my beloved Son, with whom I
am well pleased" [Mt 3.17]. If he was not united, he would not bear
the name "Jesus Christ," but rather "God the Word," which he bore
from the beginning. If this is not the case, *you* tell *me*: For what reason did the apostles not proclaim the Son of God "the naked Word,"
but rather in every instance proclaimed him Jesus Christ, and him
crucified [1 Cor 1.23, 2.2]? Is it not obvious that they did so because
of the union? The Lord Jesus Christ is Son of Man not because of
mere flesh but because of the union with holy flesh. Likewise, he is
Son of God not because of the bare Word, but because of union with
the Word. A characteristic is one thing, union another.

51   I am speaking of a mystical and unconfused union, for the
Word neither turned into flesh, nor did flesh dissolve into the Word;
rather, with the Word remaining exactly as he was and with flesh
being exactly what it is, God the Word, in accordance with the will
of God the Father, was pleased to be united with flesh in his mother's
womb. Each nature remains what it is without confusion,[26] without
either of them insisting on its own separate identity in Christ, by virtue of either the names the Lord was known by or the deeds he did.

---

[26]The term "without confusion" (in Greek, *asynchytōs*)—and its correlative,
"unconfused union" (in Greek, *henōsin asynchyton*), used earlier in this section—that
Mark uses here is one of the four adverbs used in the christological definition of
the Council of Chalcedon, where the union of natures in Christ is described as
being "without confusion [*asynchytōs*], without change [*atreptōs*], without division
[*adiairetōs*], without separation [*anchoristōs*]."

According to Scripture, the same Christ who is called "Son of Man" is also called "Son of God," for [the angel] says to Saint Mary, "The Holy Spirit will come upon you, and the power of the Most High will overshadow you; therefore the child to be born will be called holy, the Son of God" [Lk 1.35].

Do you see that the same person who was born of Mary is also called "Son of God" by means of the union effected in his mother's womb? He himself both spoke and taught; he himself both performed divine deeds and suffered human sufferings. Although it was the Word who did the divine deeds, this was nonetheless not God "stripped down," but was rather God the Word united with humanity, and even if it was a human being who suffered human sufferings, it was nevertheless not humanity divided from Divinity, but was rather humanity united with the Godhead.

52　　I am speaking therefore of the transformation of neither the Word nor the flesh, but rather am confessing their undivided union. Thus we can conceive of the impassible Word *and* believe that he is the Son of God who suffered[27] for us, since each nature, in a manner befitting God, remained integral to itself while making the properties of the other its own for us. As a result, Christ, composed of both natures, became mediator between God and humanity [1 Tim 2.5].

May he be conceived of as sole Son of God and believed in at every moment and in every place and through every powerful act and deed, in accordance with Holy Scripture.

To *Christ* be the glory, for ever and ever. Amen.

---

[27]In Greek, "impassible," that is, "not-suffering," is *apathē,* and "suffered" is *pathonta*, both from the verb *paschein*, "to suffer."

CHAPTER FOUR

Concerning Holy Baptism

Introduction

In *Concerning Holy Baptism*, Mark addresses a fundamental problem in Christian life: Why is there sin after Baptism? Mark picks
his way between the untrammeled enthusiasm of those who expect
from Baptism a remaking of the person into Edenic perfection and
the dyspeptic pessimism of those who despair at failure and thus
suppose that Baptism effects merely a superficial change. Since the
sixth century, it has been thought that Mark was addressing certain
Messalian tendencies. It is worth pausing briefly to consider what
this means. Modern scholarship has shown that Messalianism is less
a system of principles or beliefs than a typology that was generated
(rather fitfully) by heresiologists to characterize groups of ascetic
Christians who were considered objectionable for a variety of reasons.[1] For our purposes, two common accusations are salient: first,
that Messalians did not deign to work manually but insisted rather
on "spiritual work"—a claim that will be familiar from Mark's *Disputation*, because the Attorney lodged it against monks in general;
and second, that Messalians denigrated holy Baptism as being of no

---

[1]Most recently, see C. Stewart, *'Working the Earth of the Heart': The Mes-
salian Controversy in History, Texts, and Language to AD 431*, Oxford Theological
Monographs (Oxford: Oxford University Press, 1991); K. Fitschen, *Messalianismus
und Antimessalianismus: Ein Beispiel ostkirchlicher Ketzergeschichte*, Forschung zur
Kirchen- und Dogmengeschichte 71 (Göttingen: Vanderhoeck and Ruprecht, 1998);
M. Plested, *The Macarian Legacy: The Place of Macarius-Symeon in the Eastern
Christian Tradition*, Oxford Theological Monographs (Oxford: Oxford University
Press, 2004), 16–27.

benefit for spiritual progress.[2] The second theme is one taken up by Mark in *On Holy Baptism*. So it is not surprising that early opponents of Messalianism—such as Babai the Great—found in Mark's treatise a valuable weapon.[3]

As for Mark himself, he is keen to maintain that (despite any concerns to the contrary) Baptism *does* in fact result in Christian perfection. As he puts it in his *Answer* to the second question, "Holy Baptism does represent perfection—but it does not perfect someone who does not keep the commandments." Mark uses the word "perfect" generously throughout the treatise, in order to stress that nothing is lacking from Baptism. When baptized Christians sin, this is not because of a defect in the sacrament of holy Baptism; instead, it is because they voluntarily return to their sin, "like a dog to its vomit," to borrow an image from Proverbs.

Mark echoes the *Macarian Homilies* by roundly endorsing the idea that Baptism conveys a "deposit of grace" within the Christian, and that being entrusted with this deposit implies the need to cultivate it.[4] It is for this reason that Mark regularly invokes the "spiritual law" in talking about Baptism. For instance, he claims that ". . . it is clear that grace is perfect in us, but we are imperfect because of our failure to keep the commandments. Thus holy Baptism is perfect vis-à-vis us, but we are imperfect vis-à-vis it."[5] This emphasis on keeping the commandments indicates that Mark's discussion of Baptism builds on the fundamental teachings that he laid down in his double work, *On the Spiritual Law* and *Concerning Those Who Imagine That They Are Justified by Works*. Here, Mark develops his teaching further and occasionally offers up a well-turned phrase: his memorable

---

[2]See, e.g., the claims attributed to Adelphius, a leading "Messalian," in Photius' *Bibliotheka* 52 (R. Henry, ed. [Paris: Belles Lettres, 1962]) and also the characterization found in Theodoret's *Haereticarum fabularum compendium* 4.11.

[3]Babai, *Commentary on Evagrius' Gnostic Chapters* 3.85 (in W. von Frankenberg, *Eugarios Ponticus* [Berlin, 1912]).

[4]Macarius, *Great Letter* 2 (W. Jaeger, ed., *Two Rediscovered Works of Ancient Christian Literature: Gregory of Nyssa and Macarius* [Leiden: Brill, 1954], 233–34).

[5]Mark, *Answer* to Question 2.

gloss of grace as "the spiritual law inscribed in us" (*Answer* to the fourth question) is a particularly fine example.

Even though the terms that Mark uses to describe the results of Baptism are continuous with his explorations of the Christian law and Christian works, the exposition of Baptism is in many ways more sophisticated. It builds upon the claims that Mark makes in the works translated in the first volume of this collection. And this indicates that Mark, perhaps paradoxically, considers Baptism a very advanced theological subject. It may well be the fount of Christian identity, but Baptism for Mark is understood only (if at all) in retrospect. In other words, only with the benefit of experience can one begin to make some sense of what results from being initiated into the perfection of Christian life. This return to the foundations is typical of Mark's thinking—as, indeed, it is of the thinking of many monastic teachers. Through meditative and calm reflection, one learns to evaluate maturely the experiences of the Christian life and to draw from them enduring wisdom.

Concerning Holy Baptism[6]

PART ONE

First Question

Question: Some say that holy Baptism represents perfection, and rely on the Scripture that says, "Get up, be baptized, and have your sins washed away" [Acts 22.16]; and, "Wash yourselves, and make yourselves clean" [Is 1.16]; and again, "But you were washed, you were sanctified, you were justified" [1 Cor 6.11], citing many such passages as evidence. Others say that past sin is removed through spiritual struggles, and they too cite Scripture as evidence: "Let us cleanse ourselves from every defilement of body and of spirit" [2 Cor 7.1]. At the same time they also discover that the same sinful activity persists in themselves after Baptism. With regard to these two positions, what should we say, or whom should we believe?

Answer: We need to have faith in the apostolic preaching and persevere in our professions of faith, and not test God's power with human conjectures, nor voluntarily get ourselves bound voluntarily once again by the yoke of servitude [cf. Gal 5.1], but rather hold fast to our freedom by keeping the commandments; to the extent that we do this, we will discover the whole truth and clearly understand that we are controlled by sin insofar as we come up short in keeping the commandments. Because we have considered the apostolic preaching to be futile, putting our trust in idle speculation rather than in the word of God, our faith is therefore futile and we are still in our sins [1 Cor 15.17].

---

[6]Source: de Durand, *Marc le Moine*, 1:297–397.

Second Question

Question: We are not saying that the apostolic preaching is futile, but rather are seeking to learn the truth.

Answer: If we hold the preaching to be true, let us fulfill all the commandments; then we will know if we are being controlled by sin.

Holy Baptism does represent perfection—but it does not perfect someone who does not keep the commandments. Let us, then, not put our faith in human speculations but rather in Holy Scripture: "Christ died for our sins in accordance with the Scriptures" [1 Cor 15.3]; and "We have been buried with him through baptism" [Rom 6.4]; and "Whoever has died is freed from sin" [Rom 6.7]; and "Sin will have no dominion over us" [Rom 6.14]—if we keep his commandments. If we do not, we are faithless and are justifiably held in the grip of sin.

Faith consists not only of being baptized into Christ, but also of keeping his commandments. According to Scripture, it is clear that for us who have been mystically buried with him through Baptism, "he has both raised us up with him and has seated us with him in the heavenly places" [Eph 2.6; Col 2.12]; nevertheless, he has still given commandments in order that, keeping them, we may find the perfection that he has given to us. If we do not keep them, however, we make it clear that we are willingly being controlled by sin. Thus if we say that we are removing sin through works, then "Christ died for nothing" [Gal 2.21], and everything said above is a lie, and Baptism does not represent perfection.

But, for those who say they acquire perfection through spiritual struggles, the law of liberty [Jas 2.12] is useless, and all of the legislation of the New Testament is abrogated. They also present Christ as unjust since he appointed works of liberty for those who have been baptized, while those baptized are still, these others say, by their own free will "slaves to sin." And God's grace is no longer grace, but rather is a reward for our spiritual struggles: "If it is through works, it is no longer on the basis of grace, and if it is by grace, the work is not work" [Rom 11.6],[7] but is a commandment given by him who has freed us, and is a work of liberty and faith. Such words Saint Paul by divine dispensation wrote in advance to the Galatians when he also admonished them with similar statements for being unfaithful. So, we are not nullifying God's grace [Gal 2.21]. Heaven forbid!

Nor are we denying the faith that comes from preaching; but if we are held in the grip of sin even after Baptism, it is not because Baptism is imperfect, but because we neglect the commandment and by our own free will are addicted to sensual pleasures, as Holy Scripture reproaches us when it says, "The person who turns back to his own sin" voluntarily and by his own free will "is like a dog that has turned back to its own vomit" [Prov 26.11; 2 Pet 2.22]. Neither God nor Satan forces the will to do his bidding after Baptism. Have these people not heard that the commandments of Christ, given after Baptism, are a law of liberty [Jas 2.12], as Scripture says: "Act and speak as those who are to be judged by the law of liberty" [Jas 2.12]? To give another example, Saint Peter says, "Build up a supply of virtue by means of your faith" [2 Pet 1.5]—and, after saying this, he adds, "Because the person who does not have these things at hand is blind and nearsighted and forgets that he has received the cleansing of his past sins" [2 Pet 1.9].

Understand, from what has been said, that the purification that takes place through Baptism occurs mystically, but is effectively discovered through the commandments. If we who have been baptized have not been freed from ancestral sin, it is obvious that we cannot do the works of liberty either, and if we are able to do them, it is clear that we have been mystically freed from our servitude to sin,

---

[7]Rom 11.6 reads (NRSV), "But if it is by grace, it is no longer on the basis of works, otherwise grace would no longer be grace," and some New Testament manuscripts then add, "But if it is by works, it is no longer on the basis of grace, otherwise work would no longer be work," to which Mark is apparently alluding. It may be significant that the form of Rom 11.6 cited here was also known to John Chrysostom, Theodoret, and the Syriac translation of the New Testament; de Durand takes this as suggesting Mark's proximity to Antioch (SC 445, pp. 300–01 n. 1).

in accordance with what is written: "The law of the Spirit of life has set me free from the law of sin and of death" [Rom 8.2]. Because we have neglected the commandments of him who has purified us, we are controlled by sin. Whether these people demonstrate that those who have been baptized are unable to perform the commandments of liberty and, therefore, that holy Baptism is not perfect, or whether we demonstrate that the baptized have received such ability, let them acknowledge that they have been given their freedom through the grace of Christ, but have handed themselves over into the service of evil, because they do not fulfill all the commandments and because they have once again fallen under its control. Let them also accept from their own proof texts this reproach: "Let us cleanse ourselves," it says, "from every bodily and spiritual defilement" [2 Cor 7.1]. How can the person who is a slave to sin cleanse himself from every defilement, if he does not possess such liberty and ability but is instead held in the grip of sin?

If you have the ability to get control of the passions, understand that you do not possess it through your own authority but because of free will. Whatever things Holy Scripture says to us concerning purification, it exhorts us as free persons not to hold onto such defilements but to love liberty, since we have the power to incline whichever way we want, whether towards good or towards evil.

Third Question

Question: If we are made free through Baptism, why do we not see the works of liberty as do those who spiritually contend?

Answer: The pleasures that we willingly seek and our disregard for the commandments—vices that those who spiritually contend have corrected—darken our perceptions. We said earlier that a person is made free by the favor of Christ's free gift. With regard to a person's own will, where he loves there will he abide, even if he is baptized, because there free will operates without violence.[8] Thus when Christ says, "The violent take the kingdom of heaven by force" [Mt 11.12], he is speaking about one's own will, that each of us after our Baptism is constrained not to be turned towards evil but to abide in what is good. If he suffered violence at the hands of the authorities [see Jn 19.10–11], certainly God, who has freed us, can also force us not to turn towards evil.

But that is not the case now: He, through Baptism, has released us from forced servitude, and nullified sin through the cross, and laid down the commandments of liberty. He has assigned to our free will the responsibility for abiding or not abiding in his commandments. The commandments, therefore, to the extent that we show diligence in keeping them, signal our love for the one who has freed us; to the extent that they are neglected or abandoned, they demonstrate our passionate craving for pleasures.

Those who succumb to their own vain imaginings, saying, "We want to keep the commandments but cannot, held as we are under the suzerainty of sin. Consequently, we must first spiritually contend and wipe out sin in order to be able to fulfill the commandments of liberty," neither know what they are saying nor understand what they are asserting [1 Tim 1.7]; if you do not have complete liberty, you cannot fulfill the commandments either. Through what kind of spiritual contendings, therefore, do you say that you will "wipe out" sin? The "spiritual contendings" of the faithful *are* the commandments.

You will then say to me, "I cannot keep the commandments if I am not first purified through spiritual contendings." Show me, outside of the commandments, the "spiritual contendings" you are talking about, and I will be persuaded by your views. If you are talking about prayer, there is a commandment; if you are talking about fasting or keeping vigil, there is a commandment; if you are talking about sharing, or denying oneself, there is a commandment; if you

---

[8]The word here translated "without violence"—*abiaston*—also means "without being forced"; it is related to the verb that Mark used earlier when he said that neither God nor Satan "force" (*biazetai*) the will, and to the verb in Mt. 11.12 that he quotes in the next sentence.

are talking about the subjugation of thoughts, there is a commandment; if you are talking about death or the cross or any virtuous work whatsoever, there are commandments about all of them.

Thus those who have received the ability to keep the commandments because they have not turned back [Lk 9.62, 17.31] he orders to continue the fight because they are faithful—not because they have wiped out sin, but so they may no longer be turned back to sin. Moreover, these commandments, in and of themselves, do not extirpate sin—for this has taken place only through the cross—but rather safeguard the boundaries of the freedom that has been given to us. Now tell me, if you are saying that through works you are extirpating Adam's sin, how did "Christ die for our sins in accordance with the Scriptures" [1 Cor 15.3]? To this they can have no response, but merely pose questions incoherently, making everything subservient to their own suppositions and disobeying scriptural truth.

If sin is destroyed by Baptism, someone will say, why does it continue to work in the heart? We have stated the cause many times: It is not because sin has been left to do its work after Baptism, but because sin is cherished by us that we have neglected the commandments! Holy Baptism provides the perfect release; to bind oneself again because of one's evil inclinations, or to be freed from them because one keeps the commandments, is a matter of choice and free will. A longstanding thought about some pleasure or pent-up anger does not indicate that sin has been left in us, but rather signals the inclinations of our free will. Thus we have the power to defeat thoughts and, according to Scripture, "every proud obstacle raised up against the knowledge of God" [2 Cor 10.5]. An evil thought, for those who defeat it in themselves, is a sign of God's love, not a sin. The assault of the thought is not a sin; rather, the friendly association of the mind with the thought is a sin.[9] If we are not friends with

[9]Evagrius Ponticus had long since asserted that "whether or not [tempting thoughts] trouble the soul does not depend on us; but whether or not they abide, or whether or not they stir up passions does depend on us," and that "the monk's sin is agreement with the pleasure proclaimed by a thought" (*Praktikos* 6.75; A. and C. Guillaumont, ed., Sources chrétiennes 170–171 [Paris: Cerf, 1971]). See also his analysis of

the thought, why spend time with it? It is impossible for something hated by our heart to associate itself with the heart for any length of time without our complicity to do evil.

If, therefore, even a hated thought gets control of our mind—for it happens, and I will not gainsay it—nevertheless this is not a remnant of Adam's sin, but is rather the result of our post-baptismal faithlessness. When, after holy Baptism, we are able to keep all the commandments, but do not do so, then, even against our will, we are held in the grip of sin until, through repentance, we call upon God, carrying out all the commandments, and he blots out the sin caused by our faithlessness. Thus there are two sources for the operation of evil, and both are our responsibility: One operates in proportion to our failure to keep the commandments, while the other inevitably seizes hold of us because of our evildoing after Baptism; this God alone destroys by exhorting us to acts of mercy and prayer and the patient endurance of all eventualities. These very things the perfect grace given to us through Baptism provides us without our knowing it.

Fourth Question

Question: Did not Paul sin after Baptism because he was involuntarily affected by the passions? After all, he says, "I see another law at war with the law of my mind" [Rom 7.23].

Answer: This is how those who think wickedly also pervert and distort all the rest of the Scriptures. Look again at the beginning of that chapter and you will find that Saint Paul is not speaking about himself after Baptism but is, rather, assuming the character of the unbelieving and unbaptized Jews, trying to persuade them that without the grace of Christ given through Baptism it is impossible to

the evil thought into four constituents, according to which evil is found in the passion that attends the thoughts: *On thoughts* 19.

overcome sin.[10] He said, "Wretched person that I am! Who will rescue me from this body of death?" [Rom 7.24]. He then adds, "Thanks be to God through Jesus Christ our Lord!" [Rom 7.25]. Therefore he says, "The law is spiritual, but I am of the flesh, sold into slavery under sin" [Rom 7.14].

As a result, then, he also interprets everything about the Law spiritually, not wishing the Jews to be under the Law but under grace [Rom 6.14], which is the spiritual law inscribed in us. If, then, we follow closely the words of Saint Paul, "interpreting spiritual things for those who are spiritual" [1 Cor 2.13], we can, through figurative representations, learn the truth: how matters pertaining to the Law and the temple and sacrifices are fulfilled in us who have mystically received the grace of the Spirit through Baptism. He said that we are a temple of the Holy Spirit [1 Cor 3.16, 6.19] and commands us "to offer spiritual sacrifices" [1 Pet 2.5]; he is speaking of someone who is inwardly and not outwardly a Jew, and is saying that circumcision of the heart takes place spiritually, not literally [Rom 2.28–29]. Christ, the heavenly Lawgiver, through the Spirit has inscribed this same spiritual law for the faithful, "not on tablets of stone but on tablets of human hearts" [2 Cor 3.3]. Thus, just as he said that these things are inward, so too, it seems to me, each of the things that we have talked about—or, rather, each thing that takes place—takes place in a figurative way.

Since we do not yet firmly believe in Christ nor consider ourselves obligated to all his commandments nor have denied ourselves in accord with what he said [Lk 9.23], we are ignorant of the aforementioned mysteries that we have received through Baptism. When we condemn ourselves for our lack of faith and sincerely believe

[10]The interpretation of this passage, and in particular the question of how many literary personae can be identified in it, was a topic of lively discussion by the Fathers. The two best-represented strategies for explaining Paul's meaning are (1) taking him as speaking on behalf of the human race as a whole, and (2) taking him as speaking in the character of an unredeemed person. As it happens, Augustine held both positions at different points in his life: see his *Retractationes* 1.23.1; for other examples, see K.H. Schelkle, *Paulus, Lehrer der Väter: die altkirchliche Auslegung von Römer 1–11*, 2nd ed. (Düsseldorf: Patmos, 1959).

in him through all the commandments, then, undertaking the aforesaid matters in ourselves, we truly confess that holy Baptism is perfect[11] and that in it the grace of Christ is abundantly poured out. That grace afterwards waits for our obedience and expects us to keep the commandments, which, through grace, we have already received the ability to do.

Thus, those of us who have not yet kept the commandments of liberty have not yet laid hold of free Jerusalem, "for the Jerusalem above is free, and she is the mother of us all" [Gal 4.26]; she regenerates us through "the washing of rebirth" [Titus 3.5]. But we are still on the road—or perhaps while we travel, we have wandered off the path, for quarreling over things about which we are ignorant and contradicting the truth are detours on the path and do not take us in a straight line. Thus blessed Paul, seeing us loiter on our ascent[12] to perfection, says, "Run in such a way that you may attain [the prize]" [1 Cor 9.24]. If we have not yet reached the city, when will we lay eyes on the temple and, going inside, gain access to the altar?

Why am I talking about the city and the temple and the altar, when we do not even pass by "the wild animals that live among the reeds," which the prophet implored God to rebuke [Ps 68.30] in order that the firstborn of the sacrifices—which the inward Jew [Rom 2.29] has been commanded to offer in sacrifice—might not become prey caught by wild beasts? Or do you think that "the Jew" is only "inward" because of what Paul says, while the temple has not yet been built by David, nor has the mercy-seat yet been constructed by him, but rather is going to be constructed by you?

This is what you are openly bellowing, you who say that by your spiritual struggles you have abolished Adam's sin and that this has not come about through the grace of Christ which exists in us inwardly through Baptism, but will be seen when, successfully reaching the end of the road of the commandments, we present our

[11]See the First Question.
[12]In Greek, "ascent" (*anodos*) is related etymologically to "road" (*hodos*) and "travel" (*hodeuein*).

innate thoughts as sacrificial offerings to Christ the High Priest—
sacrifices that are whole and sound, not sacrifices that have been
gnawed by wild beasts! In fact, most thoughts that deviate from the
path become the prey of wild beasts—I am talking about the need
for the patient endurance of afflictions—and, leaping off the straight
path, they wander into trackless areas, all the while blaming others
instead of themselves.

Hardly any of our thoughts keep to the straight path, and when
they do it is only because they are safeguarded through prayer,
wounded by temptations, bound by faith; in this way they reach
the city and the temple and offer up their sacrifice. The city is that
joyous and lawful discernment in Christ which, when she adminis-
ters things in a faithful manner, brings both peace and responsible
living, but when she fails to do so is handed over to her enemies, to
her destruction. The temple is the sacred dwelling place constructed
by God for the soul and body, while the altar is the foundation of
hope in this temple; here a thought first-begotten in every situation
is brought forward as a sacrifice by the mind, like a firstborn animal
for the forgiveness of the one making the offering, provided that the
offering is unblemished when he offers it.[13]

This temple also has a curtained inner area "where Jesus, a forerunner on our behalf, has entered" [Heb 6.19–20], and, according
to the Apostle, dwells in us: "Do you not realize that Christ dwells
within you?—unless, indeed, you fail to meet the test" [2 Cor 13.5].
This inner area is the innermost and hidden and pure recess of the
heart; unless a universal and spiritual hope opens it by means of
God's grace, it is not possible to know with certainty the one who
dwells within, nor is it possible to know whether our reasonable
sacrifices [Rom 12.1] have been accepted or not. Just as in the former
times of Israel fire destroyed the remains [1 Kings 18.38; 2 Chr 7.1], so
too does it happen here: When the faithful heart opens up by means

---

[13]Mark's "firstborn thoughts" are similar to the "first thoughts" described by
Evagrius Ponticus, in his *Thoughts* 7; see also Evagrius, *On Prayer* 126: "The one who
prays is he who dedicates to God every first-fruit of his mind."

of the aforementioned hope, the heavenly high priest accepts the firstborn thoughts of the mind and destroys them with godly fire. With regard to this the Lord said, "I came to bring fire to the earth, and how I wish it were already kindled!" [Lk 12.49]. We said that "firstborn thoughts" are not those that arise through some kind of afterthought of the heart, but rather are those that are immediately offered to Christ when they first appear and make their appearance known—for those that a person offers because they are cluttering up his mind Holy Scripture has called "lame and blind and monstrous" [Deut 15.21], and thus they are not acceptable to God our Lord and Master.

Thus the fact that even after Baptism we are responsible for every evil idea has already been demonstrated through scriptural proofs, but if it is also necessary to establish this through ordinary procedures, once again it will be said: Friend, you say that after Baptism you are controlled by Adam's sin without its being your responsibility, and you claim that you can extirpate this sin through your own spiritual struggles. Know without a doubt that you contradict yourself and stumble over your own words. If you say "evil thoughts are Adam's sin," learn from Saint Paul that, having clothed yourself with Christ through Baptism [Gal 3.27], you have the power and the weaponry [Rom 13.12] to destroy them—"for the weapons of our warfare," he says, "are not physical, but rather have divine power to destroy strongholds, destroying thoughts and every proud obstacle raised up against the knowledge of God" [2 Cor 10.4–5]. If you have the power to oppose them, however, and do not destroy them when they first attack, it is clear that you delight in them because of your faithlessness and have joined forces with them. You are responsible for such an action, not Adam.

Fifth Question

Question: How can someone, "because of faithlessness," "delight" in thoughts or "join forces" with them if he has shut himself up in his cell, and every day fasts and practices abstinence and poverty and hospitality, and keeps vigils and sleeps on the ground and prays, and endures numerous afflictions such as these?

Answer: You are right to say that by practicing "numerous afflictions such as these" he "endures" them, for if we conscientiously and joyfully carry out some of the aforementioned virtues without being overwhelmed by them, there is no room in our minds to take delight in thoughts, for it is impossible for the person who is grieved by bodily sufferings not to meet with assaults to the same degree that he grieves, and be comforted by dislike for sufferings. If such a person did not wish this, he would not be afflicted by sufferings. We suffer this way because we do not willingly endure the good things that are to come but only fearfully endure the temptations now assailing us. As a result, we think that our own evil deed is a sin, while we say that its antecedent thought is the work of someone else. It is impossible for those who believe that this work is not their own, but belongs to someone else, to turn away from it. Thus it is when some disgusting thought, without being harbored in the mind, and being hated as a thief, unexpectedly inflicts itself upon us, forcibly overpowers the mind, and takes possession of it.

Nevertheless, understand good and well that even this thought has its origins in us, or indeed after Baptism we surrender ourselves to some evil thought until we put it into practice and, on account of this, become liable for it, contrary to our way of thinking, or we willingly seize on some "seeds of evil" and, on account of this, evil fortifies its position: the thought that, because of the seeds, has us in its grip does not depart until we hurl away these seeds, while the thought that resides with us on account of the evil we have put into practice is driven away only when we offer to God labors worthy of repentance. Thus I for my part do not attribute this sin to Adam, but rather to the person who has the seeds and puts the evil into practice.

If you say to me that even in these two cases the thought is pre-eminent and you look to see what is the cause of these two, I will also say to you that *you* are the one who has the power to purify yourself of its attacks; and, not having done so, you have continued to join forces with the thought until you put it into practice. But if, on account of the weakness of your mind, you have been completely unable to cast off this thought before putting it into practice, how, after you have done so, will you claim that you have extirpated it, especially when, on account of your actions, it has fortified its position and has justifiably laid hold of you? If you assert that, with God's help, you have extirpated it, consider for a moment that even before you had put the thought into practice, God would have helped you, if you had wanted it. And when you perceive that his help for you has filled your whole heart, you will know for a fact that grace has not come as though by transfusion from outside, but rather has been given to you inwardly through Baptism, and now works within you to the extent that you, in turn, hate the thought and turn away from it.

Thus, having freed us from all compulsion, Christ has not prevented thoughts from assaulting our hearts, so that some thoughts, hated by the heart, might suddenly disappear, while others, to the extent that we love them, might perdure, in order that Christ's grace might be shown and what the human will loves might be demonstrated: labors, on account of grace, or thoughts, on account of the pleasures they bring. And let us not be astonished that we are forcefully possessed not only by the thoughts we love but also by those we hate, so that they become like some evil kin, and their assaults work together with our evil desires: Each desire in due course hands over to its neighbor the person who has long served it, so that he is led away by the latter, even perhaps against his will, while already being forcibly dragged by habit towards the former.

Who, filled with self-conceit, will be able to escape arrogance? Or who, filled with sleep and delighting in self-indulgence, will not be seized with the thought to commit sexual sin? Or who, handing himself over to greed, is not constricted by a lack of compassion?[14] How will those who are deprived of all these things against their will not be angered and driven to distraction? Thus we ought to believe that it is the fault of each of us that we are controlled by sin, for we have been freed from forced servitude "because the law of the Spirit of life has set me free from the law of sin and death" [Rom 8.2].

We consequently have it in our power—we who have heard and learned the precepts of the Spirit—to conduct ourselves according to the flesh or according to the spirit. It is impossible for those who have fallen in love with people's praise and with fleshly indulgences to conduct themselves according to the spirit, and it is impossible for those who innately prefer the things to come over things in the present to live according to the flesh. Thus it is essential from now on that we who have strayed far from the path hate people's praise and bodily indulgences, through which evil thoughts spring up, even against our own will, and make it our intention to say with the Lord what the prophet uttered: "Do I not hate those who hate you, Lord, and waste away before your enemies? I hate them with a perfect hatred; they are enemies to me" [Ps 139.21–22].

There is no doubt that evil thoughts, which prevent God's will from taking effect, are his enemies, since he "desires all people to be saved and to come to the knowledge of the truth" [1 Tim 2.4], while evil thoughts delude us by means of evil desires and prevent our salvation. Concerning such thoughts, the Lord said that they proceed, not from Adam, but from the heart, and on account of this defile a person [Mt 15.18]; it is clear that they proceed not from a faithful but rather from a self-conceited heart. "How can you believe," he says, "you who accept glory from people and do not seek the glory that comes from God alone?" [Jn 5.44].

---

[14]Evagrius traced some similar genealogies for various temptations; see his *Thoughts* 1.

When we hate self-conceit, therefore, and put our faith in that hatred in every situation, fastening every thought to it through heartfelt and single-minded hope, then just as in the beginning of faith given to us through Baptism, when the body of Christ became food for the believer, so too the well-grounded and pure mind, by means of spiritual hope and the denial of the thoughts, becomes the food of Jesus, who said, "My food is to do the will of my Father" [Jn 4.34]. What is the will of the Father? "He desires all people to be saved and to come to the knowledge of the truth," as Paul says [1 Tim 2.4]. By "truth" he means that truth that is discovered in accordance with spiritual hope, as we said earlier; this spiritual hope is not believed in through hearsay [Rom 10.17] but because of the working of the Holy Spirit, which is, according to Scripture, "the assurance of things hoped for" [Heb 11.1]. For there is "faith through hearsay" and there is "faith that is the assurance of things hoped for." The unbaptized or self-conceited person cannot "come to the knowledge of the truth." First of all, it is mystically given to those who have been baptized in the Catholic Church and inwardly dwells in them.

Would that, in proportion to their keeping the commandments and their spiritual hope, it were thus revealed to those who believe in the Lord, who said, "Rivers of living water shall flow from the belly of the person who believes in me, as Scripture has said" [Jn 7.38]! "He said this," it says, "about the Spirit, which those who believed in him were about to receive" [Jn 7.39]. On account of this we believe that through Baptism one mystically receives liberation and purification, in accordance with what [the Apostle] says: "But now you have been washed, now you have been purified, now you have been sanctified" [1 Cor 6.11]. He wrote such things to the Corinthians, who had not yet been purified in accordance with spiritual hope through the renunciation of thoughts and had not yet been sanctified through the working of the Spirit that takes place in the heart. He was writing, rather, to those who were still evil and unjust and fraudulent—and they were all these things towards their brothers!—in order that he might demonstrate that those who have been baptized have mystically received purification and sanctification as a gift from Christ. Each person is tempted by his own lack of faith, "being lured by his own desire and enticed by it" [Jas 1.14], as it is written: "Then when desire has conceived, it gives birth to sin, and sin, when it is fully grown, gives birth to death" [Jas 1.15].

Sinful thought, therefore, comes from our own lustful desire, and this sin finds its fulfillment in action done at its behest, which Scripture terms "death." That the grace given by the Spirit, which, according to the Lord, teaches us all truth [Jn 14.26, 16.13], is in us by means of our Baptism, know again from Scripture and from facts. Look first at what blessed Peter says to the crowd in Acts: "Repent and be baptized," he says, "every one of you, in the name of our Lord Jesus Christ, so that your sins may be forgiven, and you will receive the gift of the Holy Spirit" [Acts 2.38].

Do you understand, then, how through Baptism the forgiveness of sins and the gift of the Holy Spirit are given in proportion to one's faith? Insofar as someone lacks faith, he is immediately held in the grip of sin. Look also at how Saint Paul accuses the twelve men in Ephesus who were baptized outside of the faith and says, "Did you receive the Holy Spirit when you became believers?" They said to him, "No, we have not even heard that there is a Holy Spirit." He said to them, "Into what then were you baptized?" and they said, "Into John's baptism." Paul said, "John baptized with the baptism of repentance, telling the people to believe in the one who was to come after him, that is, Jesus." When the men heard this, they were baptized in the name of the Lord Jesus. And when Paul laid hands on them, the Holy Spirit came upon them [Acts 19.1–7].

Are you convinced now that the Holy Spirit is immediately given at Baptism to those who are steadfast in the faith, while it is not given to those who lack faith or whose faith is heretical, even if they are baptized?[15] That it is we who grieve the Spirit and extinguish it in

[15]Those who are "steadfast in the faith" (*bebaiopistoi*) have faith (*pistis*), whereas the twelve at Ephesus, baptized without the Holy Spirit, were baptized "outside the faith" (*apistōs*), literally, "faith-lessly," like those here who "lack faith" (*apistois*) or "whose faith is heretical" (*kakopistois*).

us, learn from the same Apostle when he says, "Do not extinguish the Spirit" [1 Thess 5.19]; and again, "Do not grieve the Holy Spirit, in whom you were sealed for the day of redemption" [Eph 4.30]. We have cited these witnesses not in order to say that every person who is baptized and has received grace suffers no change after that and no longer has need of repentance, but rather to say that at Baptism, in accordance with Christ's gift, perfect grace is given to us as a gift in order that we may fulfill all the commandments. Afterwards, to the extent that each person who has mystically received grace falls short and does not perfectly carry out the commandments, he is controlled by sin—which is not Adam's sin, but rather the sin of someone who is negligent and careless because he has received the power to do the work but has not successfully completed it.[16] He has fallen short because of his lack of faith, and lack of faith is not someone else's sin, but belongs to the person who lacks faith. This sin afterwards becomes the mother and begetter of every kind of sin.

Thus, whether we wish to be perfected quickly or slowly, we are fully[17] obligated to put our faith in Christ and fulfill all his commandments, having received from him the power to fulfill them—and this not as though we were obliged to them one by one, fulfilling every single commandment, but rather, taking them as a whole, succinctly accomplishing each individually and, by doing this, accomplishing all of them. Some commandments are more fundamental and incorporate within themselves a large multitude of other commandments. We are obligated to *this* spiritual struggle alone: to struggle against our own lack of faith and not to neglect the all-embracing commandments; through these the grace that has been given to us is revealed to be at work. Saint Paul prays that this may be accomplished in us when he says, "For this reason I bow my

---

[16]To "carry out" or "fulfill" the commandments in Greek is literally "to work" them (*ergazesthai*, *ergasia ergon*, "work"), a concept that Mark works here and in the following paragraphs, where grace is "at work" (*energōs*) in the believer, the Holy Spirit "works [*energei*] its fruits in us," the believer is "empowered" (*energeitai*) by the fruits of the Spirit, and "discovers a certain spiritual activity [*energeian*]."

[17]*Teleiōs*, "perfectly."

knees to the Father of our Lord Jesus Christ . . . that the Lord may grant you through his Spirit the power to be strengthened in your inner being, and that Christ may dwell in your hearts through faith with complete confidence and understanding" [Eph 3.14–17].

Now would be the time, as we said earlier, to back up our testimony with an accounting of facts. See, to the extent that we believers fulfill Christ's commandments, to that same extent the Holy Spirit also works its fruits in us. The fruits of the Spirit, according to Saint Paul, are "love, joy, peace, patience, kindness, generosity, faithfulness, gentleness, self-control" [Gal 5.22–23]. Who, then, is so completely uninitiated in these activities [of the Spirit] after Baptism that he could deny having received the grace of the Spirit at Baptism? Who, once again, is continuously empowered by these fruits each day who has not yet fulfilled the commandments so that he can say, "I am perfect or unchanging"? From which it is clear that grace is perfect in us, but we are imperfect because of our failure to keep the commandments. Thus Holy Baptism is perfect vis-à-vis us, but we are imperfect vis-à-vis it.

You, then, my good man, who have been baptized in Christ, give yourself only to that work which you have been given the power to do, and prepare yourself to manifest him who dwells within you; in this way the Lord will also manifest himself spiritually, in accordance with his promise, as the Apostle himself knows: "The Lord is the Spirit, and where the Spirit of the Lord is, there is freedom" [2 Cor 3.17]. Then you will understand what has been said: "The kingdom of heaven is within you" [Lk 17.21]. It is also imperative to understand that those who partially keep the commandments enter the kingdom in proportion to the way they keep the commandments, while those who wish to reach perfection must keep all the commandments in an all-embracing way.

The renunciation of one's life—that is, death—embraces all of the commandments. To the extent that someone lives for the body and thus inadequately accomplishes this renunciation, he will be unable to withstand assault on account of the aforesaid inadequacy. Thus, if one of the faithful lives a good and faithful life by keeping the commandments, he correspondingly discovers a certain spiritual activity; let him believe that he has already received the power associated with this spiritual activity just as through Baptism he has received the grace of the Spirit, the source of all good things—I mean not only the source of hidden and spiritual things, but also the author and originator of all visible virtues.

And let none of the virtuous suppose that he has done anything good solely by means of his own ability, because the good person, says the Word, does not "produce good" on his own, but rather "from the good treasury of his heart" [Lk 6.45]. By "treasury" he means the Holy Spirit, hidden within the heart of the faithful, for "the kingdom of heaven is like treasure hidden in a field, which a person found and hid; then in his joy he went and sold all that he had and bought that field" [Mt 13.44]. This completely accords with what has already been said, for the person who knows with certainty that he has Christ hidden within him at Baptism, as the Apostle says [Col 2.12, 3.3], has cast away all the things of this world and remains within his own heart, protecting it with all diligence and seeking to leave this life in accordance with the proverb [Prov 4.23].

Therefore, one must not imagine that one extirpates Adam's sin, or even one's own sins committed after Baptism, except through Christ, "for he himself," it says, "[is at work in us], enabling us to will and to work for his good pleasure" [Phil 2.13].[18] This added phrase "for his good pleasure" shows that his "good pleasure" lies in the virtues that we do, but doing these virtues or extirpating sin is not possible without God. And what was said, "Without me you can do nothing" [Jn 15.5], and "You did not choose me; rather, I chose you" [Jn 15.16], amount to the same thing. So too, perhaps, one should understand, "All things came into being through him, and without him not one thing that has come into being came into being" [Jn 1.3], if "all things" includes things pertaining to us. Therefore the prophet did not say, "*From Jerusalem* the kings will bring you gifts

[18]In Phil 2.13 Paul says that it is God who is at work.

for your temple," which is probable and occurs, but rather the opposite: "*From your temple* kings will bear gifts to you *in Jerusalem*" [Ps 68.29]. Thus for each person a most noble[19] mind first receives from the temple of the heart good proposals from the indwelling Christ and applies them to that virtuous way of life which the Psalmist calls "Jerusalem," and then once again offers them to Christ, who, through his good care and concern, gave them in the first place.

In saying these things, we are not precluding what is to come, but are acknowledging that we have received the power to keep the commandments and have been freed from the chains of death, and thus are obligated to keep the commandments from now on. If we do not keep the commandments, the grace given to us is not revealed. How are we, who are dead because of sin, able to do good on our own if he himself has not given us life through "the washing and rebirth" and has not given us the gift of the grace of the Spirit [Titus 3.5–7]? From this we know that the grace of the Spirit that has been given to us as a gift is perfect and has been given to us so we may fulfill all the commandments. This grace receives no increase from us, but herself provides increase to us by means of growth in Christ, empowering us until death to do her works "until all of us come to the unity of the faith and of the knowledge of the Son of God, to maturity, to the measure of the full stature of Christ" [Eph 4.13], which accords with the spiritual course that we spoke of earlier.

PART TWO

Sixth Question

Question: Whom, then, does the baptized person mystically receive? Christ, or the Holy Spirit? Sometimes you have said that Christ dwells within the baptized, while at other times you have said it is the Holy Spirit.

---

[19]*Basilikōtatos*, that is, "most kingly" (*basileus*: "king").

Answer: We receive the Holy Spirit through Baptism, but since the Holy Spirit is also called "Spirit of God" and "Spirit of Christ," we receive through the Spirit both the Father and the Son.

Seventh Question

Question: So the Spirit is the Trinity?

Answer: We are not saying that the Spirit, as one person, is the Trinity; but since the Spirit is not separated from the Father and the Son, we acknowledge the Trinity in it, according to one and the same divinity. For just as the Son and the Spirit are in the Father, and again, just as the Father and the Spirit are in the Son, so too are the Father and the Son in the Spirit—not by a confusion of the three hypostases, but rather through the union of the single and selfsame will and divinity. As a result, we name either the Father as a single entity, or the Son, or the Spirit; we name the Trinity with one name, in accordance with the reasoning we have already given.

Eighth Question

Question: How does Scripture say that Jerusalem is "heavenly" [Heb 12.22], while you have said that it is "in the heart"?

Answer: Not only Jerusalem. We know also that whatever other good things the righteous are going to receive at the time of the resurrection will take place on high, but the foretaste of these and the first-fruits are at work spiritually from this point on in the hearts of those who are steadfast in the faith; as a result, fully assured concerning the things to come, let us pay no attention to all the things of the present and love God until the day we die. Thus he did not say, "You are going to draw near," but rather, "You have come to Mount Zion and to the city of the living God, the heavenly Jerusalem" [Heb 12.22].

All of us, then, are capable of receiving these things from the time of our Baptism, but, out of our number, the only ones considered worthy to do so are those who are steadfast in the faith, those who, through the love of Christ, die each day [1 Cor 15.31]—that is, those who transcend every conception of life here on earth and who give no thought to anything but the time when they will attain the perfect love of Christ, which is an inner opening of the heart "where Jesus, a forerunner on our behalf, has entered" [Heb 6.20].

Saint Paul, seeking to make this central, said, "but I press on to make it my own, because I have been made Christ's own (that is, in order that I may love because I have been loved)" [Phil 3.12]. After making this love his own, he no longer allowed himself to think about anything else, neither things that afflict this body of ours, nor the wonders of creation, but refrained from almost all thought, not allowing himself to be deprived of the activity of the Spirit for even one hour. He made clear whatever things he was renouncing on account of the love of the Spirit and said, "Who will separate us from the love of Christ? Will hardships, or distress, or persecution, or famine, or nakedness, or danger, or sword?" [Rom 8.35]. And again, "I am convinced," he says, "that neither death, nor life, nor angels, nor rulers, nor authorities, nor powers, nor things present, nor things to come, nor height, nor depth, nor anything else in all creation, will be able to separate us from the love of God in Christ Jesus our Lord" [Rom 8.38–39]. To the extent that he allowed himself to think about none of these things, he persevered in his intentions.

Ninth Question

Question: How could you say a little while ago that the Spirit perfectly dwells within us and accepts no increase from us, while the Apostle says the opposite, that we have the first fruits of the Spirit [Rom 8.23]? He does not say that the Spirit is perfect.

Answer: When the Apostle spoke of "first fruits," he was not suggesting that they are some part of the whole, nor that they are some portion of the Spirit, for the Spirit can be neither divided nor altered. He was pointing out, rather, that we are worthy of the Spirit, not that we have the capacity for doing all the work of the Spirit, except through the perfect commandment, that is, through death—if indeed death for the sake of the truth of Christ is also one of God's commandments. Thus, since he is perfect, just like the sun, he imposes his own perfect and simple and equal grace on everyone; afterwards, each person, to the extent that his eye has been purified, to that same extent he also receives at Baptism the solar light.

In the same way, at Baptism the Holy Spirit also makes those who believe in it capable of receiving all of its activities and gifts. Afterwards, however, it does not bestow[20] its gifts equally, but gives to each person what he deserves, in proportion to the way he keeps the commandments, insofar as he bears witness by means of his good works and demonstrates the extent of his faith in Christ [Rom 12.3]. Therefore the Apostle says, "God has sent the Spirit of his Son into our hearts, crying, 'Abba, Father!'" [Gal 4.6]; and, "That very Spirit bears witness with our spirit that we are children of God" [Rom 8.16].

Inasmuch as no one extirpates from himself Adam's sin, but rather Christ alone does this in proportion to one's faith in him, listen to what the Apostle says: "Christ died for our sins in accordance with the Scriptures" [1 Cor 15.3]; and again, "God proves his love for us in that while we were still sinners Christ died for us" [Rom 5.8]; and again, "We have been buried with him through Baptism so that, just as Christ was raised from the dead, so we too might walk in newness of life" [Rom 6.4]; and, "Whoever has died is justified and freed from sin" [Rom 6.7]; and, "By grace you have been saved, and not by works, so that no one may boast" [Eph 2.8–9]; and again, "For once you were darkness, but now you are light in the Lord. Live as

---

[20]*Energei*; see n. 5 above. The Spirit bestows its gifts in proportion to the way someone keeps (*ergasias*) the commandments, a crucial point for Mark.

children of the light" [Eph 5.8]; and again, "You are children not of the slave but of the free woman. For freedom Christ has set us free" [Gal 4.31–5:1]; and again, "[As servants of God, live] as free persons and do not use your freedom as a pretext for evil" [1 Pet 2.16].

Do you see how Scripture calls the spiritual struggles that you say extirpate sin works of "newness" and of "freedom" and of "light"? It also clearly shows that the errors you call "the sin of Adam" are errors due to free will, for Scripture talks about "using your freedom as a pretext for evil" [1 Pet 2.16], and "grieving the Holy Spirit" [Eph 4.30], and "enacting the desires of the flesh and of the senses" [Eph 2.3], and "having started with the Spirit, are you now ending with the flesh?" [Gal 3.3], and "we are debtors not to the flesh, to live according to the flesh" [Rom 8.12]. Holy Scripture recognizes that these verses and others like them show that it is up to us whether we do them or do not do them. Therefore it is not Satan, nor the sin of Adam, but us that Scripture blames.

If you wish, pay attention and I will sum everything up for you. You say that the forms that thoughts give rise to are the sin of Adam. But look: Paul clearly and obviously charges us with the responsibility for this perversion when he says, "Do not be conformed to this world, but be transformed by the renewing of your minds" [Rom 12.2]. If these things are not due to our own will, but are caused by the tyranny of Satan and are the fault of Adam's sin, why then are we blamed by Scripture if we are unwillingly controlled[21] by sin and tyrannized by Satan? Are we going to be punished without cause? Or perhaps, as far as you are concerned, God is unjust, since he ordered nature to be this way and asks us to do things beyond our ability? But this is not the case. God forbid!

Now it is my turn to ask you a question, and I want you to give me an answer [cf. Job 38.3?]: Are we obligated to offer to God each day

---

[21]*Energoumenoi* (see notes 5 and 8 above). In monastic thinking, *energeiai*, supernatural "influences, agencies, or activities," can be of angels or of demons, hence "possession." Thus human beings can actively "carry out" or "fulfill" (*energazesthai*) the commandments or can be passively controlled (*energoumenoi)* by demonic influences.

whatever ability for godliness nature gives us? Yes or no? Undoubtedly you will say "Yes" to me, since God has given us this gift by nature and in accordance with his power has laid down commandments. Therefore the good we daily offer to him is a daily debt gratefully offered. Show me, then, the recompense for past sin, either yours or Adam's, and I will tell you that not only are you not able to show this, but you are also unable to make perfect recompense each day. And why is this obvious? Because one is never discovered with the same virtues. Insofar as you advance in virtue today, to that same extent you will be rebuked as a debtor for what you have failed to do as you demonstrate the abilities that nature has given you. It has been shown through daily progress that yesterday's deficiency is not because of nature but because of will, and on account of this we are controlled by sin.

Tenth Question

Question: Grant that it is as you say. Nevertheless, there is one thing I do know: if Adam had not transgressed, I myself would not be tempted by evil assaults.

Answer: You have not gotten even this right. Not being tempted by evil assaults indicates a nature unaffected by sin, not human nature.[22] If we and Adam share a single nature, it necessarily follows that his nature accords with ours, and ours with his. Therefore let that first human person himself convince you that he was neither unaffected by sin nor particularly inclined toward evil, but was, rather, inclined to follow his own will; he was not forced to transgress the commandment because of his nature, but rather wanted to do so of his own free will. Thus just as Adam was susceptible to Satan's assault and had the power to obey or not to obey, so too do we.

[22]Mark's claim here can be expressed by borrowing from the categories used by Augustine at *City of God* 22.30: Mark is claiming that there is an important difference between "not sinning" and "not being able to sin." So even if Adam had not sinned, that would not mean that we would therefore not be able to sin.

Eleventh Question

Question: Perhaps now I can tolerate what you are saying because you are not doing away with Satan's assault.

Answer: In what I have previously said, I have not ever "done away with" Satan's assault. I know for a fact that Job was tempted by the Devil [Job 1.12, 2.6] and that Scripture says, "Our struggle is not against blood and flesh but against the rulers, against the authorities, against the cosmic powers of this present dark age, against the spiritual forces of evil" [Eph 6.12]; and again, "Resist the Devil, and he will flee from you" [Jas 4.7]; and elsewhere, "Like a roaring lion, your adversary the Devil prowls around, looking for someone to gobble up" [1 Pet 5.8].

But since you people believe that your evil thoughts are not your responsibility but are the responsibility of certain others, saying sometimes that they are the sin of Adam, while at other times saying they are due to Satan himself, and at still other times calling them "the assault of Satan," we say that Adam's sin is something altogether different again, as is Satan's sin, as is "the assault of Satan," and our evil thoughts are something altogether different too, even if they have as their starting point an "assault." Satan is the very substance and being of the Devil, which even tried to tempt the Lord [Mk 1.13]. The sin of Adam is the transgression of the commandment by the first human being [Rom 5.14]. The assault of Satan is the manifestation in a single thought[23] of an evil deed; this manifestation, along with the deed, comes creeping up on the mind on account of our lack of faith.

We have received a commandment not to worry [Mt 6.25–33], but to keep a complete watch over our own hearts and to seek the kingdom of heaven, which is within us [Lk 17.21]. When our mind

---

[23]*Monologistos*, an important term for Mark; see Lampe, 882B, who suggests two definitions: "of single thought" and "in thought alone." As Mark uses the term, it is often difficult to distinguish between the two meanings.

withdraws from the heart and from the aforementioned search, it immediately makes room for the Devil's assault and becomes susceptible to evil suggestions. But not even then does the Devil have the power to set our thoughts in motion, but since he shows us no quarter, he coercively introduces every kind of evil thought and allows us to think nothing good.

The Devil has only the power, by the use of thoughts alone, to suggest evil deeds to the forefront of our mind, in order to test our inward disposition. Where will our thoughts incline? Towards what the Devil suggests, or towards what the Lord commands? These are antithetical to one another. As a result, with regard to the things we love, we immediately rouse our thoughts towards the Devil's suggestions and are eager to have our minds keep company with what has been suggested. With regard to the things we hate, unable to continue associating with them, we hate even the assault itself. (But even if this hated assault persists—it does happen—it does not happen because of a recent disposition; rather, the assault gets confirmed through an old predisposition.) Thus it stops in its tracks without advancing and is concentrated in a single thought, prevented by the heart's disgust for it from progressing into a multitude of distracting thoughts and passions.

Such one-sided manifestations of nature, when they are hated by the person observing them, are not able by means of their own force to carry away the mind into the passion of a multitude of considerations except through the heart's love of sensual pleasure alone. Consequently, if we abstain completely from love of sensual pleasure, not even the manifestation of predispositions concentrated in a single thought will be able to harm us any longer, even if it does condemn our conscience to uncertainty about the things to come. When the mind recognizes the ineffectual opposition of the predisposition and confesses to God its original fault, even this temptation is removed.

And once again the mind has the power to attend to the heart and through prayer to safeguard and preserve it, attempting to enter into the heart's inner chambers, which are undisturbed by the passions; within those precincts no winds comprised of evil thoughts violently shove both body and soul towards the cliffs of sensual pleasure and throw them down into bitumen pits [Gen 14.10], nor is there some kind of wide and spacious highway strewn with the words and designs of worldly wisdom and enticing those who follow its path, even if they are very intelligent. The pure inner chambers of the soul and the home of Christ admit of no unvarnished thought imported from this age, whether rational or irrational, only the three qualities of which the Apostle spoke: faith, hope, love [1 Cor 13.13]. Thus someone who is a lover of the truth and who wants his heart to suffer afflictions cannot be driven out by predispositions that accord with the sequence of events that I described earlier; rather, he can turn his attention to his heart and advance into the interior and draw near to God alone, in order not to shrink from the afflictions brought on by diligence and perseverance. It is impossible for the person who pays attention to distracting thoughts and carnal pleasures not to suffer afflictions, but circumscribing himself each day, not only on the outside but also inside, he ponders those things he does both in thought and in deed.

From this we know that the assault that comes in a single thought is coercive, because it persists even though it is hated, and we know that easy familiarity with thoughts that come upon one is freely chosen. Those who do not sin in a fashion similar to Adam's transgression [Rom 5.14] also demonstrate this: Although they are unable to prevent the assault, they completely repudiate easy familiarity with it and thus avoid the accompanying evil desire.

Twelfth Question

Question: Therefore have we not by necessity received Adam's transgression, that is, sin occasioned by our thought?

Answer: It is not Adam's transgression but rather a reproach directed at each of us for our love of pleasure. But not even then have we inherited the transgression since, if that were the case, we would all be transgressors because of what we had inherited by necessity and would not be accused by God of being transgressors because of what was inherently due to our own nature. But this is not the case at present: We do not all transgress the commandment, nor do all of us keep it. From this it is clear that transgression is not the result of necessity but is the result of the love of pleasure. If you say that the Lord came because of this transgression, why did he not remove it through Baptism? No, it is still a fact that each of us now has it in his power to transgress or not to transgress.

Thus, since this transgression is something freely chosen, as has been demonstrated, no one has inherited it by necessity but we have, as a result of it, inherited death, which is compulsory. Death is alienation from God. When the first human being died, that is, when he was alienated from God, we too were unable to live in God. On account of this the Lord came in order to give us life through the washing of new birth [Titus 3.5] and to reconcile us to God [Rom 5.10; 2 Cor 5.18], which he has done. Therefore, we have not inherited transgression, since even Adam himself was not forced to transgress, but did so willingly. We have by necessity inherited death, since death by necessity prevailed over Adam. Death ruled even over those whose sins were not like the transgression of Adam [Rom 5.14].

Thirteenth Question

Question: Let us grant that Adam transgressed willingly and, on account of this, since we share the same nature with him, that we too fall willingly. But was not the first assault forced on him?

Answer: Yes, indeed, that assault was forced on him. But that assault is neither sin nor righteousness; rather, it is a condemnation of what we choose to do out of our own free will. Thus God allows us to encounter assault in order to show that those who incline toward keeping the commandment wear crowns of victory as the faithful, while those who incline toward pleasure are condemned as faithless. We also need to understand this: we are judged "approved" or "reprobate" not simply because of each turn we make; when we are approved by means of the assaults we endure throughout our life in the flesh, as victors and vanquished, as those who fall and are raised up again, as those who keep to the path and also wander off it, then, on the day we leave this world, all of us are counted up together and are judged accordingly. Therefore the assault is not sin. God forbid!

If matters seem to indicate that we are by necessity compelled by a single thought, we have nevertheless received in the Lord the power to do spiritual work; it is up to us, when an idea first enters our head, to immediately test whether it is harmful or helpful and to reject or accept thoughts, which multiply not by necessity but because of our disposition. Let us propose, as you have, that these thoughts present themselves out of necessity and inheritance. Why then does Holy Scripture condemn us for our own evil thoughts? Or how can we shut out those thoughts that harass us out of necessity and inheritance? If you say to me, "We can do this through the grace that we received at Baptism, in accordance with the Scriptures"—understand that even so we ourselves are still responsible, because we have power from God to shut out these thoughts when they first appear and spring up. If someone says that someone else is responsible for his own sins, not only does he sin without restraint but he also blasphemes against God, as if God had without reason allowed war to be waged against human beings.

Fourteenth Question

Question: Why, then, although I have been baptized, and call upon God, and invoke his grace, and wish with my whole will to be saved and set free from evil thoughts, am I unable to do so? It is clear that Adam's transgression has made this heritage inevitable for us!

Answer: As rational beings, we need to understand what we are hearing. Since the soul, darkened by love of pleasure and self-centeredness, has plunged into the depths of ignorance, it no longer pays attention to either scriptural commandment or real consequences or the authority of experience, but follows only its own opinions. Who, believing in Holy Scripture and keeping the Lord's commandments, does not find corresponding relief from thoughts and complete assurance that they have no hold over him, but rather have authority over us only because of our lack of faith and failure to keep the commandments? Thus all of us neither share an equal condition, nor are we driven by the same understandings, since the motivations for our thoughts are freely chosen. If they were coerced on account of Adam, all of us would do similar things and would inevitably be ruled by the same things; controlled by natural heredity and not by a willful love of pleasure, we would have no need of either scriptural authority or apostolic admonition. But this is not the way things are now. God forbid!

Look, we can see that not everyone is controlled by thoughts the same way, nor by the same opportunities, nor by the same things. On the contrary, to the extent that each person has faith in the Lord concerning the good things to come and pays no attention to human fame and enjoyments, such a person has shut off thoughts and is more at peace than the person who delights in enjoying himself.[24] Because of this, each of us differs from the other both in the thoughts we have and in the way we live our lives. Therefore most of us also deceive ourselves about the truth in this matter and do not seek to practice faith in Jesus, that is, to keep his commandments, nor trouble our hearts with poverty and humility in order to extinguish

[24]In saying that such a person is "more at peace" (*hēsychesteros*), Mark is appealing to the concept of quietude (*hēsychia*) that was already important in monastic literature and would increasingly become central to Byzantine piety.

our thoughts; instead, because we have a secret love for enjoyments (I mean for self-centeredness and people-pleasing), both for arrogance and a love of show and ostentation, of superiority and pride, and other vices similar to these whose success multiplies our desires and whose lack of success multiplies our irascibility—because of this, we are powerless.

Why, then, accepting the causes, are we tempted to reject without cause the effects that naturally follow? If what I have said is false and we are controlled by thoughts without any personal responsibility, let us carefully consider matters as though we were making our confession to God. Who does not know that in word and in deed and in thought we are enticed each day by the aforementioned passions, and that we love those things that cooperate with us as we do benefactors, and turn away from those things that impede us as we do from enemies? If we love the aforementioned passions in this way, even to the point of openly defending them, how will we hate the assault brought on by them, which comes with a single thought? Once we have accepted the first thought, how do the thoughts that complete it not follow?

Fifteenth Question

Question: Even if we admit that things are this way, in the Gospels did the Lord not promise all the same "to grant justice to those who cry out to him night and day" [Lk 18.7]?

Answer: The Lord did not tell the parable to those who are voluntarily addicted to pleasures, but rather to those who are warring only with superficial things and who do not give their assent to them.[25]

---

[25]The word translated as "superficial things" is *proslēpseōn*, which according to H. G. Liddell and R. Scott, *A Greek English Lexicon*, 9th ed. (Oxford: Clarendon Press, 1996), *s.v.*, is related to the word for "outer garment" (*proslēmma*). It would seem, then, that Mark is contrasting people who have cultivated bad habits and people who are, so to speak, draped with a temptation.

Thus he promised to grant justice to those who are wronged as though by enemies, but he accuses those who reject the help offered by a commandment, saying, "Why do you say to me, 'Lord, Lord,' and do not do what I say?" [Lk 6.46]. He also compares them to the fool who built his house upon the sand of his own desires and not upon the rock of the Lord's precepts [Lk 6.49; Mt 7.26].

Do not therefore rely on your own shaky mind and irrational counsel for all your opinions, as though these were true. Never say, "I have been baptized, and I call upon God and draw on his grace, desiring with my whole will to be saved from evil thoughts—but I am unable to do so, because I am held subject by my thoughts without being responsible for them." You are waiting at some point for the justice that the Lord promised to grant in the Gospels, while you are always saying that you are not responsible for anything. What incredible blasphemy! I will nevertheless ask you where you get this high opinion of yourself from, and I expect you to give me an answer. I know that, constrained by the truth, you will either speak even more pridefully, or you will confess your own responsibility for things. When the Lord said that he would quickly grant justice [Lk 18.7], why does he not quickly do so, but instead delays and has abandoned you to evil thoughts, even though you pray wholeheartedly and singlemindedly, as you have said?

Sixteenth Question

Question: But he said, I believe, that he would delay for no other reason than to give me patient endurance [Col 1.11]. Insofar as someone patiently endures being warred upon, he will also be glorified.

Answer: I was thinking of responding only to the presumptuous opinion that you insist on clinging to, but now you have also added blasphemy to your presumptuousness. In order to claim for yourself a false "patient endurance," you have brought the Lord forward as a false witness to bolster what you are saying. You maintain that, according to Holy Scripture, evil thoughts no longer lead to wickedness and love of sensual pleasures and all sorts of sin that, according to the word of the Lord, come from the heart and defile a person [Mk 7.20]; rather, they are sources of patient endurance and procure for us the glory that comes from God!

I myself have never found those controlled by wicked thoughts applauded by Holy Scripture, neither in the Old Testament, nor in the New; rather, they are deplored and condemned because they have only themselves to blame: Just as God hates wicked thoughts, he also hates the heart that gives birth to them. Therefore, we who have these thoughts ought to mourn for ourselves because we are lovers of sin, and not become puffed up with conceit as though we were waging war against evil foreigners. So, my friend, understand this well: The Lord observes everyone's heart [see 1 Chr 28.9]. He immediately defends those who hate the first impulse of evil thoughts, just as he promised, and does not allow a swarm of mental distractions to rise up against them and defile their mind and conscience. On the other hand, with regard to those who renounce the first outbursts of wicked thoughts not on account of faith and trust in God, but rather, inclined toward the love of pleasure, do so, clearly, out of a desire to closely observe and test those thoughts, because they lack faith and look only to themselves for help, God allows them to be repeatedly accosted and pursued by thoughts. He does not do away with such thoughts, then, because he sees that we cherish the suggestions preceding them and do not hate their first manifestations.

If someone, after such a clear explanation, does not believe what I have said, he can learn the truth by putting it into practice. If he neither believes in Scripture nor wishes to satisfy himself of the truth by putting into action what I have said, it is clear that he loves the pleasure that his own opinions bring, for what is more voluptuary than this: to suppose that sinful thought is alien to oneself, and to pride oneself on this and be puffed up about it, rather than to prepare oneself to confess and show sorrow for one's wicked decisions?

Seventeenth Question

Question: You said earlier that we have not inherited Adam's transgression, but rather death. Since death rules, wicked thoughts also rule.

Answer: Lord preserve us from such perverse belief! Why do you think the Lord came in the flesh [1 Jn 4.2] if it was not—clearly—to die for everyone, according to the Scriptures [2 Cor 5.14], and to nullify the one who has power over death, that is, the Devil [Heb 2.14]? If you believe that Adam's death still holds sway, which is a perversion of our faith, it is clear that you are also denying the Lord's advent and hold that Baptism is defective, while those who have been baptized are ruled over by ancestral death without any responsibility on their part. Therefore, my friend, listen how, by the grace of Christ, you have become a new Adam [1 Cor 15.45, 47] and are forced to bear nothing of the old Adam—unless it is your own perverse belief and transgression!

The Lord came *on our behalf*; he died for us; he freed us from ancestral death; he cleanses and renews us through Baptism; he places us in the paradise of the Church; he allows us to eat from every tree in paradise [Gen 2.9], that is, to love everyone baptized in the Church, and to patiently endure failures, and not to search for each person's deviations from the path and love those we think are good while hating those we believe are evil, which is the tree of the knowledge of good and evil [Gen 2.9]: the mind that tastes of this tree immediately falls into the same failures and discovers its own nakedness [Gen 3.7] through the evil it discovers against its neighbor; it did not recognize this discovery at first, veiled as it was by compassion.

Therefore, the Lord commands those placed in the paradise of the Church, saying, "Do not judge, lest you be judged; forgive, and you will be forgiven" [Lk 6.37]. He sums up these things when he says, "In everything do to others as you would have them do to you, for this is the law and the prophets" [Mt 7.12]. The law says, "You shall love your neighbor as yourself" [Lev 19.18], while the prophets say, "As you have done, so shall it be for you" [Ob 15]. How often have we besmirched the commandments! How often have we heartlessly condemned our neighbor! How often have we hated or even mistreated someone who has done us no harm! If this is the way things are, why do we still blame Adam for the evils we do? If we have also fallen into a death like his, it is because we in similar fashion have voluntarily transgressed the commandments, just as he did.

Adam, therefore, confronted three situations and not one, as you believe; these were: an assault that took place according to divine dispensation, a transgression that took place because of Adam's own faithlessness, death in accordance with God's just judgement. Death did not naturally follow from the assault that took place according to divine dispensation, but rather followed from the transgression that took place because of Adam's faithlessness. We therefore have inherited only death: We were unable to come back to life from the dead until the Lord came and gave life to all who believed. By divine dispensation we have an "initial thought,"[26] just as Adam did—and we can will to disobey it or not disobey it, just as Adam could. And the following words of the Apostle convince us that any transgression we commit on account of our thoughts takes place because of free will and not by necessity: "those whose sins were not like Adam's transgression" [Rom 5.14]. If then those who followed Adam were able not to sin as Adam did when he transgressed, it is clear that we too are able to do so. Why, then, do we make excuses by wishing away our sins, and why do we prattle about the injustice of God, as though God unjustly allows us to be warred upon by the evils of others?

We therefore ought to understand clearly that all of Adam's guilt has been wiped away by the Lord. If each of us suffers any kind of

[26]Evagrius also uses the term "initial thought" (*prōtonoia*) to describe the mind's first movement: *On prayer* 126. Mark's use of it seems to imply a renewed state from which we can respond to diabolic assaults with the same equipoise that Adam had enjoyed in Eden.

evil, he suffers it because of his own doing: On account of his own faithlessness or, to be sure, on account of his love of pleasure, he has rejected the perfection that he received mystically in Baptism. Even if a person does not yet know what he has received because his faith is imperfect and he is defective in works, God has nevertheless given perfection as a gift, for it says, "Every perfect gift is from above, coming down from the Father of lights" [Jas 1.17]. This perfection does not simply happen in and of itself, nor can someone discover it, even if he brings to bear upon it human wisdom and all worldly understanding, *unless he keeps Christ's commandments*, and this takes place proportionately: The gift of perfection is variously revealed to us according to the various ways we keep the commandments. Let no one, then, commend himself with words or rhetorical figures without having that understanding, for it says: "The person who commends himself is not approved, but rather the person whom the Lord commends" [2 Cor 10.17].

Even the person who receives commendations from the Lord ought to hold the proper opinion and correctly know this: to the extent that someone has waged spiritual battle against his own lack of faith, and has made progress in the faith, and has arrived at some good, not only through mere knowledge *but also by keeping the commandments*, he has discovered—or will be able to discover—nothing more than what he has already received mystically through Baptism; that is, Christ: "As many of you," it says, "as were baptized in Christ have clothed yourselves with Christ" [Gal 3.27]. Christ, being perfect God, has given the perfect grace of the Spirit as a gift to those who have been baptized.

We have not received this grace, which is something given to us, by our own doing; it is revealed and manifested to us in proportion to the way we keep the commandments and it serves to increase our faith, "until all of us come to the unity of faith, to perfect maturity, to the measure of the full stature of the fullness of Christ" [Eph 4.13]. If, then, as those brought to new birth, we bring anything to him, this was already concealed in us by him and from him, as it is written:

" 'Who has known the mind of the Lord, or who has been his counselor? Or who has given a gift to him and expected to receive a gift in return?' From him and through him and to him are all things. To him be the glory for ever and ever. Amen" [Is 40.13; Rom 11.34–36].

Jerome the Greek,
Works Useful to Every Christian

INTRODUCTION

Georges de Durand includes in his critical edition of Mark's works the following brief document, entitled, *Works Useful to Every Christian*. The author—an otherwise unknown Jerome—argues forcefully that the proof of salvation is found in the effect (in Greek, *energeia*) that Baptism has in the life of the Christian. Jerome stresses the inner experience of this effect, and he underlines his point by devaluing the importance of Baptism as such. As for the former, Jerome likens this effect, which is nothing other than the movement within the heart of the Holy Spirit, to the quickening of a babe in its mother's womb. When queried, Jerome asserts that this experience is the "true and inerrant proof" that one has been baptized, and he explicitly disparages arguments, analysis, and rationalization as attempts to build up comparable assurance.

Indeed, as his explanation develops, Jerome comes to qualify Baptism itself. He is conspicuously ready to stipulate that a "right" Baptism is prerequisite, by which he seems to mean a Baptism performed with the Trinitarian formula. But he may go further than this, since he specifically notes that sacraments are available to the unworthy, the unbelievers and the heretics—and all these groups are known to take part in the sacraments of the Church. It is at this point that Jerome's warmly pietistic endorsement of spiritual experience begins to seem somewhat ominous. Jerome himself does not unambiguously divide the Church into a coterie of the worthy on the one hand and those on the other who have not had the experience of the Holy Spirit's effect; but the implication is there to be taken up by an unconvinced reader. And it is possible that Mark was precisely such an unconvinced reader.

Even if Mark did not know Jerome's *Works Useful to Every Christian*, de Durand was surely right to include it in his volume because it corresponds neatly to the perspective that Mark addresses in *On Holy Baptism*. In our introduction to the latter writing, we pointed out some of the difficulties associated with using the term "Messalian" to characterize Mark's opponent. It is easy to see that the term "Messalian" would be difficult to apply with confidence to Jerome, or his writing. Even so, there are trajectories of thought evident in Jerome's work that can be compared to Messalian ideas, e.g., about the inefficacy of the sacraments and the importance of prayer. For this reason, and without wishing to commit to the view that Mark was directly responding to Jerome, it seems good to include Jerome's treatise in this appendix.

Works Useful to Every Christian
By the blessed Jerome[1]

1   *Question:* "How is it that you are a Christian?"
Answer: "Because I believe in Christ, the Son of God."

2   *Response:* "Your answer is ignorant and irrational, since I did not ask you how it is that you are *called* a Christian, but rather what is the actual *property* that makes you a Christian. If I had asked, 'Why are you called a Christian,' you would rightly have responded, 'I believe in Christ.' But I am trying to find out the reason why you are a Christian. The question may appear trivial and simple, but few people answer it fittingly when they are asked. And even if the one asked should say, 'God willed it and so I am a Christian,' the answer is not correct. Even if one should say, 'I willed to be a Christian,' the answer is not right."

[Answer:] "But because God willed it, and I wanted to do God's will!"

3   *Question:* "Does willing make you a Christian, or not?"
Answer: "If I say yes, I would be lying; if I say no, I am not telling the truth—for I was an infant then. I neither refused nor consented."

4   *Question:* "I would like to know, then, how you know that you were baptized at all. Perhaps you were dropped along the way by your parents, who were secretly pagans who never really wanted you to be baptized. That sort of thing has happened often, and it still happens to this day!"

---

[1]Source: de Durand, *Marc le Moine*, 2:338–49; N.B. "the blessed Jerome" is in the title as it is presented by de Durand and is not the invention of the translators.

Answer: "[I know] by its effect. Isaiah says, 'By fear of you, Lord, we conceived in the womb and were in pain and bore a spirit of salvation' [Is 26.17–18]. Thus, he shows that we who have been illuminated by Baptism conceive the Holy Spirit. Again, through the prophet God says about those who have been baptized, 'I shall dwell among them and walk in their midst' [2 Cor 6.16], and 'I will pour out my Spirit upon all flesh' [Joel 3.1]. So as many as have conceived the Holy Spirit in the womb by holy Baptism, inwardly—within their very heart—are fully confident in their heart, from the leaps and goadings and joyous transports and activities and (if I may say so) bounds of the Spirit's grace, that they have been baptized.

No one on this earth who has not been baptized abounds in this kind of grace and activity, nor has ever experienced it, not even if he has fulfilled all of God's righteous commandments. Only they do who have been reborn of water and the Spirit [cf. Jn 3.5], who have conceived in their womb the grace of the Spirit, who have protected it pure and undefiled. In the same way that a woman who has conceived feels the leaps of the babe within her, these people likewise know from the joy, happiness, and exultation rising in their heart that the Spirit of God dwells within them, whom they received in Baptism. Concerning this grace of the Holy Spirit, Christ said, 'The kingdom of heaven is within you' [Lk 17.21], and again, 'I have come to cast fire upon the earth, and would that it were already kindled!' [Lk 12.49]."

5   *Question:* "So then will everyone, whether educated or not, know that he has been baptized from this proof alone, and never by any other method?"

Answer: "The true and inerrant proof of being a Christian is this one. Listen to what Paul says when he accuses some people: 'Or do you not know that Jesus Christ dwells in you? If not, then you are unapproved' [2 Cor 13.5]. As I have said, one who has conceived in the womb knows with certainty that she has, not from words, but from actions and from the leaps of the babe. Likewise, the true

Christian should have complete assurance that he has received holy Baptism and that he has been counted worthy of the Holy Spirit, not from his parents saying that they had him baptized or from any other method, but from his own heart. This is why Paul said to certain people, 'Do not quench the Spirit' [1 Thess 5.19]—that is, do not drive away the Spirit—and, 'Do not sadden the Holy Spirit, by whom you were sealed on the day you were set free' [Eph 4.30], and again, 'You have not received the spirit of slavery, but of freedom' [cf. Rom 8.15].

When David had lost this grace through adultery, he cried out to God, saying, 'Restore in me the gladness of the Savior and renew an upright spirit in my inner parts' [Ps 50.14, 12]. You see that the Holy Spirit dwells inside the faithful. Furthermore, according to the extent that one protects the purity of the house that is his heart, he will be illuminated and will perceive the divine fire dwelling within himself through tears, through joy, through gladness and consolation and happiness. Particularly at the time of feasts, liturgical gatherings, and Baptisms, when the Holy Spirit is present, the Spirit's joy which dwells in the person's soul will also leap and thus the person will be completely assured that he is truly a Christian and has received holy Baptism.

"What I have said should not seem strange or unacceptable. Even the prophets, who slept with women and were immersed in this life of involvement with people and things, had this grace of the Holy Spirit—and not just the men, but the women, too, who prophesied. For the Holy Spirit does not flee or feel loathing for the union of an honorable marriage. How is it that even many who are in the world experienced the actions of this grace of the Holy Spirit? I am talking about those who are present at the altar and those who approach to partake in the mysteries of Christ. All of a sudden, they are filled with tears and joy and happiness. How is it that the Christian has complete confidence to partake, not of mere bread and wine, but truly of the body and blood of the Son of God that are sanctified by the Spirit? For we never experience any such thing, such joy and activity[2] or the sweetness or compunction, when we simply eat bread and wine at our own table, even if the bread is nicer and the wine is older and better than the bread and wine that are offered on the altar.

"The Christian should know all these things, for there is nothing else in all our faith, in all the Church and in all the Holy Scripture more necessary than this thing, and nothing else like it. From it, one has complete confidence that God is in him and with him. From it, one knows that there truly is no other faith on earth except for that of the Christians, even though a great number of other people also have the Scriptures, churches, sacrifices, teachers, books, partial knowledge of God and some good deeds, feasts and changes of vestments, prayers, memorial services and priests. But nobody on earth ever receives this grace which is hidden in the Christian's heart and activity of the Holy Spirit, except for those who are rightly baptized into the Father, Son, and Holy Spirit and who have received them in faith. About this wealth of ours, the Lord says, 'The kingdom of heaven is like a treasure hidden in a field' [Mt 13.44], that is, the Holy Spirit who hides in us on the day of our divine Baptism. Paul also said about this, 'We have this treasure in earthen vessels' [2 Cor 4.7], that is, in our bodies of clay, and again, 'Do you not know that your bodies are the temple of God and the Spirit of God dwells in you?' [1 Cor 6.19, 3.16].

These considerations necessarily bring us to the central question: In what way should a Christian know that he has received holy Baptism and that he is a true Christian? Entering into the Church is not the sign of being a true Christian: Many who are unworthy enter along with us. Making the sign of the cross is not the sign of being a true Christian, either, nor is partaking of the body of Christ. It is possible that even the faithless and the heretics take Communion,

---

[2]Jerome uses the word *energeia* (here, "activity") to describe the work of the Spirit within the Christian and the consequences of that work, which include the Christian's perception of the Spirit at work. He also uses it in the *Answer* to Qu. 4, where we have translated it as "effect."

and do everything else that we do. Instead, as I have already said, the sign of a true Christian which God graciously bestows upon the Christian does not come from outside; it is not given on tablets of stone, but on the fleshly tablets of the heart [cf. 2 Cor 3.3].

So then let us feel around within ourselves and see if we have there the sign that God gave us at Baptism and the gift, the grace, and the treasure. The Gospels, prophets, apostles, and teachers have orally taught us the faith of God by hearing, but God teaches a person whether he is a Christian, not through the hearing of words, but through substantial things present in the soul. That is why Paul says, 'Faith is by hearing' [cf. Rom 10.17] *and*, 'Faith is the substance of things hoped for, the evidence of things not seen' [cf. Heb 11.1]. And so we have learned what the sign of the Christian is, which nothing on this earth other than faith procures. Blessed, then, are those who receive and keep it and depart this life with it, for theirs is the kingdom of heaven [cf. Mt 5.3, 10]."

Select Bibliography

Mark's works

Marc le Moine. *Traités I*. Georges de Durand, O.P., ed. Sources chrétiennes
    445. Paris: Cerf, 1999.
Marc le Moine. *Traités II*. Georges de Durand, O.P., ed. Sources chrétiennes
    455. Paris: Cerf, 2000.

Other primary sources and translations

Apophthegmata Patrum, alphabetic collection. PG 65.71–440.
Athanasius of Alexandria. *On the Incarnation*. Charles Kannengiesser, ed.
    Athanase d'Alexandrie: Sur l'Incarnation de la Verbe. Sources chré-
    tiennes 199. Paris: Cerf, 1973.
Athanasius of Alexandria. *Life of St Antony*. G. J. M. Bartelink, ed. *Athanase
    d'Alexandre: Vie d'Antoine*. Sources chrétiennes 400. Paris: Cerf, 1994.
Augustine. *Retractationes*. P. Knöll, ed. *Sancti Aureli Augustini, Opera* I.ii.
    CSEL 36. Vienna: Tempsky, 1902.
Babai. *Commentary on Evagrius' Gnostic Chapters*. Wilhelm von Franken-
    berg, ed. *Euagrius Ponticus*. Abhandlungen der Königlichen gesellschaft
    der wissenschaften zu Göttingen. Philologisch-historische klasse, N.F.
    13.2. Berlin: Weidmanssche Buchhandlung, 1912, 8–471.
Mishna Sukka. Isidore Epstein, ed. *The Babylonian Talmud: Seder Mo'ed* 6.
    London: Soncino Press, 1938.
Clement of Alexandria. *Stromateis*. O. Stählin, ed. *Clement Alexandrinus:
    Werke*, 3rd rev. ed. 3 GCS 17. Berlin: Akademie, 1970.
Epiphanius. *Panarion*. K. Holl, ed., J. Dummer, rev. *Ancoratus und Panarion*.
    GCS 31. Leipzig: Hinrichs, 1980.
Epistle to Barnabas. B. Ehrman, ed. & trans. *The Apostolic Fathers*. Loeb
    Classical Library, 2 vols. Cambridge MA: Harvard University Press,
    2003.
Eusebius. *Ecclesiastical History*. K. Lake, ed. & trans. Loeb Classical Library,
    2 vols. Cambridge, MA: Harvard University Press, 1989.

Evagrius Ponticus. *On the Eight Spirits of Evil*. PG 79.1145–64.

Evagrius Ponticus. *On the Thoughts*. Paul Géhin et al., eds. *Évagre le Pontique: Sur les pensées*. Sources chrétiennes 438. Paris: Cerf, 1998.

Evagrius Ponticus. *Praktikos*. Antoine and Claire Guillaumont, eds. *Évagre le Pontique: Traité pratique ou le moine*. Sources chrétiennes 170–171. Paris: Cerf, 1971.

Evagrius Ponticus. *On Prayer*. Simon Tugwell, OP, ed. *Evagrius Ponticus: De oratione*. Oxford: Faculty of Theology, 1981.

Ignatius of Antioch. *Romans*. B. Ehrman, ed. & trans. *The Apostolic Fathers*, Loeb Classical Library, 2 vols. Cambridge MA: Harvard University Press, 2003.

Macarius. *The Great Letter*. W. Jaeger, ed. *Two rediscovered works of ancient Christian literature: Gregory of Nyssa and Macarius*. Leiden: Brill, 1954.

On Melchizedek. Birger Pearson and Søren Giversen, eds. *Nag Hammadi codices IX and X*. Nag Hammadi Studies 15. Leiden: Brill, 1981.

Photius. *Bibliotheka*. René Henry, ed. *Photios: Bibliothèque*. Paris: Belles Lettres, 1962.

Pistis Sophia. Carl Schmidt, ed., Violet Macdermot, trans. & notes. Nag Hammadi Studies 9. Leiden: Brill, 1978.

Testament of the Twelve Patriarchs: A Critical Edition of the Greek Text. M. de Jonge, ed. Studia in Veteris Testamenti Pseudepigrapha 1.2. Leiden: Brill, 1975.

Theodoret. *Haereticarum fabularum compendium*. PG 83.336–556.

Secondary studies

de Jonge, M. and A.S. Van der Woude. "11Q Melchizedek and the New Testament." *New Testament Studies* 12 (1966): 301–26.

Fitschen, Klaus. *Messalianismus und Antimessalianismus: Ein Beispiel ostkirchlicher Ketzergeschichte*. Forschung zur Kirchen- und Dogmengeschichte 71. Göttingen: Vanderhoeck and Ruprecht, 1998.

Lampe, G. W. H. *A Patristic Greek Lexicon*. Oxford: Clarendon Press, 1961.

Liddell H. G. and R. Scott. *A Greek English Lexicon*, 9th ed. Oxford: Clarendon Press, 1996.

Pearson, Birger. "Melchizedek (NHC IX, *1*)." *The Anchor Bible Dictionary* 4:688–89. New York: Doubleday, 1992.

Plested, Marcus. *The Macarian Legacy: The Place of Macarius-Symeon in the Eastern Christian Tradition.* Oxford Theological Monographs. Oxford University Press, 2004.

Schelkle, K. H. *Paulus, Lehrer der Väter: die altkirchliche Auslegung von Römer 1–11,* 2nd ed. Düsseldorf: Patmos, 1959.

Stewart, Columba. *"Working the Earth of the Heart": The Messalian Controversy in History, Texts and Language to AD 431.* Oxford Theological Monographs. Oxford University Press, 1991.

POPULAR PATRISTICS SERIES

ST VLADIMIR'S SEMINARY PRESS
1-800-204-2665 • www.svspress.com